THE SEEDS OF TERRORISM

Mohammad Amir Rana

A NEW MILLENNIUM PUBLICATION

Published in 2005 by
NEW MILLENNIUM
34, South Molton Street
London W1K 5RG

Printed and Bound in UK
for New Millennium Publication

THE SEEDS OF TERRORISM

THE SEEDS OF TERRORISM

Table of Contents

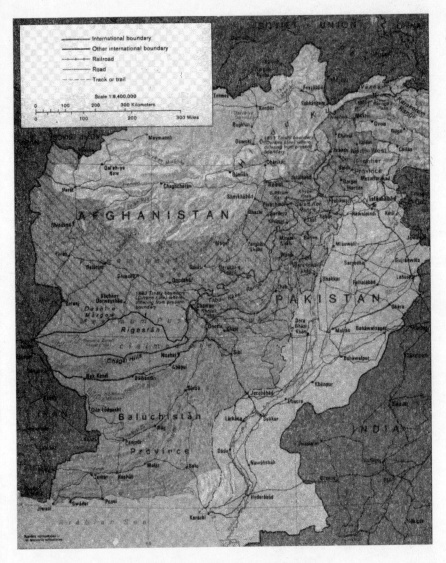

Map of Pakistan-Afghanistan border areas

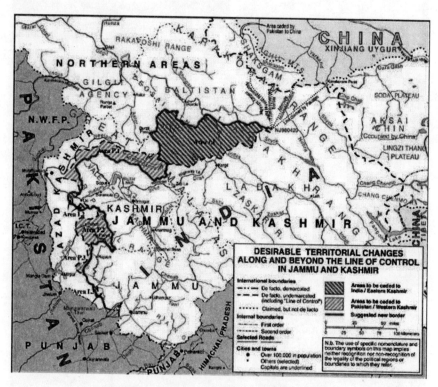

Map of Pakistan-Kashmir/India border areas

INTRODUCTION

Amir Rana is a brave man. He is a journalist working in Pakistan for *The Friday Times* in Lahore, in Pakistan, the very heartland of the al-Qaida and Islamic jihadi movement in the world. As a journalist, he has studied the rise of the world jihadi movement, which is to be distinguished from the Israel/Palestine struggle, in his own country over the past twenty years and this, his second book on the subject, is the result. The author is a young married man, a Muslim, who curries favour from no quarter. Not from his own military government or its present leader, General Musharraf, or from Pakistan's infamous ISI (Inter-Services Intelligence Directorate) which has, does and will torture, murder or terrorize individuals like him who annoy them too much, or who just cross their path. He does not pander to America or its leader, President Bush, or to European, Indian or Arabian governments or institutions, and he certainly seeks no favours from Osama bin Laden's al-Qaida or any of the many other jihadi and Islamic militant groups operating, some openly, in his country today.

Amir Rana is under surveillance. He has been 'leaned on' by state 'officials' and has been threatened by jihadi leaders because he continues to expose duplicity in the affairs of his own government and other participants in the so-called 'war on terror' which has been fought since the September 2001 atrocity in the US. He insists on writing about these things because he cares. He abhors violence and wants to see a peaceful world. He hopes to raise a family in peace. He despairs of seeing young men being encouraged to go on an adventure, to join the jihad to fight for God, and then meeting their bereaved families later.

His study of the present establishment of the Islamic jihadi movement and the history of that movement is very detailed, necessarily, because a proper understanding of the forces at work cannot be gained without an appreciation of that detail and the complexities of the issue. The author's access to insiders in the jihadi movement as well as the ISI and the Pakistan Army and bureaucratic establishment has enabled him to accurately record the realities of the situation on the ground and that provides his readers with the ability to distinguish between the fact and the fiction in the war on terror.

This work explains how al-Qaida came into existence. Its origins are traced back to the anti-Soviet jihad conducted by Afghan mujahideen with the support of the CIA and the ISI in the early 1980s. It explains how foreign elements, including Osama bin Laden, were recruited for the Afghan jihad by the CIA and how the ISI began its meteoric rise in power in Pakistan because of its proxy management of the jihad on behalf of America and Saudi Arabia. It shows how America then lost interest in the jihadi movement it had created after the Soviet withdrawal from Afghanistan and how it turned a blind eye to the ISI's redirection of that jihad against India in Kashmir.

The work deals extensively with incidents and events in Pakistan after a Pakistani based jihadi group attacked the Indian parliament in December 2000, bringing the two nuclear powers very close to war, and after New York was attacked in September 2001, bringing Pakistan very close to civil-war. It describes the difficulties faced by Musharraf's government when he tried to curb the activities of the hundreds of different jihadi groups operating in Pakistan against the Northern Alliance government in Afghanistan, against the Indians in Kashmir and against their other perceived enemies of Islam around the world. The author records the divisions that emerged in Pakistan's political/military hierarchy as well as the conflicts of interests in the mujahideen, their internal feuding and the ambivalent attitude of the ISI towards the new anti-terrorist policies Musharraf is trying to pursue.

This book also describes in detail the war of words, mostly exaggerated or distorted, being fought by the propagandists of the Islamic militant movement in Pakistan and the sophistication of their propaganda machinery. This alternative press in Pakistan plays a key role in the fund-raising and recruitment drives of the jihad movement and, as the author points out, they may invent, distort or exaggerate issues, but there is enough truth in their claims of duplicity in American foreign policy towards the Muslim world to enable them to persuade masses of people of the righteousness of their cause. Optimistically, however, he lifts the reader with hope when he describes the loss of popular appeal that affected the recruitment drives and fund gathering activities of the jihadi movement when Musharraf joined the anti-terrorist camp after the attack on US in September 2001. Then, he depresses again when he describes the resurgence of anti-American, pro-jihad, sentiment when Iraq was invaded in 2003.

However, the author also gives the reader some hope that there may be a solution to at least one of the problem areas where jihad is going on, in Kashmir. He gives an outline of the moves towards peace being made between the two nuclear powers who are locked in an undeclared war for control of that unfortunate state. Further, at the end of his comprehensive analysis of the modern jihad, he offers a simple formula for the solution of the main causes of jihad in the world today. If only there was a will.

Amir Rana is a member of that Muslim majority who want to live in peace but who have great difficulty making their voices heard over the strident tones of the jihadi propaganda machine and over a western press that seems to prefer Islamophobic and Zenophobic sensationalism to moderate Muslim opinion or an acknowledgement of some home truths about the behaviour of western interests in the world today. Those readers who want to see the issue of the 'war on terror' from a moderate Muslim perspective will learn a lot more from this book than from any newspaper or other media source in the west.

Tom Deegan
London, September 2004

Chapter 1
11 SEPTEMBER 2001 (9/11) AND PAKISTAN

In an interview in *Newsweek* in March 2000, the President of Pakistan, General Pervez Musharraf, said: "I cannot pressurize the Taliban to arrest Osama bin Laden. The Taliban lead a free country." The jihadi weekly, *Zarb-e-Momin* (Karachi) published an extract from that interview. It reported the president saying; "No jihadi organisation in Pakistan is involved in terrorism. They are now working against India in occupied Kashmir after completing their jihad against Russia in Afghanistan." Yet, on 12 December 2003, while answering a question in a program on the BBC, President Musharraf was claiming that, to date, his government had arrested or killed five hundred terrorists.

Is this change in the views and intentions of President Musharraf a result of some progressive transformation in his thinking? Analysts are of the opinion that this transformation took place after the 9/11 World Trade Centre attack when the American President phoned him and asked whose side he was on. Anxious to avoid confrontation with a raging America, President Musharraf decided to say a goodbye to the terrorists which Pakistan had created, nurtured and protected for many years and to join the opposite anti-terrorist camp immediately. Terrorism had got out of hand!

A equally fateful, albeit contrary, decision by the government of Pakistan was taken by General Ziaul Haq (Zia) in 1979 when, on the urging of the Americans and in collaboration with the CIA, Saudi Arabia and other Islamic states, he established a mujahideen army based in Pakistan to take on Soviet Russia, seen then as the biggest enemy of Islam, in the hills of Afghanistan. That decision of General Zia culminated in the 9/11 attacks against America. Frankenstein's monster had returned to haunt its creators.

The Afghan Jihad – First Nursery for Militants

The relatively ineffective anti-Soviet opposition activities carried out by militant groups in Afghanistan up to 1979 were changed into a much more serious and effective jihad by America, Saudi Arabia, and Pakistan. After Soviet military forces entered Afghanistan, three million Afghans moved to Pakistan. Thus, America's Central Intelligence Agency (CIA) through its ally, Pakistan's Inter-Services Intelligence Directorate (ISI), gained control of a huge contingent of mujahideen.

Until the early 1980s, the aim of the CIA was just to keep Soviet forces engaged in a Vietnam-type conflict. To this end, mujahideen groups were based, trained, armed and provided with financial resources in Pakistan. The ISI ran the show in all practical respects.

However, when the decision was made to actually defeat the Soviets in Afghanistan, Saudi Arabia and Pakistan made efforts to recruit young men from all over the Islamic world for the jihad. According to one estimate, about thirty-five thousand mujahideen recruits from forty different countries arrived to take part in the Afghan jihad during the period 1982 to 1992. Osama bin Laden was one of them. He reached Afghanistan after receiving his training at the Islamic Centre in New York which was run under the patronage of the CIA. Who could have guessed then that this young man, sent to Afghanistan by America, would be the cause of an atrocity that would result in a new, massively belligerent, American foreign policy that led to hundreds of thousands of people being killed, maimed or displaced in two wars and which would affect the political map of the entire world.

Referring to the memoirs and lectures of the well-known Islamic scholar Dr Iqbal Ahmad, David Barsamon wrote in his book, *Terrorism: Theirs and Ours* that Dr Ahmad met Osama bin Laden in 1986 after the CIA had drawn him into the jihad and arranged his placement in Afghanistan. Dr Ahmad says that Osama was then an American confidante but he turned against America when it sent its forces into Saudi Arabia, the sacred land of Islam, during the Gulf War: "Dr Ahmad said that bin Laden's code of ethics was tribal and consisted of two words: loyalty and revenge. 'You are my friend. You keep your word and I'm loyal to you. You break your word, I will go on my path of revenge.' For him (bin Laden) America had broken its word. The loyal friend had betrayed him. Now they're going to go for you. They are going to do a lot more. These are all the chickens of the Afghan jihad coming home to roost."

An interesting point to be made here is that former President George Bush Sr had a close personal relationship with Osama bin Laden's family because the Bush and bin Laden families have been closely associated in business. George Bush Sr had earned the first million dollars of his life in a deal with an oil company and that deal had been struck with Osama's older brother, Saleem bin Laden. According to the BBC's *Newsnight* television program on 6 November 2001, both families had also been associated in arms dealings.

The mujahideen won the war against Soviet forces in Afghanistan with the help of Israeli arms and donkeys from Brazil and Egypt. American author George Crele's book *Charlie Wilson's War* (2003), brought to light the fact that Israeli arms had reached Afghanistan with the consent of General Ziaul Haq who had entered into an agreement with Israel and American. The book was based on the memoirs of Charlie Wilson, a friend of Pakistan and a member of the American Congress. The fact is that thousands of donkeys and mules were brought in from Egypt and Brazil to carry Israeli arms into the hills of Afghanistan.

Mujahideen from all over the world, along with donkeys and mules, Israeli arms, the assistance of the CIA and Pakistan's secret service, the ISI, as well as revenue from Saudi Arabia and other Arab states, converged in an alliance to defeat and expel Soviet forces from Afghanistan. However, after the success of this great mission, this new mujahideen remained in existence, most of the Afghan mujahideen returned to their homes, but the foreign, Pakistani and Kashmiri mujahideen stayed on with a new agenda, to free Muslims from their perceived American, Israeli, and Indian oppression in the Middle East, Palestine and Kashmir respectively. When, through the ISI, the Americans armed and financed the mujahideen for the jihad against the Soviets in Afghanistan they were creating an army of thousands of young jihadis who would come back to attack them. After the success of the jihad in Afghanistan, the Pakistani and foreign mujahideen continued to receive the assistance of the ISI and the ISI continued to receive the assistance of the CIA, but the jihad was now concentrated against the Indians in Kashmir. Leading elements in the ISI believed the recently unemployed mujahideen could be used to repeat the Afghan success in Kashmir, the whole of which could then be incorporated into Pakistan. The Americans turned a blind eye to the activities of the jihadis in Indian-held Kashmir.

The Role of the ISI (Inter-Services Intelligence Directorate)

The ISI played a most significant and prominent role in the Afghan jihad. Once the Pakistan Government agreed to establish mujahideen for the jihad in Afghanistan, the ISI was made responsible for organising Afghan mujahideen groups; providing bases, training them, providing them with material resources, reinforcing them with Pakistani volunteers

21

and ensuring the support of the people of Pakistan for the jihad in Afghanistan, all paid for by America and Saudi Arabia. When the ISI made its cold-war contribution in the 1980s by organising the mujahideen's armed resistance to Soviet rule, America's interest in this jihad grew and the CIA and ISI began a close collaboration. A team led by General Abdur Rahman, ISI, gave new covert warfare ideas to the ISI and centred its attention on the jihad of Afghanistan. This was just the beginning of the ISI's real growth in power in the country. They had been in existence since independence in 1947 but their successful management of the jihad in Afghanistan enabled them to do almost anything they wanted in the country. Their influence cannot be overestimated. Thankfully perhaps, only the regular army is a more powerful force in Pakistan today. Within a period of just four years, the ISI had made Afghanistan ungovernable for the incumbent government and its Russian allies. The Russians felt disillusioned by the end of 1987 and, four months into 1988, the matter reached Geneva and to Russia's withdrawal from Afghanistan. During the period 1979 to 1988, the military wing of the ISI had successfully spread the impact of the Afghan jihad all over the world. By this time the ISI had become a massively powerful and influential factor in Pakistan.

An expert journalist of military affairs, Hamidullah Abid, has to say the following in this reference: "The area of ISI's operation should have shrunk after 1988 but, on the contrary, its policy planners gave it a boost in a surprising manner. After Kabul, the new centres of jihad emerged in Srinagar, Bosnia, Chechnya, and Palestine. Mujahideen who had collected from all over the world, especially the Muslim dominated countries, went to join centres closer to their homes. However, mujahideen from Saudi Arabia, Yemen and a few other countries stayed on in Afghanistan. Among those were Osama bin Laden and more than a thousand mujahideen belonging to al-Qaida."

It is important to note here that when Osama bin Laden was driven out of Somalia and Sudan he went to Afghanistan where he was provided shelter by the incumbent government of Hikmetyar and Rabbani. Later, when the Taliban took over, Osama joined them.

The Creator of the Taliban

The interim administration of Afghanistan fell into the hands of the Mujahideen after the expulsion of Soviet forces. Soon afterwards, the Mujahideen began feuding among themselves and caused a civil war in the country. Conditions were such that Professor Burhanuddin Rabbani, who was made President of Afghanistan during the interim period, tried to hold on to power even after his term had expired. Kabul was under the control of Rabbani's ally, Minister of Defence, Ahmad Shah Masood, and the new Prime Minister, Hikmetyar, was in no position to enter Kabul.

Under these circumstances, Pakistan came up with a new policy regarding Afghanistan. This was the Taliban Policy, the credit for which is claimed by the former Interior Minister of Pakistan, Nasirullah Babur. He asserts that considering the internal condition of Afghanistan, it was only appropriate to give political power to the Pushton people because the mujahid leaders had started to act strangely in their relations with Pakistan. This strained relationship has been recorded several times in the electronic and print media. However, the former chief of the ISI, Jawaid Ashraf Qazi, has asserted that he had made his first contacts with the Taliban through Mullah Rabbani at the time when the Taliban had already initiated their efforts to take over. According to him, Mullah Rabbani had come with a request that Pakistan should stop aiding and assisting the Afghan mujahid commanders and that he did not need any military or financial assistance except permission to purchase petrol from Pakistan. (Interview in *Dawn*, 5 November 2002)

Later, while giving an interview on Pakistan's State TV channel, PTV, in November 2002, Ashraf Qazi shed light on the background of the Taliban leadership and said that Mullah Omar was a teacher in a village madrasa of Sangisar near Kandahar who said that the mujahid commanders had created a hell in the entire region and nobody's life or property was safe. One example of the abuse of power described how a mujahid commander had kidnapped a young boy from his madrasa and sexually assaulted him. In reaction to this, Mullah Omar, now a prominent al-Qaida leader, attacked the headquarters of the offending commander along with the students of his madrasa. After the success of this operation, the people of Kandahar also came to join him. He took a vow that he would save

Afghanistan from the oppression of the warlord mujahid commanders.

Jawaid Ashraf Qazi denied the statements of General Nasirullah Babur that he had been in contact with the Taliban since the very beginning. He said that not only General Nasirullah Babur but also Maulana Fazlur Rehman, the chief of Jamiat Ulema-e-Islam, an Islamic fundamentalist jihadi group, had made contacts with the Taliban through the ISI. In an interview in the *Daily Express* (Lahore: 11 January 2004), General Nasirullah Babur said: "I did not only brief Laghari (the then President of Pakistan), Benazir Bhutto the PM, the Director General of the ISI, and the Foreign Secretary on the current Afghan situation but they also used to give me their advice. I had organised the Taliban in my own way and I did not want to have other Afghan organisations or Rabbani, Hikmetyar and Masood chased out by the Taliban. Let me also tell you that in the beginning even the Americans used to meet the Taliban and considered them reasonable people. The Taliban also wished to have cordial relations with the Americans."

Apart from these claims and counterclaims by Pakistani leaders, there are research reports and testimonies from the Taliban and their allies among the Pakistani mujahideen that help us draw the conclusion that the Taliban were the creation of the ISI. And the ISI was proud of this fact. A former ISI agent who was active in the Afghan jihad until 1992 said that it was almost impossible for the Taliban to occupy the ninety per cent of Afghanistan which they controlled without the help of the ISI. He said the ISI not only provided arms to the Taliban but also gave large amounts of money to bribe the commanders who had kept different areas under their rule. In this way, several towns were taken over by the Taliban without waging any kind of war against them. For example, a very large sum of money was paid to Gul Agha, the Governor of Kandahar, to lay down arms. The commander of Hizb-e-Wahdat of Bamiyan was won over with a payment of eight million dollars. Confirmatory reports of this bribery were also published in the monthly *The Herald* (Karachi: November 2001).

Quite contrary to the statement of Jawaid Ashraf Qazi, the former Chief of the ISI, a student from Baluchistan who was active along with the Taliban in Afghanistan says that the Afghan students were properly trained in the madrasas in the art of warfare before they were sent to Afghanistan. According to a report of the Human Rights Watch of New York, one of its representatives met with Pakistani technicians in Kabul in September 1996 who revealed that they were laying telephone cables for the new government. According to that Human Rights Watch representative, the most surprising thing was that a senior officer from the ISI was supervising the project. It was in the presence of this representative that the officer gave instructions to a Taliban leader regarding the laying down of arms.

Regarding assistance to the Taliban, in November 2001 *The Herald* recorded: "...there have been frequent reports of Pakistani military units offering training to the Taliban and other jihadi groups in more than 10 training camps across Afghanistan. One such unit was dispatched by the ISI's Afghan Bureau to the former Afghan Army base at Rishkhor, near Kabul, in September 1996. The suggestion that there was earlier UN support for the Taliban remains disputed but analysts point to some circumstantial evidence to show that such support was indeed offered in certain major areas. In Herat, for instance, the Taliban switched from jihadi-style hit-and-run operations to a more innovative 'mobile warfare'. The transformation came months after a 6,000 strong Taliban army was routed by the forces of Herat governor, Ismail Khan, in April 1995. In September, the Taliban employed 4 x 4 pick-up trucks to outflank opposition forces and cut them off from their rear-area supply depots. The retreating forces of Ismail Khan failed to establish defence lines and Taliban mobile units repeatedly outflanked their new positions by leaving the road at will and driving across open country and hilly terrain.

"A similar flair for speed and flank attacks characterised the battle for Kabul in September 1996 and that for Mazar-e-Shareef in August 1998. On both occasions, credible reports confirm the presence of Pakistani military advisors in the Taliban ranks. Significantly, say analysts, Taliban military effectiveness disappeared when they embarked on operations alone. For instance, the Taliban's abortive attack on Herat in April 1995 was carried out without the approval of the ISI. During the fighting for Mazar, Taliban forces floundered after Pakistani advisors were pulled out in the wake of the crisis sparked by the killing of Iranian diplomats.

"The presence of professional Pakistani fighters became most obvious during the Taliban's attack on Taloqan, the capital of northern Takhar province in September 2000. There were also reports that Pakistani aircraft were used to rotate Taliban troops on the Taloqan front line. The frequency of such reports forced the UN Secretary General to implicitly accuse Pakistan of interfering in Afghanistan. The US government was also obliged to issue a démarche to the Pakistani government asking for assurances that Pakistan had not been involved in engineering, the fall of Taloqan."

The New York Times of 8 December 2001 claimed that Pakistan's secret services agency, the ISI, continued supplying arms to the Taliban until 12 October 2001. Quoting Egyptian and Pakistani officials, the report said: "Pakistani border guards at a check point in the Khyber pass on 8 October and 12 allowed passage to convoys of trucks loaded with rifles, ammunition and rocket-propelled grenade launchers hidden under their tarpaulins headed into Afghanistan.

"A senior Pakistani intelligence official acknowledged that the 8 October shipment did contain arms for the Taliban. But the official also said it was the last officially sanctioned delivery and that Pakistan had since been living up to its commitment to the anti-terror war."

The Herald wrote further regarding the supply of arms to the Taliban by the ISI in the earlier quoted issue: "The shipment of fresh weapons supplies to the Taliban from Pakistani territory continued through subsequent years. During 1994–96, these supplies passed through the Kurram Agency (a tribal area) and were delivered at various locations up to Khost in southern Afghanistan.

"Later, the route shifted to the main border crossing on Torkham and the deliveries were made directly to the central corps headquarters in Kabul. The Taliban officials responsible for receiving these supplies included Ajab Gul, Mullah Sulaiman and Maulavi Mohammad Salam."

Jihadi sources claim that the Taliban had allowed Afghanistan to become a second home for Pakistan. Most Afghan government departments were under the control of the ISI and Pakistanis were running the affairs of state. Sources have confirmed that Pakistani military forces had also transferred their units there. According to these sources:

1. The Pakistani Consul General in Herat was a member of the ISI and he was also the political and military advisor to the Taliban government.

2. Faizan, the military advisor to the southwest group of the Taliban, and Mohammad Gul, the military advisor at Kandahar, were also associated with the ISI. The subunit commander of Mazar-e-Shareef, Jawaid Ahmad, was also a member of the Pakistan Army and Pakistani military advisors were also present at the Bagram airbase.

3. Two hundred suspected terrorists from the Pakistani sectarian organisations, Sipah-e-Sahaba and Lashkar-e-Jhangavi, were present in the Rashkor area of Kabul under the leadership of Riaz Basra. Three hundred members of the Pakistani militant organisation, Harkat-ul-Mujahideen, were also

present in the Naglu Settlement of Kabul. The centre of Hizb-ul-Mujahideen, a Kashmiri militant organisation, was at the New North Road in Kabul. Two thousand young men of the Pakistani student organisation, Islami Jamiat Tulaba, who were members of Pakistan's Afridi tribes were part of the Taliban forces.

4. Apart from these, Pakistanis held important positions in the Taliban forces. These included Mullah Mohammad Nabi (from Quetta), Mullah Israil of Intelligence (from Chaman), Field Commander Mullah Abdullah (from Chaman), Mullah Mohammad Akhtar of Rashkor 7th Division, and the head of Kabul security, Mullah Abdur Razzaq (from Quetta).

The Assistance of the CIA

It was not only Pakistan and its ISI which were involved in the creation of the Taliban. That old friend of the Afghan jihad, America and its CIA, were equally involved. Many reports that shed light on the role of the CIA have already appeared.

According to a report in *The Herald* in November 2001, the American government had assisted the Taliban with four hundred thousand dollars to purchase arms. The same issue had an interview with Nasirullah Babur in which he had said that America supported communist leaders like General Momin and General Rasheed Dostam in the first phase when announcements regarding the establishment of Islamic rule were made after the exit of Soviet forces and when there was no unanimity concerning the intended form of government among the mujahideen. These communist leaders were given a red carpet reception in Washington, Ankara, and Islamabad. The reasoning behind this was that they could prevent the mujahideen unifying as a fundamentalist Islamic force. Nasirullah Babur also said: "America projected Zahir Shah during this period but, when the mujahideen refused to go ahead with the communists, the Americans left them midway. The warlords then started dealing in arms and narcotics and began extracting taxes from the public by force. Kandahar was the most badly affected where as many as five commanders ruled at the same time. They were commanders Najibullah, Agha, Haji Ahmad, Ameer Ali, and Ustad Abdul Ali. In October 1994, about five hundred people took arms against them. These were the people who were later known as the Taliban. When the Taliban were on a firmer footing, they received American assistance to dislodge the mujahideen. Millions of dollars worth of arms and narcotics were sent to the Taliban through smugglers." However, the Americans did not expect the Taliban to gain military success so quickly. They were greatly surprised when the Taliban started capturing other provinces after taking on Kabul.

What could America gain by assisting the Taliban? *The Herald* wrote in this regard: "Over the last few years, there has been speculation about a US-UK nexus in the politics of oil pipelines in Central Asia and the Caucasus region. The ISI is being used as a catalyst in this scheme. Says Michael Chossudovsky, professor of Economics at the University of Ottawa: 'In a cruel irony, while the Islamic jihad – featured by the Bush administration as a "threat to America" – is blamed for the terrorist assaults on the World Trade Centre and the Pentagon, these same Islamic organisations constitute a key instrument of US military-intelligence operations in the Balkans and the former Soviet Union.'

"Like the Taliban, the Chechen and Central Asian militants have been trained and bank-rolled by the ISI and through them the Anglo-American oil conglomerates have sought to control pipeline corridors out of the Caspian sea basin. These conglomerates are indirect beneficiaries of the war in Chechnya. In addition, the Afghan drug trade has been funding both the Bosnian Muslim Army and the Kosovo Liberation Army, two instruments of American strategic interests in the Balkans. In other words, says Chossudovsky; 'backed by the ISI, which is in turn controlled by the CIA, the Taliban Islamic State has largely been serving American geopolitical interests'."

11 September 2001 (9/11)

A conflict of interests developed between America and Pakistan's ISI regarding assistance to the Taliban when Osama bin Laden and his associates made Afghanistan their base of operations. It is believed by many knowledgeable Pakistanis that the ISI was using the al-Qaida network all over the world for its own ends. Those included getting funds from private welfare organisations and wealthy individuals, mainly oil money, for the Taliban Government and also meeting certain goals concerning the external affairs of Pakistan, the details of which remain secret. Although the ISI had a very strong influence over the Taliban Government and al-Qaida, it is fairly certain that Osama bin Laden did not confide in them about the intended atrocities of 9/11. It may also be the case that Osama bin Laden's al-Qaida did not confide fully their intentions in New York to the Taliban leadership because the result of such atrocities against American civilians would be very predictable, bearing in mind the earlier American cruise missile attacks on suspected al-Qaida bases in Afghanistan. Some evidence of this lack of knowledge can be assumed from Mullah Omar's offer to extradite Osama bin Laden to a neutral country if proof of his guilt was forthcoming. Impractical, inadequate, half-hearted or otherwise, this offer suggests the Afghan leadership may know exactly what al-Qaida were planning to do in America in September 2001.

Pakistan's interest in Taliban ruled Afghanistan was much more geopolitical than ideological and its support for the mujahideen was continued as an instrument with which to drive the Indians out of Kashmir, to be annexed by Pakistan. Only the mandarins of the Pakistan State can reveal the intended game plan but Pakistan's leadership had no great difficulty in suddenly withdrawing support for the Taliban and the mujahideen immediately after 9/11. Ideology could not bind Pakistan with Islamic fundamentalism and Pakistan's geopolitical interests could be temporarily shelved or redesigned as circumstances dictated.

Confirming this view, Jessica Stern wrote in the American *Foreign Affairs* magazine' in December 2001: "Pakistan has two reasons to support the so-called mujahideen. First, the Pakistani military is determined to pay India back for allegedly fomenting separatism in what was once East Pakistan and which in 1971 became Bangladesh. Second, India dwarfs Pakistan in population, economic strength, and military might. In 1998 India spent about two per cent of its $469 billion GDP on defence, including an active armed force of more than 1.1 million personnel. In the same year, Pakistan spent about five per cent of its $61 billion GDP on defence, yielding an active armed force only half the size of India's. The US government estimates that India has 400,000 troops in Indian-held Kashmir – a force more than two thirds as large as Pakistan's entire active army. The Pakistani government thus supports the irregulars as a relatively cheap way to keep Indian forces tied down."

Apart from this major consideration, Pakistan had access to a huge area in Afghanistan from where, according to some sources, the ISI and the Pakistan Army could develop their aims and objectives including, possibly, nuclear experiments, missile testing, and exercises in military training and technology development.

However, 9/11 changed everything. Because of the absence of any strong or widespread ideological relationship between the Taliban and the mujahideen on one side and Pakistan's military and civil establishment on the other, Pakistan wasted no time in withdrawing from the Taliban and prosecuting a crackdown on the mujahideen. As previously, when General Zia allowed Pakistan to become an American instrument in defeating the Soviet Union in Afghanistan in 1979, after 9/11, geopolitical pragmatism being the only sensible course of action, Pakistan again allowed itself to become an instrument of America against the Taliban and the mujahideen and it provided all forms of significant logistical support to America in this connection. After all, what were the alternatives? A cold war with America like the one that ruined the Soviet Union which possessed massive industrial and technological resources? No serious statesman, or religious leader, would cause their people to suffer the international hostility, the sabotages, the poverty and deprivations, and the ultimate inward collapse of a nation that would result from another cold-war embargo. The likelihood of war developing from such a Pakistani confrontation with America and most of the other nations on earth would be very strong and, if the jihadis had their way, possibly even a nuclear war. Pakistan could not morally protect and support a group of misguided fanatics who deliberately planned and carried out an indiscriminate slaughter of more than three thousand men, women and children, of all faiths and cultures from all over the world.

As a civilised nation, Pakistan had only one option in those circumstances. It made itself available to the American military machine. According to a jihadi magazine: "Pakistan supported the allied forces in a big way. As many as 57,800 war flights were flown from the Pakistani land. Two thirds of the airbases and secure sea docks were under the occupation of the allied forces. 420 foreign terrorists were arrested. The military kept a watch on bases and places used by the Americans. Nobody from the allied forces ever received any injury (in Pakistan)."

The following was said in a report issued by the American Central Command. "Pakistan provided five airports and airbases to America. This apart, it gave permission to land on any of its airports or bases in times of emergency. The American planes were also provided with approximately forty thousand litres of oil. Air passage from Pakistan to Afghanistan was also provided. In this way, Pakistan offered two-thirds of its air facilities to America to be used by its airmen and army. As a result of this, Pakistan had to divert its own civil and army aviation. New routes had to be set for commercial flights. The Pakistani Navy had to provide space for American ships in its docks and helped them disembark the forces. It had to make adjustments to its own programs to facilitate the American and allied forces. According to the American *Marine Corps Gazette* (2002), the operation to disembark allied forces at Pasni was greater than the one in Korea fifty years earlier. 8,000 navy personnel, 330 vehicles and 1350 tonnes of material were landed there. The number of applications sent for this was 2160, completed operations 2008, operations underway 152. As many as 99 police raids were carried out in Pakistan after 11 September. 420 foreigners were arrested, 332 were handed over to America. 134 persons were sent back to their respective countries, 38 were let off, and 16 persons are still under interrogation in Pakistan. Included among the most wanted foreigners who were arrested was al-Qaida's Abu Zubaida and Ramzi bin Shaiba. They were arrested and handed over by Pakistani agencies. Abu Zubaida was the second important person in the al-Qaida rank. Ramzi bin Shaiba was a suspect in the 11 September attack."

These are the statistics issued by a jihadi organisation, Jamiat al-Furqan, which they had published in their organ called *Tadbeer-e-Nau* (June 2003).

Efforts at Rapprochement

After the post-9/11 telephone call from President Bush to President Musharraf, Pakistan tried to find a peaceful solution to the problem. It sent the ISI chief General Mehmood with a delegation of ulema (Islamic scholars) to Afghanistan so that Mullah Omar and other Taliban leaders could be persuaded to extradite Osama bin Laden to America. This contingent flew to Afghanistan on 16 September 2001 but came back disappointed two days later. According to Pakistani government sources, Mullah Omar put forward three conditions for the handover of Osama bin Laden: (1) that they would hand him over to a neutral country where proceedings against him would be carried out with justice (2) that the UN would lift sanctions against Afghanistan, and (3) that the world community would come forward to make good the losses caused by the war and would reconstruct the concerned nations.

This offer was made by the Taliban leadership to other mediators but the ulema who were a part of the delegation asserted that they did not even mention the handing over of Osama to America. A similar report was also published in the Pro-Taliban jihadi weekly, *Zarb-e-Momin* (5 October 2001): "The Shaikhul Hadeeth of Darul Uloom Haqqania, Akora Khatak and the beloved leader of the mujahideen, Maulana Dr Sher Ali Shah has claimed that when our delegation reached Kandahar, we made Justice Mufti Mohammad Taqi Usmani our spokesperson. We spoke to Mullah Omar for three to four hours. His faith is so strong that it will weigh heavier than those of our faiths put together. He was repeatedly reciting an ayah (prayer) from the holy Koran. He said that America wants to destroy Afghanistan entirely and if we yield even a little, Islam shall be defeated. About the release of eight Christian missionaries he said that he would have no objection if the court chose to release them. Seeing his firm faith, Maulana Salimullah Khan's eyes moistened and all the ulema in our party were deeply moved. Maulana Mufti Taqi Usmani said then that these are the people of the first centuries. Dr Sher Ali Shah said that a poisonous propaganda was started by the print and electronic media in Pakistan and other countries after our meeting that the ulema had asked Mullah Omar to handover Osama to America although nothing like this was ever said."

General Mehmood might have a different account but, in any case, the effort on the part of Pakistan to bring about a rapprochement was unsuccessful. *Asia Times* wrote in its edition of 30 August 2003: "It is an open secret that this delegation that had gone to consult the Taliban, had gone there to issue instructions as to how best they could preserve their arms and how could they be saved in the event of an American bombardment. Sources in five or six jihadi organisations assert that Pakistan wished to buy time by sending this delegation so that it could transfer its military set-up back into Pakistan safely. America had co-operated in this effort."

The New Role of the ISI

Apart from the report in the *Asia Times* that Pakistan had actually bought time to retrieve its arms, material and personnel by sending this delegation, secret service sources also claim that, even though they had provided correct information about Taliban deployment and locations to the Allied forces, some officials of the ISI had also played a role in providing information and safe passage to the Taliban. It is not known, however, whether they did so in their individual capacity or if they were given instructions to do so. It is understandable that many ISI officers had developed sympathies and friendships for their Taliban and mujahideen proteges over many years and suffered a conflict of loyalties when the Pakistan Government switched sides.

Regardless of orders from above, the ISI maintained a soft attitude towards the Taliban in any case. According to an official of the ISI, when the Americans bombed Kunduz, he wept bitterly. He said: "We could not have done anything at that point of time although those of our associates and officers who had done their stint with the ISI in Afghanistan supported the Taliban fully."

The Roots of Al-Qaida

Pakistan had become so deeply involved in the international jihad movement before 9/11 that, when it wanted to extricate itself from involvements after those atrocities, the 'establishment' did not fully appreciate how deep its own mujahideen roots had really gone. For example, when America put a ban on an Islamic defence organisation called the Rabita Trust in October 2001 and impounded its properties on a charge of aiding and abetting Osama bin Laden and al-Qaida, it came to light that President Musharraf was also the President of this trust.

On 14 October 2001, America demanded that President Musharraf should disassociate himself from this trust. Amazingly, President Musharraf did not even know he was a patron of the Rabita Trust! He denied any association immediately. Later investigations, however, showed that the trust was created in 1988 during the regime of General Zia (Ziaul Haq) and he was its founder and chairperson. The stated aims of the trust was to help Pakistanis who were coming back home from newly independent Bangladesh. According to the rules and regulations of the trust the chief of the Pakistan government had to be its patron and all presidents from Zia onwards had been its patrons.

The link between the Rabita Trust and al-Qaida was established when an important Libyan member of al-Qaida, Abdur Rahman was killed in Peshawar on 14 August 2003 by Pakistani law-enforcement agents. A document recovered from his house showed how the al-Qaida network operated in Pakistan. The more significant point in this connection was that it transpired that he was the son-in-law of the Rabita Trust Chairman, Abdul Hai, a former bureaucrat who had served as Deputy Secretary in Pakistan's Defence Ministry from 1973 to 1976.

Not only has al-Qaida and Osama bin Laden been involved in foreign actions but he has also been playing a role in the making and undermining of governments in Pakistan. Osama collected financial resources used to help to topple the Benazir Bhutto Government and he also played a part in bringing down the Nawaz Shareef Government. Former Home Minister, General Nasirullah Babur, in an interview in the Urdu *Daily Express* (Lahore: 11 January 2004), spoke in this connection: Q: "Benazir Bhutto has alleged that Osama bin Laden gave money to topple her government. What do you have to say on this matter?"

Nasirullah Babur replied: "The anti-narcotics force raided a spot in Khyber Agency and photographs of Osama were recovered from there. I had to say that the money raised from this narcotics business was being spent against the Benazir government. Nawaz Shareef had not spent a single paisa of his own. Osama and his associates were against the Benazir Government also because they thought that any governance provided by a woman was illegitimate."

The weekly *Nida-e-Millat* of 21 August 2001, published an answer to a question as to whether the

Pakistan Government would be unstable if Osama was killed. The answer was given by Maulana Samiul Haq who was quite close to Osama: "The government had planned to damage relations between Pakistan and the Taliban. A pact was reached in Washington on Kashmir and Kargil. That government of Nawaz Shareef had to go."

Did the ISI Play a Double Game?

In the post-9/11 phase and after the attack by American and allied forces on Afghanistan, western media published regular reports claiming that the ISI was still supporting the Taliban and that the agency had not provided accurate information to America regarding Taliban addresses. The American Government, however, broadcast differently and President Bush publicly stated his appreciation of the assistance received from General Musharraf.

How was it possible for an organisation such as the ISI, that had fomented and led the jihad for twenty-two years, take such a U-turn so quickly? America had played a very important role in making the ISI into a stable and effective instrument for the recruitment and running of a massive mujahideen force during the cold war. Could the ISI then be expected to abandon its original aims and objectives so soon? Doubtless, it needed time to adjust to the new policy being pursued by Pakistan's rulers. And those ISI people, probably the majority, who were committed to the previous policy of sponsorship and support for jihad, along with the ideological sympathies which inevitably 'rubbed off' over the decades, needed time to adjust. Many of the leading elements in the ISI were not sure how Pakistan could join the American camp against terrorism without admitting pure hypocrisy. However, pragmatism easily triumphed over ideology because these same elements were also very anxious to ensure that America did not make Pakistan its next target for cruise missiles and B52 bombers, possible based in an American allied India.

Two indicators of political thinking in Pakistan after 9/11 can be extracted from a popular pro-jihadi magazine and from a world news service report: "Pakistan was included in the list of 'possibly terrorist' countries apart from those countries actually denounced as terrorist. It was kept under a close watch. This amounted to keeping an eye on the activities and plans of the ISI. The Americans, rightly or wrongly, began to see the face of the ISI in several hostile activities; the hijacking of aeroplanes, rebellions within Afghanistan, the power of the Taliban, the al-Qaida network, the oppositional movements of Hamas, Palestinian suicide attacks, bombings in Srinagar and such other happenings. It is said that the CIA and the FBI had collected evidence of their suspicions but decided not to use it immediately, rather to wait for another more appropriate occasion. It was during this time that America declared some jihadi organisations, who were just establishing their base camps, as terrorists and put a ban on them. However, nothing was said against their supporters. The Americans got a good opportunity after 9/11. They demanded that the Pakistan Government put a check on the ISI and they decided to break its network. The result was that the ISI, without which nothing could happen in Afghanistan during the previous twenty years, was routed out of Afghanistan in three months and it reached such a state that its well-wishers had no space for themselves there. The policy planners know that this has to happen in Srinagar after Kabul. Ways and means are being found so that a retreat with some respect would be possible. Now the question is being raised as to how Pakistan became a haven for jihadi forces? Who is responsible for all this? The new policy makers of the ISI have to answer these questions. Those answers are being prepared. In the first phase, officials, starting from the chief to the lower ranks were compulsorily retired or suspended. In the second phase, announcements for disassociation with jihadi organisations were made. In the third phase, action shall be taken against those policy makers who remained in power for the period 1979 to 2002." (The weekly *Friday Special*, Karachi, 1 March 2002)

A well-known international news agency published an interview with a senior officer of the ISI in January 2004 which is interesting for its strategic and ideological revelations. The report explained that conditions were imposed by the ISI. "'Come alone. No names revealed, No tape recorders, no mobile phones and definitely no cameras.' After giving these rules, the Pakistani bureaucrat chuckled as he explained how to find the Inter-Services Intelligence Directorate (ISI). 'Everyone knows it. It has got high red walls and a black gate that is never open.'

"Like any secret service, the ISI is allergic to too

much light. Down the years, coups and clandestine wars have been plotted from within its largely windowless inner sanctum on Islamabad's Zero Point Roadway. But, in a rare briefing for a foreign journalist, a senior ISI official sought to set right the agency's appalling image as the former friends of al-Qaida and enemy of democracy.

"'People who thought this was a fundamentalist army were very mistaken,' said the urbane uniformed officer recalling a decade of estrangement with the United States. In the 1980s, the ISI was buddies with the CIA in helping the mujahideen, including Osama bin Laden, drive the Soviet Union's Red Army out of Afghanistan. Then it soured as Pakistan pursued nuclear arms and became more deeply involved with the Taliban and, according to diplomats, other shadowy Islamist groups. The ISI officer, an avowedly moderate Muslim, said his agency only kept company with the likes of the Taliban for strategic reasons, never ideological ones.

"'This person did not believe in theocracy,' he told Reuters, raising his arm reverentially toward a portrait of the founder of Pakistan, Mohammad Ali Jinnah. 'He wanted a progressive Muslim nation and had great faith in adopting democratic traditions.'

Jinnah would be disappointed. Generals have ruled for most of Pakistan's fifty-six years since independence and each of Pakistan's first three democratically elected prime ministers learned to fear the ISI.

"'There's no Western intelligence agency like the ISI. The nearest comparison is the KGB.' remarked one Islamabad-based western diplomat, referring to the ruthless Soviet-era secret police agency.

"Reform: President General Pervez Musharraf is seeking an image makeover for an army saddled with a reputation for religious zealotry since the Islamisation of the armed forces by another President, the late General Ziaul Haq, more than twenty years ago.

"One army officer, in a career-damning move, dubbed the ISI, 'the invisible soldiers of Islam.' Present and former spy masters say there are no such cabals, stressing military officers can serve a one-time only three-year attachments in the ISI and discipline is rigorous. Any rogue elements, they say, among the ISI's thousands of personnel amount to no more than a handful of individuals.

"But two assassination attempts on Musharraf last month raised questions about the depth of loyalty in an army whose motto is, 'Jihad is the Way of Islam.' Musharraf dismisses those doubts, saying discipline is more powerful than any dissent engendered by his decision to join the US led war on terror in 2001.

"Under pressure from Washington after the 11 September attacks on the United States, Musharraf withdrew support for Afghanistan's Taliban after eight years of backing the ultra-fundamentalist regime that gave refuge to al-Qaida.

"As the first US bombs fell on Afghanistan, Musharraf replaced his ISI chief. The new man is Lt. Gen. Ehsanul Haq who shares Musharraf's more progressive outlook. General Haq purged around fifteen ISI officers.

"'Within six months General Haq didn't have anyone who could have any contacts or linkages with the Taliban,' the ISI officer recalled.

"Musharraf has made enemies. In the eyes of some militants, he has compounded the sin of selling out the Taliban and al-Qaida by sending peace feelers to India.

"Retd General Mirza Aslam Beg, the army chief during the 1980s predicted jihadis will wage war in Kashmir whatever Islamabad and New Delhi decide, just as Palestinians do regardless of Egypt and Jordan's peace with Israel. These (peace) talks can be sabotaged any time, sure. Musharraf has selectively banned some radical Islamists militant groups. Diplomats say these same militants, some of whom shared Afghan training camps with al-Qaida, were encouraged for years by the country's political and military establishment as they ran covert operations in both Afghanistan and India." (Reuters, 7 January 2004)

Fundamentalists in the Army and the ISI

Apart from what the Reuters report has to say, it is true that the jihadi culture has greatly influenced Pakistani society and the army is an integral part of that society. As the modern jihadi culture was created, nurtured and groomed in Pakistan, its effect on the many senior people involved in that process, coupled with the massive public support which was state sponsored, should not be underestimated. The psychological trauma involved in changing sides cannot easily be washed off.

A member of a secret service department who was reluctantly involved in an operation against al-Qaida in Lahore said that he had no alternative and had to carry out his orders, but his sympathies lay with jihad and the jihadis. Under these sorts of circumstances, it is understandable that Military Intelligence (MI) was given a new role to play and several areas of responsibility formerly the prerogative of the ISI were entrusted to it.

The jihadis have many supporters in Pakistan's army and secret services. It is extremely unlikely that none of them would be 'helping out' their former friends and allies. Many examples of this will appear in the following chapters. An important report in this connection was published in *Asia Times* of 30 August 2003 according to which the FBI were given permission to interrogate army personnel anywhere and at any time regarding their connections with the jihadi network. *Asia Times* states that, in the first phase of the FBIs extra-jurisdictional authority, Lt. General Khalid Abbasi, Adjutant and Quarter Master posted to Kohat in Frontier Province, has been taken into custody.

The Daily Times also published a report on 31 August 2003 claiming that twelve lower-ranking officers of the Pakistan Army along with some non-commissioned officers have also been detained. However, the army's Inter-Services Public Relations branch (ISPR) said in its statement about the matter that the number was only 'three or four' and that they had been taken into custody only to establish if they actually had any relations with extremist organisations.

The report published in *Asia Times* also brought to light the fact that the FBI had also been given permission to open and staff small units in the operations offices of the ISI to monitor the directorates workers. According to the report the FBI discovered, by electronic bugging devices, that the Pakistan Army has been ineffective in stopping some ISI operatives from helping the jihadi network and that the ISI has been in constant touch with the Hizb-e-Islami commanders of Gulbaden Hikmetyar. Commenting on this, the report said: "The arrest of Pakistani military officers possibly linked to former Taliban and former al-Qaida operatives just before the second anniversary of the 11 September terrorist attacks are the first visible signs of latent support for extremists within the country's military. The officers hailed mostly from the Northwest Frontier Province, a stronghold of Pakistan's religious parties that are sympathetic to the Taliban and al-Qaida. These parties have led a movement to force Pervez Musharraf to give up either his presidency or the post of army chief. President Musharraf faces a credible threat from Islamic extremists and pockets of their supporters within the army. A high level military officer privately admits there have been three assassination attempts by suspected Islamic militants against Musharraf since Pakistan became a US ally in the war against terrorism. One Western diplomat in Pakistan said: 'The arrests show a glimpse of the dark side of the ISI (Inter-Services Intelligence) and the Pakistan army.'"

No doubt, President Musharraf and his secularly pragmatic colleagues are under threat from some pro-jihad elements within the establishment but the geopolitical reality is such that the new anti-terrorist policy of the current Pakistan leadership is an imperative for the future well-being of the people and the country simply because the alternatives would be disastrous.

Musharraf's New Agenda

After deposing Nawaz Shareef and his government and re-establishing military rule in Pakistan, President Musharraf started appointing religious people in the army and the administration. In this way, he was favouring Islamic militants and jihadi organisations. His U-turn after 9/11 changed everything for good. He drove backwards and emerged with a reputation for being a 'deft driver'.

President Bush eulogizes Musharraf and issued statements of appreciation on him. However, some sections of the American administration still have their doubts about him and these may be gauged from the Executive Summary of America regarding Pakistan: "In the wake of 11 September, bilateral relations have dramatically improved and Pakistan has become a valued partner in the war on terrorism. But, as in the past, US and Pakistani policies only partially coincide. US interests in pursuing the war on terrorism conflicts with Pakistan's continued support for Islamist terrorists engaged in 'jihad' against India in the disputed territory of Kashmir. (Pakistan considers many of these militants to be 'freedom fighters' and Pakistan's failure to prevent pro-Taliban elements from using the Pashtun tribal areas as a base to attack Afghanistan. Islamabad's dissatisfaction with the status quo in Kashmir continues to fuel dangerously high tensions with India (with which the United States is seeking better relations) and has caused concern about reported nuclear commerce with North Korea. America has a major stake in friendly and long-term ties with Pakistan. A positive relationship, however, will be difficult to sustain unless Islamabad firmly turns its back on terrorist group and plays by non-proliferation rules. In his seminal speech of 12 January 2002, President Pervez Musharraf said that he wanted to make Pakistan 'a modern, progressive, and dynamic state.' Achieving this laudable goal will not be easy given the country's unstable political institutions, its weak economic and social development, and the uncertain commitment of its military leadership to reform. The Task Force, at this juncture, believes that Pakistan can pursue the reform agenda; supporting this effort should be the principal aim of US policy over the medium term. Washington should, however, adopt a much more nuanced approach than that followed by the Bush administration.

"In the economic and security assistance arena, the United States should:

- Obtain early congressional approval for a five year, $3 billion assistance package, but the package should be revised so that two-thirds ($400 million annually) is allocated for economic development and one-third ($200 million annually) for security assistance, instead of the fifty-fifty division proposed by the executive branch.
- Conditional release of aid above a base line level ($1.5 billion over five years or $200 million of

economic assistance and $100 million of security assistance annually) on Pakistan's progress in implementation of a political, economic and social reform agenda: its cooperation in the war on terrorism and its prevention of leakage of sensitive nuclear technology and material.

- Make education the principal focus of US assistance, with high priority also for projects to aid Pashtun areas.
- Boost economic and technical support for institutions for which good government rests – the courts, parliament, police, democratic political parties, and revenue collection.
- Continue to use appropriated funds to buy back Pakistan's official debt to the United states and
- Ease restrictions on Pakistani textile imports into the United States and avoid new barriers after the multifibre agreement comes into effect in 2005.

"To promote democracy, the United States should:

- Urge publicly as well as privately an enhanced civilian and a reduced army role in governance.
- Oppose continued involvement of the Inter-Services Intelligence Directorate (ISI) in the electoral process and
- Provide increased assistance in bolstering civil society.

"To promote regional stability, the United States should:

- Press President Musharraf to make good on his pledge to stop infiltration across the line of control

(LoC, the de facto border between Indian administered and Pakistani administered parts of Kashmir) permanently;

- Press Musharraf not permit the use of Pakistani territory as a base for neo-Taliban attacks on Afghanistan and
- Make clear that Pakistan's failure to do a better job of preventing the use of its territory by terrorists will reduce US assistance levels."

Apparently, President Musharraf is following this agenda but he has his own agenda as well. This is proving beneficial politically and economically to Pakistan as well as helping him personally.

1. After 9/11, President Musharraf was successful in convincing the world that Pakistan is an important party in the war against terrorism and that this war cannot be fought without its help. That is why Pakistan must be helped in every way.

2. The jihadi network is very strong in Pakistan and has links with the worldwide terrorist network. Pakistan's policies and the lives of its leaders are under threat from them.

3. The influential Pakistani religio-political body called Majlis-e-Ittehad has become a challenge to him and are against his reform agenda and thereby against American interests even though Muttahida Majlis-e-Amal (a powerful alliance of six religious parties with 64 seats in the National assembly) has emerged as his major ally.

4. America has no options in Pakistan apart from his administration and if he is not there the American

agenda in Pakistan will suffer. In order to maintain this impression, he has taken legal steps (by constitutional amendment) to keep Benazir Bhutto and Nawaz Shareef outside the country so that they may not return to their homeland to become rivals. If they do choose to return, they will face charges of corruption against them. Further, there is no one in the army as enlightened as him who would implement this agenda. Under such circumstances, America can have no options in Pakistan except Musharraf.

5. The nuclear program of Pakistan is not secure. If Muttahida Majlis-e-Amal, which is growing in influence in the country, comes into power, these weapons could become a threat to India and America, or the technology might be passed on to some other country.

The following chapters discuss conditions in Pakistan after 9/11, Pakistan's role in the modern jihad, the jihadi background of the ISI and fundamentalists in the army, and the political successes of Muttahida Majlis-e-Amal. They will also take into consideration: (a) whether or not President Musharraf can keep to his stated agenda; (b) how many of the claimed dangers to that agenda are real and how many are imagined; (c) how sincere he is in helping to quell al-Qaida, and to what extent the army and the ISI may be obstructive in this regard.

Chapter 2

JIHADIS UNDER FIRE

It was late at night on 21 December 2000 when President Pervez Musharraf was approached by the country's intelligence supremo who wished to discuss a matter of grave urgency. It transpired that Pakistani intelligence had picked up credible signals from across the border that the Indian Air Force was planning a major retaliatory strike, possibly in Azad (Free) Kashmir in response to a terrorist attack. Pakistan was in touch with Washington minutes later and what followed was a flurry of night-long diplomatic activity that ultimately convinced India to back off. A major war, if not a catastrophe of epic scale, had been averted in the subcontinent.

The Jihadi Attack on the Indian Parliament

The Herald in January 2002 reported: "On 13 December 2000, suicide attackers hit the Indian parliament. Jaish-e-Mohammad, a Pakistan based jihadi group, claimed responsibility although, later, under Pakistani government pressure, one of their spokesmen denied any involvement by this group. Nevertheless, this terrorist attack left the peace of the South Asian region in jeopardy. India was outraged and ready for war.

"After the 9/11 outrage one year later, Pakistan joined the international coalition to curb terrorism. India continuously accused Pakistan of patronising and encouraging those militant organisations which were aiding and abetting terrorist activities in Indian Kashmir and in India itself. This incident (the Indian Parliament attack) provided grounds for India to move its troops up to the borders of Pakistan. In these circumstances the government of Pakistan made a formal decision not to let any jihadi group operate against India from anywhere in Pakistan. To achieve this end, it was decided that senior security officers would further increase their various contacts with the jihadi leadership to convince them that their activities were not in the best interests of Pakistan.

"A series of measures aimed at eliminating the activities of jihadi groups were discussed at a top-level meeting held in December 2001 under General Mohammad Aziz Khan, the Chairman of the Joint Chiefs of Staff Committee. Besides General Khan, Vice Chief of the Army Staff, General Mohammad Yusuf, Chief of the Air Staff, Air Chief Marshal Mushif AU Mir, Chief of the Naval Staff, Admiral Abdul Aziz Mirza, and the heads of the intelligence services also attended the meeting. The meeting was called to make key strategic recommendations to President Musharraf on the geopolitical situation in the region with particular reference to the massive build-up of Indian troops on Pakistan's borders.

"General Aziz Khan, who had some experience of dealing with religious groups during his tenure at the ISI, was now playing a leading role in the government's decision-making on military and strategic affairs. He was also actively involved in matters relating to US-Pakistan co-operation in the war against terrorism. Soon after his December meeting with the other heads of services, General Khan made a brief visit to US troops at Jacobabad and US General Richard Meyers flew especially to Rawalpindi in mid-December 2001 to have an in-depth discussion with him.

"The Pakistan Government, having taken a formal decision to ban the activities of all jihadi groups, meant that its officials would maintain emphatically that the decision was in line with the country's security interests. However, continued Indian accusations against Pakistan-based jihadi groups were actually forcing Pakistani officials not to directly confront any of the jihadi groups as that could be interpreted as a policy taken under Indian pressure. 'Not only the General Pervez administration but no Pakistani government would like to be seen as succumbing to Indian pressure,' observed a senior Pakistani official. 'As a matter of fact, the Indian statements had undermined our resolve to launch a crackdown against the extremists groups in Pakistan.'"

The December meeting headed by General Khan deliberated on the possible fallout from a confrontation between Pakistan's government agencies and the extremist groups, particularly Jaish-e-Mohammad and Lashkar-e-Taiba who were singled out in the more widely publicised Indian accusations. President Bush appeared to have joined India against Jaish-e-Mohammad and Lashkar-e-Taiba when he asked

President Musharraf to take action against both of these groups because they were included in the US list of extremist organisations. Another Pakistan based jihadi group, Harkat-ul-Mujahideen, had been on the US list of terrorist organisations since October 2001 and was charged with sending mujahideen fighters to Afghanistan to join al-Qaida and Taliban groups.

The News (Lahore) in its edition of 24 December 2001 had indicated that any efforts of Pakistan's military government to root out jihadi groups might only have a superficial success because almost all of the groups which were likely to be targeted had already changed their names and decentralised their operations into smaller cells. They had 'gone underground'.

While President Musharraf was trying to deal decisively with the religious extremist groups at home, his government was going an extra mile to impress upon the international community that Pakistani agencies had absolutely no role in the alleged activities of some Pakistani groups in Indian cities. *The News* quoted a Pakistani official in this connection. "If Americans, French, and British can join al-Qaida, no one should be surprised to see some Pakistanis confronting Indians, but it does not mean that our government has sent them to bomb places in India." Despite this official denial, the monthly *The Newsline* (Karachi, June 2002), quoting a jihadi leader, reported that the ISI was continuously engaged with the jihadi groups to convince them that their militant operations in Kashmir should be minimised. *The Newsline* wrote: "The atmosphere in the room was grim. A sense of unease gripped the meeting as a senior ISI officer told the leaders of various jihadi groups assembled there that the launching of fighters across the line of control had to be stopped. 'We don't have a choice in the prevailing situation. There is tremendous pressure on Pakistan,' he was reported as saying. The meeting ended on a bitter note and the jihadi leaders left disgruntled, declining the officer's invitation to join him for a meal. 'Everyone was dejected by Pakistan's turn around,' said a participant."

A jihadi leader later told this writer that the ISI had guaranteed that small-scale operations would be allowed once the situation became normal. In order to control the jihadi actions and provocations against Indian-held Kashmir, the ISI and the army had planned to engage them in diversionary operations of the 'semi-military' kind. They were told that they were required to act as a guerilla army to hit Indian forces from behind if they attacked Pakistan. "This was the strategy to minimize the jihadi operations, otherwise there was no threat of war," a jihadi leader had said in August 2003. He also claimed that, after this decision, jihadi groups held back their mujahideen for this purpose even though this had affected their local operations.

The ISI had also put a restraint on the jihadi groups from issuing press statements about their operations and organisational activities and they were told to strictly implement this policy. According Mohammad Iqbal, a Harkat-ul-Mujahideen office worker in Kotli, a district of Azad Kashmir, the ISI had also decided that only specific news agencies would be issued with reports of mujahideen activities but in none of these news reports would the name of the organisation be mentioned. The ISI also took an important step towards restructuring the jihadi group in Kashmir. As a result of this, different jihadi organisations such as; Jaish-e-Mohammad, al-Umer Mujahideen and Jamiat-ul-Mujahideen, were merged and it was decided they would use the name of Jamiat-ul-Mujahideen in Indian-held Kashmir but they would retain their original identities in Azad Kashmir and Pakistan.

One Hizb-ul-Mujahideen activist revealed that this policy of merging various jihadi organisations was formed especially for the Pakistani groups. However, this created further divisions within them as no organisation was ready to work under any other group. Some groups had clearly objected that they would not be able to work under smaller or rival organisations. This was a delicate time for Pakistan to announce a ban on the jihadi organisations. The ISI had completed its task within the given time and all jihadi groups were ready to act according to the new demands.

This new strategy helped Pakistan to meet a major demand made by the US and other western countries. Pakistan had been stopped from using any of its areas to promote any guerrilla activity in Indian controlled Kashmir. When these developments were under way, the chief of Lashkar-e-Taiba, the militant jihadi wing of Markaz-ud-Daawa-Wal Irshad, Professor Hafiz Mohammad Saeed, called a press conference in Islamabad on 24 December 2000. He renamed the organisation from Markaz-ud-Daawa-Wal Irshad to Jamaat-ud-Daawa, and its jihadi wing, Lashkar-e-Taiba, was now restricted only to Azad Kashmir. He stepped down and the new General Council, headed by Maulana Abdul Wahid Kashmiri, took over and accepted to run Lashkar-e-Taiba.

Professor Saeed rejected the claim that the government had pressed them to take these decisions. Three days after his press conference, he was arrested and later kept under house arrest. However, although Professor Saeed denied that the government had pressed them to take these decisions, some knowledgeable sources in Islamabad were not ready to believe his claim. These sources claimed that Lashkar-e-Taiba was the most powerful Pakistan-based jihadi group which had been projecting its activities openly and, after the attack on the Indian parliament on 13 December, it was on the 'hit list' of India. The army also believed that Lashkar-e-Taiba was the only organisation capable of launching powerful protests in Pakistan after the government's decision to ban the jihadi groups.

After dealing with the jihadi groups, on 12 January 2002 President Musharraf announced a ban on certain other organisations and made a public address on television and radio. This address of his was declared a milestone in the history of Pakistan by the national and international media. In his broadcast to the nation the President talked about sectarian violence, terrorism and bigotry and expressed his resolve to create an atmosphere of tolerance and brotherhood in the country in the light of the teachings of the prophet Mohammad (peace be upon him) and the guidelines set by the Qaid-e-Azam (the Great Leader, Mohammad Ali Jinnah) and Allama Iqbal (the founders of

Pakistan).

President Musharraf said that Jaish-e-Mohammad, Lashkar-e-Taiba, Sipah-e-Sahaba, Tereek-e-Jafaria and Tanzeem-e-Nifaz-e-Shariat-i-Mohammadi were banned forthwith and added that Sunni Tehreek was put on a watch list. "No party in future will be allowed to be identified with words like Jaish, Lashkar, or Sipah," (words which refer to private armies) the President warned. He pointed out that 400 people were killed in violent activities the previous year. In his hour-long speech, he said that foreign students and teachers would have to be registered with the concerned government agencies: "And if they are found without valid documentation and permission from their respective governments by 23 March they will be deported." President Musharraf went on to say that he would soon be announcing 'speedy trial courts' to be set-up to try those who were involved in terrorism and sectarian killings. The sanctity of mosques and imambargahs would be restored and the writ of the government would be established at all costs.

The President also said that the use of loudspeakers in mosques would be limited to Friday sermons only. "And if this facility is misused, it will also be banned." He had announced. He appealed to religious leaders to preach religious tolerance and to make the country prosperous by imparting both religious and worldly education. The President repeatedly said that the civil governance had weakened and that the time had come to take serious measures to rehabilitate institutions by halting the activities of religious extremists and other criminals. Without mentioning the name of any country, the President said: "We should stop interfering in the affairs of others and stop using violence as a means to thrust our point of view on others." He said that people should convince others to change their ideas rather than use the language of threat.

He made it clear that the government of the day alone was qualified to give the call for jihad as was very much enshrined in the teachings of Islam and the prophet (peace be upon him) and that no individual or party had the right to do so. "What kind of Islam are you preaching when you go against the interests of your own Muslim brothers here or in Afghanistan; and how could the Taliban justify the killings of the Muslims of the Northern Alliance?" he asked emphatically. He declared that Pakistanis would not be allowed to carry out any territorial or subversive activities in or outside the country. He warned those foreign Muslims who were using Pakistan as their centre of activities against foreign governments: "No way, we will not tolerate this any more." He spoke categorically.

After his speech, nearly two thousand activists of different jihadi and sectarian organisations were arrested in the crackdown and hundreds of offices of banned organisations were sealed.

Challenges and New Games

President Musharraf had taken these decisions under international pressure, especially from the US and India, to avoid further tension on the borders and he successfully de-escalated the tension in the region. The jihadis were constrained from operations and Kashmiri jihadi sources confirmed that, after the President's speech, communication links between jihadi guerrilla fighters inside Indian-held Kashmir and their bases on the Pakistani side of the border had been cut off. "Many of our colleagues are stuck across the border without reinforcements and supplies," said one jihadi commander.

Tráining centres inside Azad Kashmir were also closed down. The Pakistan government's clampdown on terrorism came as hundreds of fresh guerrillas were waiting at their base camps in Azad Kashmir to cross the border. It was the time of year when large-scale infiltration usually took place. According to one jihadi commander: "The volunteers are becoming increasingly upset over the delay. They have not been informed about Pakistan's ban on their activities." But many jihadi leaders were very hopeful that these new restrictions would not be imposed on them or would not endure.

While Pakistan's military commanders were still shaping the contours of their first ever push purge of Islamic militants, the underground leadership of jihadi groups such as Jaish-e-Mohammad, Lashkar-e-Taiba and Harkat-ul-Mujahideen had altered their identities and selected new locations as bases for their future secret activities. There were many challenges and problems ahead for the government to identify and keep track of these newly 'gone underground' jihadis.

The News, an English daily paper, taking its cue from leading banned groups of Jaish and Lashkar activists the day after the President's speech, had claimed that secret conferences were under way among militant Islamic groups to cobble together a unified militant Islamic front with the aim of strengthening their cause in Indian Kashmir and Afghanistan.

According to the report, instead of recruitment through public campaigns, many jihadi groups had formed underground cells of experienced supporters who would henceforth conduct secret recruitment and fund collection activities for jihadi causes all across Pakistan. To maintain their existence, the five better known militant groups had already moved their public operations to Pakistan administered Kashmir (Azad Kashmir) where the authorities there had decided to let them operate as pro-Kashmir political freedom groups under their new names.

On the other hand, Pakistani interior ministry and other official sources were claiming that the crackdown was going very successfully and they were even trying to implement section 11 (B) of the ATA (Anti-Terrorism Act) which prohibited the activities of a proscribed organisation even if it operated under a different name. The government also reproduced certain sections of the ATA, as amended on 14 August 2001, to remind the outlawed parties that action against them would be taken under the Act. This anti-terrorism legislation had been on the statute books for many years before 9/11 but had never been rigorously enforced except by one governing political party against rivals. The mujahideen were largely unaffected by this Act until after 9/11.

The ATA allows banned parties and groups to file review petitions with the relevant authorities to appeal against the government's banning decision. Even if the banning decision was not reviewed, the party could approach the federal government for a lifting of the ban three years after the date of proscription and the government, if satisfied with the policy explanations of the party in question, could lift the ban.

The government said it could take other measures against banned organisations: (a) their offices, if any, would be sealed; (b) their assets and accounts would be frozen; (c) all literature and electronic media material would be seized; (d) the publication, printing or dissemination of press statements, press conferences, or public utterances by or on behalf of, or in support of, a proscribed organisation would be prohibited. The proscribed groups would also be required to submit accounts of their income and expenditure for their political and social activities and disclose all funding sources to those relevant authorities designated by the federal government.

Jihadis Transformed

Before committing themselves to strong official action, rare in the country's history, against militant Islamic groups, Pakistan's interior ministry had estimated that at least 50,000 religiously motivated Pakistanis trained in guerilla warfare were registered with five key militant groups in Pakistan.

When this writer asked a jihadi group leader of Harkat Zubair Bhai from Muzaffarabad, why the jihadi organisations were still frightened of the government's action against them when everything had been settled with the intelligence agencies he replied; "But we could not believe in the agencies because this is just the first step. American pressure will come on them again to do the same with us as they are doing with the Taliban." He said that there were jihadi sympathizers in the government's ranks who had cautioned them that, despite all the assurances given, the government was looking to completely eliminate the jihadi outfits, at least from Pakistan. "So we asked our mujahideen to go into hiding and not to come out until favourable circumstances were created," he said.

The News on 13 January had quoted a 22-year-old former Karachi University student who gave his name as Abu Hafsa. "We have learnt lessons from the blunders made by al-Qaida and the Taliban and they will never be repeated in Pakistan. In future, each one of our registered activists will use a cover name." Abu Hafsa said he belonged to Maulana Masud Azhar's Jaish-e-Mohammad and he had participated in five guerrilla operations against the Indian army in Baramulla and other districts in Indian Kashmir. Hafsa's parents had moved to Muzaffarabad in Pakistani Kashmir from the other side of the border about 15 years ago.

About the capability of jihadi organisations, Abu Nisar, an activist from Lashkar, told *The News* that; "In Afghanistan it was not possible, but here we use all means of communication including short messaging services on mobile phones, chatting through the internet, central messaging through bulletin boards on the net and electronic paging are some of the means that can't be tapped easily." Abu Nisar adds, "A lot of us have a separate web-based e-mail addresses. So, we don't have to communicate through fixed or mobile telephones." He says that many trained computer operatives were available to Jamaat-e-Islami backed Hizb-ul-Mujahideen and, although Pakistani intelligence services had the equipment to intercept landlines and cellphones, they lack equipment and trained manpower to tap into more modern means of communication.

These few examples of the reaction of some jihadi groups to the new anti-jihadi policies and purges being carried out by the Pakistan Government indicate the difficulty faced by the relevant authorities in trying to suppress the jihadi movement in the country. The militants have sympathisers among the military and civil establishment and, as the following text will demonstrate, they are not short of men, money or guns.

The Human Resources of the Jihadi Groups

Until 9/11, there was no restriction on Pakistani citizens taking part in jihad activities. Pakistanis of all ages and from all walks of life were participating in the jihad.

A Harkat activist reported that Mullah Omar had sent instructions that only men between twenty and fifty years of age should be recruited for the jihad. One would imagine that most of those planning to take part in the holy war would be from the militant cadres of the jihadi organisations. However, it has become patently obvious that this modern version of the David and Goliath fable has an emotive appeal across the spectrum of Pakistani society. Many people, even those who do not agree with the Taliban's obscurantist version of Islam, have found inspiration in the obdurate refusal of one of the world's poorest Muslim countries to give into the demands of the only remaining global superpower. A 16-year-old boy who had been studying for his 'O' levels at a city school branch in Karachi and whose father is a production manager with the FM-100 radio station made his way into Afghanistan. He left armed with nothing more than a mere 3500 rupees in his pocket and the vague notion of helping the Afghan people. His mother, who says she sent him off with a tearful blessing, insists that as he had no training in weapons and had been studying at a madrasa for only three months, his aim was solely to provide humanitarian assistance. He had written to his family informing them that he was at the Chaman border near Quetta in Pakistan along with a group of 300 other volunteers. Two members of the Taliban, he said, were in charge of their contingent.

A 63-year-old retired civil servant and ex-army man from Lahore, left his wife reeling with shock when he announced that he was going to join the war effort in Afghanistan. Another man, Zafar Iqbal Memon, who is in his late thirties, is also preparing to leave for Afghanistan. An erstwhile playboy turned born-again Muslim, Memon says; "Life is an amanat (something given for temporary safe keeping) from Allah and it does not matter if we sacrifice it while fighting for His cause." As for the fate of his three young children and his wife in the event of his death in Afghanistan, he simply shrugs and says; "It is God who takes care for people."

It is not only semi-educated youth who form the core support of these jihadi groups. Hundreds of educated people, including some high profile officials of the government, had also joined militant groups to fight in the jihad. A close relative of a Deputy Director of Pakistan's Federal Investigation Agency (FIA) confirmed news that the Deputy Director took leave from his office in November 2000 to join the Taliban in their battle at Kunduz. After the fall of Kunduz, the FIA official made a safe return to Pakistan and rejoined the service. In another case, a respectable Karachi businessman disclosed to *The News* that his brother, a middle ranking official in a ministry of defence organisation, took three months leave last year to secretly join Lashkar, and headed for the jihad in Indian Kashmir,

However, the ban on certain jihadi organisations brought some results in Pakistani society. Firstly, before 9/11, public schools and colleges were the main source of manpower for the jihadi organisations. After the ban, jihadi organisation activities were limited only to mosques and religious seminaries and many schoolboys were thus saved from the jihadi's influence. In March 2002, an al-Badr Mujahideen member from Lahore, Abdul Khaliq, said that after the ban very few people were joining the jihadi organisations. He also pointed out a crucially important factor, that this problem of declining recruitment applied mainly to those organisations, such as al-Badr, who did not have networks in the seminaries. But Deobandi and Ahl-e-

Hadis jihadi organisations were less affected in this regard because they have their own seminaries and deep roots in other seminaries as well. Secondly, jihadist campaigning and propaganda in the public arena has been limited by the crackdown and this has created a communications gap between the people and the jihadis.

The Financial Backbone of the Jihadi's

Financial resources was the real backbone of the jihadi organisations and the government had not done much to curb the sources of finance despite the bans and talk of asset seizures. In January 2002, one Lashkar-e-Taiba man in Muzaffarabad told this writer that before the imposition of the ban on collecting the funds from the public, Lashkar had installed 250000 fund-collecting boxes all over the country and the daily income was about 12 billion rupees from these boxes alone.

The ban on collecting funds had reduced the financial resources of these organisations but it did not affect them very much. Pakistani intelligence officials confess that it would be impossible to track down the financial assets of many militant organisation because most of them had transferred their funds into the care of legitimate business interests in Karachi, Lahore, and Peshawar. These legitimate business interests make regular contributions to militant organisations. For this reason, little or no money was in deposit in the bank accounts of Lashkar-e-Taiba, Jaish-e-Mohammad and Harkat, when the State Bank of Pakistan responded to the ban against these groups by freezing their accounts.

This is a very important factor which helps to frustrate the Anti-Terrorism Act because most of the other jihadi and militant groups have also invested their money in legitimate businesses such as; commodity trading, real estate dealing, the production of consumer goods and farming. Establishing a new madrasa or mosque is also considered a beneficial business as one Jaish worker, Akbar from Sargodha, explained how investment in new madrasa is profitable because this produces new mujahideen recruits and also generates funds through public donations.

The militant organisation Jamaat-ud-Daawa invested huge amounts in madrasas, schools, hospitals and agricultural lands. In 2002 Jamaat-ud-Daawa had invested 300 million rupees in Hyderabad Division by purchasing twenty-five plots of land to set-up their seminaries, mosques and training centres. Khalid Raja, who once worked closely with the banned Harkat organisation told *The News*: "The custodians of our money are the big Pakistani taxpayers with absolutely no record of involvement in financial or moral corruption. Foreign donations were also a major source of income for jihadi groups." According to an international Crisis Group Report: "In one year, 2002, Lashkar and Jaish collected $1.5 million in British mosques." To restrict these sources, Pakistani and American authorities made an agreement that all remittance flows of over one thousand dollars must be reported to the authorities. But jihadi groups had adopted alternative ways for the transfer of money. Hawala channel and Forex Exchange (companies like Western Union operating in Pakistan) were used in this way.

On 10 January 2004, in an effort to further restrict the flow of foreign money and curb the financial resources of the jihadi groups, the government approved an amendment to the Anti-Terrorism Act (1997) which increased the punishment for offences related to the financing of terrorism.

Armaments Equals Ornaments

Because of the jihadi culture, directed first against Indian-held Kashmir, that existed in Pakistan from the birth of the nation and its massive expansion in popularity and geographical range during the Afghan jihad, Pakistan's civil society was replete with guns and weapons. Jihadi culture refers to these weapons as 'the ornaments of all Muslims. Pakistani security officials say that supporters of key militant groups generally do not keep their weapons in Pakistan, most of their weapons being located in secret depots in the high mountains and caves of Indian Kashmir. Nevertheless, they concede that many of them keep 'small arms', such as Kalashnikov rifles, at their bases in Pakistan. But, after the bans and crackdown on the jihadi organisations, huge amounts of heavier, more powerful, weapons, including rocket launchers and explosive devices, were brought back into Pakistan and it is believed these were used in terrorist attacks on foreigners and anti-Jihadi forces in the country in recent times. Deobandi jihadi organisations were involved in most of the terrorist attacks in Pakistan during 2002 and 2003.

However, most of the Kashmir based jihadi organisations, such as Hizb-ul-Mujahideen and al-Badr Mujahideen, are still following the rules that they should not bring their weapons into Pakistan. "We were under strict instructions not to carry or use weapons anywhere in Pakistan," said one al-Badr activist. Militants attached to Islamic groups insist that the insurgency in Kashmir would remain central to their mission and they would not be interested in opening a front with the Pakistan authorities.

Nevertheless, there is no shortage of illegal weapons in Pakistan which could be used to start a civil war. Arms manufacturing is the main business in the federally administered semi-autonomous tribal areas bordering Afghanistan, especially the Afridi tribal area. The town of Dara Adamkhel in this region is a major supplier of illegal weapons but the authorities play down the significance of this source for fear of the negative publicity any revelations would generate. Estimates vary, but the country's interior ministry believes that some 1.2 million unregistered Kalashnikovs are available to various militant Islamic, political and criminal groups in Pakistan. Even more complex was the network that allowed various militant and sectarian groups to acquire even more deadly hardware and use it in different parts of the region.

Al-Qaida – Still Legal in Pakistan

Regardless of the imposition of the ban on militant organisations, some Pakistani laws actually support the jihadis and this creates difficulties for the government in its efforts to extirpate terrorism. The United Nations Resolution 1371 declared al-Qaida to be a terrorist organisation but, in Pakistan, al-Qaida is still legal and it requires new legislation, or an amendment to the law, for it to be pronounced a terrorist organisation.

This situation was confirmed by Pakistan's Supreme Court in July 2003 when it heard an appeal by the federal government to keep the Khwajas behind bars. Ahmad Jawaid Khwaja, his brother, Ahmad Nawaid Khwaja, and their sons, Mohammad Usman, Omar Karrar Khawak and Khizr Ali were picked up by the Lahore police accompanied by American law enforcement agents in connection with their links to al-Qaida. Many other Pakistanis were detained on the same charges but were released by the courts on this legal ground. When this issue was raised publicly, Federal Interior Minister, Faisal Saleh Haayat, in his press statement said that the government was seriously considering declaring al-Qaida as a terrorist organisation. But his words are still awaiting the practice.

According to one law-enforcement agency official, after the ban some two-thousand jihadis from various militant and sectarian organisations were arrested, a large number of whom had links with al-Qaida or other international terrorist networks, but most of these were freed by the courts on the grounds that al-Qaida is not a banned organisation in law.

Up to the middle of 2004 these problems still existed despite all of the government's efforts to curb terrorism. All military, civil and bureaucratic planning and action has failed to achieve the halting of jihadi activity and this creates new challenges and threats for Pakistan. The country had averted a major war with India in 2002 but, if the jihadi movement, which is the primary cause of the tensions, remains unchecked, the danger from religious terrorism could easily recreate those tensions with the possibility of a major catastrophic war despite all the positive developments in relations between India and Pakistan and the support of America.

The jihadis are still very active and are now becoming increasingly dangerous to Pakistan's civil society. The assassination attempts on the President have been followed more recently, in August 2004, by an attempt on the life of the Prime Minister designate, Shaukat Aziz, in which seven people were killed by an al-Qaida suicide bomber. Murderous attacks have also been carried out against off-duty Pakistani soldiers and civilians. Some jihadi groups now appear to be trying to start a civil war in Pakistan.

Chapter 3
THE RETURN OF THE JIHADIS

On 30 January 2002, several newspapers received a leaflet from an organisation called al-Saiqa. It declared Pakistan to be Dar-ul-Harab (the home of war) and Dar-ul-Kufr (the home of infidels) and gave a call for people to wage a jihad against Pakistan and its army.

A few days before this development, a contingent of the Frontier Constabulary were attacked while on patrol at a place called Thakot Batgram in the Frontier Province. They suffered heavy losses but were successful in capturing some of the attackers. Apart from some weapons, five or six handwritten pamphlets were also recovered from those arrested. The pamphlets were in Urdu and bore the name of al-Saiqa. The text demanded that the Pakistan government should stop interfering with the religious seminaries and deny the Americans any assistance against the jihadis with a declaration that the Islamic Mujahideen would continue their jihad against Pakistan until these demands were accepted.

No organisation called al-Saiqa had been known before this attack. Later, government law-enforcement agencies opined that these could be disaffected mujahideen fighters from various jihadi groups who had chosen to react like this because of the sudden change in government policy regarding the Taliban.

However, no report regarding the interrogations conducted with the arrested attackers was ever made public.

Since then, a Christian church was attacked in Bahawalpur and a few days later Urdu newspapers in Multan received a fax in which a new jihadi organisation called Lashkar-e-Omar claimed responsibility for this attack. Later, an attempt was made to blast the convoy of President Musharraf on 26 April 2002 in Karachi. Then followed a series of attacks: on the bus of French engineers on 8 May 2002, on the American consulate on 14 June 2002 and the dastardly killing of Daniel Pearl of the *Wall Street Journal*. Attacks on churches and Christian missionaries in Karachi, Takedar, and Murree and on the church situated in the diplomatic area in Islamabad, can be seen as ugly indicators of the terrorist history of Pakistan. Responsibility for all of these attacks was accepted by organisations involved in terrorist activities. Law-enforcement agencies considered these attacks to be reactions against Pakistan's current policy regarding the jihadis and the Taliban.

The network of religious terrorists reasserted itself with greater force after 9/11. This led to an increase in religious sectarianism and terrorism. This happened in spite of the fact that more than fifty terrorists of Lashkar-e-Jhangavi involved in religious terrorism were arrested over a two-year period in 2002 and 2003. These included some of the most ill-reputed men such as; Akram Lahori, Ishaq Malik, Qari Abdul Hai and Ata. Dangerous terrorists like Riaz Basra and Asif Ramzi were killed in various police encounters. In spite of these losses by the jihadi, as many as forty-seven bombing operations were carried out from 1 January 2003 to September 2003 in which 28 persons were killed and 110 were injured. In the Gilgit arsenal explosion case, forty-three persons were killed and seventy-three were injured. Ninety persons were killed in terrorist attacks in Quetta and two hundred rockets and shoulder-fired missiles were fired in Punjab and Baluchistan.

A report in *The Friday Times* brought to light the network of Lashkar-e-Jhangavi and its ways of operation and asserted that it would not be easy to break them: "21 Lashkar-e-Jhangavi and other militants that were hiding in Afghanistan and who the former Taliban government refused to handover to Pakistan after Islamabad gave Kabul a list of terrorists and miscreants. Top of the list was Lashkar-e-Jhangavi chief, Riaz Basra. Basra was killed in an encounter in the Punjab last year when he sneaked into Pakistan following the ouster of the Taliban government. Some others on the list, most of them wanted and carrying head money, included Basra's deputy, Zakiullah, Mohammad Ajmal alias Akram Lahori, Mohammad Aslam Muawiya, Tariq Mehmood, Shakeel Ahmed, Jawed Ahmad, Rustam Ali Khan, Mohammad Tanweer Khan, Abdul Aziz alias Katona, Ghulam Shabbir alias Fauji, Amanat Ali, Dilawar Hussain, Hafiz Mazhar Iqbal, Shabbir Ahmed, Ehsanullah, Asghar Ali, Shariq, Qari Asad, Akhter Muawiya and Qari Saifullah Akhtar, who headed Harkat-e-Jihad-e-Islami with its base in Afghanistan and was wanted for his alleged role in the unsuccessful attempt to dislodge the government of former Prime Minister Benazir Bhutto. Major General

Zahirul Islam Abbasi and Brig. Mustansir Billah were tried and convicted by a military court in the same case. Most of the accused on the list have either been killed in the police encounters or have since been captured. So far, police have arrested or detained over fifty suspects in Quetta, some of whom have confirmed the identity of the attackers after the team from Karachi put names on the faces. The Taliban government had provided shelter to a number of sectarian and jihadi militants on their soil and told Islamabad to stop pressing the point. They (the Taliban) denied that these persons had taken refuge in Afghanistan. The Pakistani government remained unconvinced but most of the sectarian criminals had to sneak back into Pakistan after the Taliban rout at the hands of the US led allied troops and the capture of Kabul by the anti-Taliban Northern Alliance. An official in Karachi told *TFT* that these terrorists would enter Pakistan, mount attacks on the Shias and indulge in other criminal activities before going back to Afghanistan. They used different entry and exit points every time and were involved in bank robberies and sectarian related killings. 'We now know that these terrorists also carried out the Bahawalpur bank robbery a couple of years ago,' he said. According to police reports, armed men had robbed the bank of rupees eight million. Says another police officer of their modus operandi: 'After entering Pakistan they would disperse to engage targets in various parts of the country as per their plan. This is why when we finally got to the leaders, Riaz Basra was killed and Aslam Muawiya arrested from the Punjab while Akram

Lahori and Qari Asad were arrested from Karachi. Police sources say that the Lashkar-e-Jhangavi factions led by Akram Lahori and Asif Ramzi have not yet lost their strength despite Lahori's arrest and Ramzi's mysterious death sometime ago in a blast at a chemical warehouse in Karachi's Korangi suburb.'"

The wave of terrorism that followed 9/11 did not emanate from Lashkar-e-Jhangavi alone. The faces of several other jihadi groups were also unveiled at that time.

Terrorist Organisations Operating in Pakistan

In the Daniel Pearl murder case, apart from Maulana Masood Azhar, the Chief of Jaish-e-Mohammad, and Mushtaq Zargar of al-Umer Mujahideen, British born Ahmad Sayeed Sheikh and others were sentenced to death. At the time of Pearl's murder Omar Sheikh was in Lahore but he was considered to be the main instigator of the murder. The relationship between Omar Sheikh and Jaish-e-Mohammad is no secret and sources in Jaish also claim that he had made financial contributions and offered his advice on the establishment of the organisation. He was also associated with the al-Qaida network According to the Lahore weekly *The Independent* of 11 September 2001, Omar Sheikh had sent $15,600 to Mohammad Ata, the main player of the 9/11 incident using the Hawala channel and this money was used in planning and preparation for the attack.

Responsibility for the attacks on President Musharraf, the French engineers and other attacks in Karachi was claimed by Harkat-ul-Mujahideen-al-Alemi. On the other hand, Jaish was held responsible for carrying out attacks in Bahawalpur, Islamabad, Murree and Takedar. Lashkar-e-Jhangavi also claimed responsibility for several other incidents. The association between several jihadi groups, their association with al-Qaida and the involvement of Ahmad Omar Sheikh in the Daniel Pearl murder case made the situation quite complex. However, there was greater clarity in the way things were taking shape after the assassination attempt on President Musharraf.

Assassination Attempts on President Musharraf

The third attempt to kill President Musharraf was made on 25 December 2003. This was more dangerous than the earlier two attacks. As a result of this latest attack, eighteen persons along with two attackers were killed and more than fifty people were injured.

Only ten days before this attack, another effort to kill the President was made by blowing up the bridge in Rawalpindi. The first attack on his life was made in Karachi on 26 April 2002 when a vehicle full of ammunition was parked on Shahrahe Faisal, the road he was supposed to take. The intention was to kill him by detonating the explosives by remote control. Mercifully, the remote control did not work. Had it worked, the effect would have been devastating with a possibly huge number of casualties. Later, three persons namely, Mohammad Irfan, Mohammad Haneef, and a man called Sharib, who were involved in the attack were arrested and sentenced to ten years of rigorous imprisonment and a fine of one-hundred thousand rupees by the Special Court set-up for the purpose of eliminating terrorism. These three were associated with Harkat-ul-Mujahideen-al-Alemi. While giving an interview to *Ghazi* (Karachi) for its February 2003 issue, the widow of Asif Ramzi, the terrorist associated with Lashkar-e-Jhangavi said, regarding the first attack: "This attack was also made by Asif and only he had planned the attack but the remote button did not work at the right time. Asif was very sad about this and kept on telling me in anger; 'It is sad, the greatest enemy of jihad is saved.'"

This confession and the punishment given to the terrorists of Harkat-ul-Mujahideen-al-Alemi surely proves that Lashkar-e-Jhangavi and Harkat are two different names for the same organisation, or they have a close working relationship. The blame for the second attack made in Rawalpindi on 15 December 2003 was also put on Harkat-ul-Mujahideen-al-Alimi while, according to the reports of security services, Harkat-ul-Mujahideen-al-Alemi was established by those people who had parted company with Harkat-ul-Jihad-ul-Islami, Harkat-ul-Mujahideen, Jaish-e-Mohammad, Jamiat-ul-Mujahideen-al-Alemi and Lashkar-e-Jhangavi. These groups had definite contacts with the al-Qaida network of Osama bin Laden. The initial reports on the second attempt on the life of President Musharraf showed that the same explosives were used there as in the bombings in Bali, Indonesia.

The Daily Times of 24 December 2003 reported that many of those involved in the November 2001 attack were from Pakistan. According to sources in the Arab media, a senior leader of the al-Jihad Islamic

Movement in Mozambique had instructed his jihadi groups to attack Pakistan embassies. This organisation had turned against Pakistan because several of its activists were killed during operations against al-Qaida in Northern Waziristan and several other important activists were captured by Pakistani forces and handed over to America. An earlier threat made against President Musharraf by Ayman al-Zawahiri, an important activist in al-Qaida, was considered as part of the background of these attacks.

Those involved in the third attack were identified. According to Sheikh Rasheed, Pakistan's Minister of Information, Kashmiri and Afghan extremists were involved in this attack. One of them was from Pakistan and the other from Afghanistan. The one from Pakistan came from Rawalakot and he had been associated with various jihadi groups at different times. He began his jihadi career with al-Jihad and received his training in the camps of Lashkar-e-Taiba and he also spent time at a camp in Afghanistan. At the end, it was said that he was associated with the Jaish. He was caught by American forces near the end of the war against the Taliban regime. Later, he was released and sent to Pakistan by the new Karzai Government of Afghanistan along with 129 other jihadis after being held for a year. A few months before this third attack on the president, he had been absolved of all charges of being involved in anti-national activities.

On 31 December 2003 two terrorists from a suburban village called Manehar Chatta of Gujranwala in Punjab were arrested. They were under suspicion of being associated with the plot to kill President

Musharraf. Before this, a preliminary report regarding the attack of 15 December on the president was given to Ashfaq Pervez Kiani, a Pakistan Army Corp Commander of Rawalpindi and which recorded, according to *The Daily Times* of 25 December 2003, that forty-five people, including some officials of law-enforcement agencies, were arrested in connection with this particular attack. After the attacks on the president, evidence came to light about contacts between the Deobandi jihadi organisations and the Taliban and al-Qaida. A new activist group of terrorists had been identified.

New Relationship Between Jihadi and Terrorist Groups

According to sources in the jihadi movement, confirmed by secret service agencies, during the last three months of 2003, the al-Qaida and Pakistani jihadi organisations formed a working group to counter the new anti-jihad policies of the Pakistan government. Its aim was to undertake actions that would compel the government to change its anti-jihad policy and to attack President Musharraf and other pro-America personalities and western interests in Pakistan. These sources confirm that many organisations, including Jaish, Lashkar, and Jamiat-ul-Ansar, offered to provide martyrs ready to sacrifice themselves for their cause.

A report published in the January 2003 issue of *The Herald* (Karachi) examines these developments. "It was a combination of sophisticated technology and sheer good luck that saved Pakistan from yet another political upheaval last December. Security officials entrusted with investigations into the two (assassination) attempts on General Pervez Musharraf within a space of 11 days are now trying to put together the pieces of what looks to be an extremely complicated jigsaw puzzle.

"Having examined the evidence recovered from the scene of the 14 December attack – five detonators, a control box and the channel leading to the explosives – investigations have succeeded in unravelling some pieces of the puzzle. Well-placed sources told *The Herald* that there is a strong possibility of the involvement of some al-Qaida operatives who may have been acting in collusion with some local militant outfits. Sources in the Pakistani intelligence network say that the 14 December attack may have been a follow-up to the threats hurled at General Musharraf by a top al-Qaida leaders a few months ago. Osama bin Laden's deputy, Dr Ayman al-Zawahiri had called upon the Pakistani security forces to topple General Musharraf for 'betraying Islam'. This was communicated via two separate messages aired by Arabian TV channels, al-Jazeera and al-Arabiya, on 10 September and 28 respectively. The two channels reported that al-Zawahiri's message was received through an anonymous phone call, possibly from Pakistan. Those investigating the December attempts believe that al-Qaida became more active in Pakistan after al-Zawahiri's message was aired.

"According to their information, one of the FBI's most wanted al-Qaida operatives, Hadi al-Iraqi, is currently operating from the North Waziristan Agency on the Pak-Afghan border along with a Pakistani named Amjad Farooqi, who is wanted for his suspected involvement in the brutal murder of American journalist Daniel Pearl. These circles believe that Hadi al-Iraqi may have travelled to several Pakistani cities, of late coming as far south as the port city of Karachi. Despite being an Arab, say these sources, Hadi speaks fluent Pushto and some Urdu, and can easily pass as a Pathan. As such, conclude these sources, Hadi may well have come down to Rawalpindi to plan the 14 December attack. Similarly, initial investigations into the two-pronged suicide attacks on General Pervez Musharraf on 25 December have hinted at the possible involvement of Brigade 313, a loose alliance of five militant organisations including; Jaish-e-Mohammad, Harkat Jihad-ul-Islami, Lashkar-e-Taiba, Lashkar-e-Jhangavi and Harkat-ul-Mujahideen-al-Alemi. The alliance came into being shortly after the US started to bomb Afghanistan in October 2001. The leadership of this alliance has pledged to target key Pakistani leaders who, in its opinion, are 'damaging the cause of jihad' in order to 'further the American agenda in Pakistan.'

"According to investigators, the two suicide bombers responsible for the 25 December attacks have been identified as Mohammad Jamil, a Jaish-e-Mohammad activist from Azad Kashmir and Hazir Sultan, a Harkat-ul-Jihad-al-Islami operative from Afghanistan. Jamil, 23, was a resident of Torah Androot in the Poonch district of Azad Kashmir. Sources claim that his identity was established after a detective rummaging through the debris came across his national identity card amidst some human remains. Jamil, say sources, had gone to Jalalabad via Torkham in January 2001 through an Afghan cloth merchant in Azad Kashmir for the purpose of acquiring military training. Afterwards, he moved to Kabul and started living in the Darul Aman area on the outskirts of the Afghan capital.

"However, Mohammad Jamil was seriously injured and eventually captured by the Northern Alliance when the latter entered Kabul after the fall of the Taliban. He was shifted to a Kabul hospital where he remained under treatment for 15 days. He was later handed over to Pakistan under an agreement between the Afghan and Pakistan governments. Jamil, along with 30 other militants, was flown to Peshawar in a military aircraft. They were taken into custody and charged with immigration offences. But after being interrogated in April 2002, Jamil was set free as nothing incriminatory was found against him.

"The second suicide bomber, Hazir Sultan, 42, was affiliated with the Harkat-ul-Jihad-al-Islami and belonged to the Panjsher Valley of Afghanistan. Intelligence agencies have arrested five close aides of Hazir Sultan all of who have identified his body. Hazir was camped in South Waziristan Agency and was apparently there during the Wana operations on 2 October. Investigators believe he had moved to Rawalpindi a few days prior to the 25 December attacks, apparently to finalize the plans of the assassination attempt.

"Following the identification of Jamil and Hazir, investigators turned their attention to other components of Brigade 313. Going through the various interrogation reports of militants arrested earlier, they started putting the picture together piece by piece. The arrested leader of Lashkar-e-Jhangavi, Akram Lahori, has revealed during interrogation that over a' hundred members of Harkat-ul-Jihad-al-Islami had taken an oath on the Koran in May 2002 to physically eliminate General Musharraf at any cost. Lahori's revelation later led to the arrest of three hard-core Harkat activists – Mohammad Imran, Mohammad Hanif and Sheikh Mohammad Ahmad – for their alleged involvement in the 26 April attack on General Musharraf in Karachi.

"A day after the 25 December attacks in Rawalpindi, security officials also arrested Maulana Masood Azhar's younger brother and the deputy chief of the defunct Jaish, Mufti Abdul Rauf, from Rawalpindi. Intelligence sources confirmed to *The Herald* that Maulana Abdul Jabbar and Maulana Abdul Rauf were being questioned to ascertain whether their factions had any links with the al-Qaida network. A manhunt has already been launched for Maulana Masood Azhar who went into hiding after the government re-banned his group in November 2003.

"Among other things intelligence agencies are trying to determine is the number of suicide bombers raised by various components of Brigade 313. In this connection, they have intensified their hunt for at least five members of Jaish-e-Mohammad and Jamaat al-Furqan suicide squads. These include; Abbas Haider of Sibi, Naim and Safir from Bhakar and Adil and Tahir of Mailsi. Five of their associates died in 2002 while carrying out suicide missions in Islamabad, Murree, and Taxila. These were among the first major suicide missions carried out by religious militants in Pakistan in the wake of Pakistan's policy shift after 9/11. Investigators now believe that suicide bombers pose the single largest threat to Pakistan's security.

"Information Minister, Sheikh Rashid Ahmad, has made several statements since 25 December regarding the possible identity of General Musharraf's would-be assassins. According to the minister, Kashmiri and Afghan militants may have come together in a bid to eliminate General Musharraf. He has also described the terrorists network as 'huge' with its 'tentacles reaching from Kashmir to Afghanistan.' Sheikh Rashid said most of these terrorists may also have linkages outside Pakistan. Of the five components of Brigade 313, at least one – Harkat-ul-Jihad-al-Islami – a purely Afghanistan-based outfit under its leader, Qari Saifullah Akhtar, fled Kandahar when the US bombing of Afghanistan began in October 2001. Harkat was initially allied to Afghan leader Nabi Mohammad but became Kandahar's most prominent militant outfit following the rise of the Taliban. In the late 1990s, Harkat was credited with providing Pakistani fighters to the Muslim militant formations fighting in Chechnya and other places in central Asia. Qari Akhtar left Kandahar to settle in Pakistan where he eventually became a member of Brigade 313."

It must be clarified here that *The Herald* report is slightly off-centre in its explanation of the composition of Brigade 313, describing it as a conglomerate of various organisations with Qari Saifullah Akhtar being presented as one who came from Kandahar to join

Brigade 313. The reality, however, is that Brigade 313 is not an alliance of various groups but is the name of the Kashmir wing of Harkat-ul-Jihad-al-Islami. Several jihadi groups could and did amalgamate to form new brigades for operations in Indian-held Kashmir but Brigade 313 was constituted purely of Harkat-ul-Jihad-al-Islami and Qari Saifullah Akhtar was included in the first contingent to go from Pakistan to join the jihad in Afghanistan. He was a founder of Harkat-ul-Jihad-al-Islami and, after the killing of Maulana Irshad Ahmad, was made the Chief of the Harkat. A separate wing of Harkat is working in Kashmir under the guidance of Maulana Muzafar but this has nothing to do with Brigade 313. According to Kashmiri jihadi sources, Ilyas Kashmiri and some 350 of his mujahideen were arrested at the Kotli militant camp in January 2004 but were released in the last week of February.

Did Mullah Omar Order Terrorist Activities in Pakistan?

Apart from al-Qaida and the Pakistani jihadi groups, Mullah Omar and Afghan jihadis are now being blamed for terrorist activities in Pakistan after 9/11. What were the actual forces behind the terrorist wave that struck Pakistan after the fall of the Taliban Government in Afghanistan? Some evidence has come to light in this regard. The most important element behind this uprising is said to be Mullah Omar who called upon jihadi groups to attack western interests in Pakistan to force its government to disengage from supporting America. Informed people in the secret services in Pakistan believe that Pakistani based jihadis acted on the instructions of Mullah Omar. Evidence collected during the interrogations of arrested terrorists bear this out. However, it is also suggested that they might only be using the name of Mullah Omar as a form of iconic, rallying, figurehead because of the admiration for him that undoubtedly exists among Islamists.

Different jihadi circles reacted in their own way when public revelations were made about their activities and leadership. Several groups started a game of mud-slinging, making accusations against each other. For example, in the 22 June issue of a magazine called *Wujood* (Karachi) that represented al-Furqan, a breakaway faction of the Jaish-e-Mohammad group, Maulana Masood Azhar was said to be the organiser of terrorist attacks in Pakistan.

The following extracts from jihadi publications throw light on the involvement of the jihadi groups in carrying out terrorist activities in Pakistan: "Maulana Masood Azhar had played a strange game with the secret services of Pakistan and the Taliban itself after 9/11. Instead of going into great details of this crucial period, only a few of those details are being given here. When the Pakistan government buckled under American pressure after 9/11, the mujahideen in Pakistan got very anxious and they started reacting sharply to this development. Making use of this opportunity Maulana Masood Azhar, on the one hand, tried to convince the Pakistani security services that the mujahideen would not act adversely and, on the other hand, sent a message to the Taliban that they should organize such activities in Pakistan so that the government would be compelled to revise its opinion about its support to America.

"The Taliban leaders met in Kandahar to discuss these matters and (the meeting) was attended by two representatives of Maulana Azhar. Maulana Azhar had already taken Mullah Nuruddin Turabi, the Taliban Minister of Justice, into confidence. Therefore, he supported the program of activities to be carried out in Pakistan. He had the support of two other ministers in this matter. Before the meeting, Maulana Azhar had told Mullah Turabi in a meeting that his influence in the Pakistan Army had considerably increased and an officer had gone to the extent of falling down on his feet and begging to let him do anything that he wanted. When these matters were reported in the meeting, Maulana Azhar was not taken too seriously; he was, rather, taken as a 'pretender'. There were important Taliban ministers like Maulavi Jalaluddin Haqqani, Mullah Obaidullah, Maulavi Abdul Kabeer and Maulavi Wakeel Ahmad Mutawakkil who were opposed to the proposals for terrorist activities in Pakistan. The Afghan Ambassador to Pakistan, Mullah Abdul Salam Zaeef was invited especially to attend this meeting. All these leaders decided against the proposed terrorist activities in Pakistan because it would weaken Pakistan. Subsequently, Maulana Azhar lost respect among the Taliban leaders and he was marginalised for his pretentious claims. Some senior leaders were aware of this condition but they preferred to maintain silence as the scenario was changing very fast. Later, Maulana Azhar made strange remarks about the Taliban. He grew so indifferent that he turned his back on those Afghan leaders with whom he made friends and sought their assistance in opposition to the other senior Afghan leaders. The talk between Maulavi Hamdullah Zahid and him is an eye-opener but it may not be proper to put it on paper. In this manner, Maulana Azhar tried to mislead the Taliban from one angle and the secret services in Pakistan from a different angle."

A jihadi magazine, *Al-Tahreer* (Lahore) edited by Tahir Ashrafi, an advisor to the Punjab Government, wrote in its issue of October 2003: "According to reliable sources, a Pakistani delegation met Mullah Omar in Kandahar during the last days of the Taliban government, and, assuring him of its complete support, said that since Pakistan was favouring America against the Afghan interest, we might answer this move together by acting against the foreigners, minorities, and the government officials. This proposal was rejected by Mullah Omar who said that he would not repeat the mistake that Pakistan has committed by aligning with America."

Sources close to the secret services are of the opinion that when the ISI chief went to Kandahar to meet Mullah Omar and came back disappointed, it was deliberated upon that Mullah Omar should now be relieved of his responsibilities and some such person should take over who might be more sympathetic to the American demands. The sources said that removing Mullah Omar could save the Taliban government and Osama bin Laden could be handed over to America. However, no suitable person to take over could be identified among the Taliban, nor did the Taliban agree to this possibility.

It is also claimed by these same sources that this proposal on the part of Pakistan was the cause of Taliban hatred of Pakistan and it is on the strength of this that the claim is made that Mullah Omar gave orders to attack American and European interests in Pakistan and keep the Pakistan government under pressure so that it would revise its stance.

The IC 814 Hijacking Case

Flight IC 814 from New Delhi to Katmandu was hijacked by five jihadis on 24 December 1999. It was first taken to Amritsar, then to Lahore and, after refuelling in Lahore, to Kandahar. On the demand of these hijackers, the Indian Government released Maulana Masood Azhar, Mushtaq Zargar, and Omar Sayeed Sheikh from Indian prisons. The details about these hijackers and the hijacking have not come fully to light so far. However, some information started surfacing after the fall of the Taliban. The mujahideen, the Taliban and, according to some reports, certain institutions of Pakistan were involved in this hijacking. In its issue of November 2003, *The Herald* wrote: "Determined to unmask the masterminds behind the hijacking, the FBI has since set-up a field office in New Delhi. The Indian Central Bureau of Investigation (CBI), meanwhile, is particularly interested in the record of messages received by Air Traffic Control in Kandahar because it suspects that the hijackers were receiving directives from Pakistani officials. Indian intelligence agencies believe that the log of incoming communiqués will expose the links between the Taliban, the hijackers and their alleged sponsors in Pakistan. During the hijacking drama, Islamabad vehemently denied its involvement and went to the extent of offering to negotiate on New Delhi's behalf. However, the fact remains that Abdur Rauf Asghar and Yousuf Azhar, the younger brother and brother-in-law respectively of Masood Azhar, were among the hijackers. Masood Azhar, whose release from a Srinagar jail was successfully demanded by the hijackers and who subsequently founded the Jaish-e-Mohammad, was soon seen leading victory processions in Pakistan.

According to well-placed intelligence sources, the CBI informed the FBI that Mutawakkil, (the negotiating Taliban minister) went back on several commitments made during negotiations with the hijackers, leaving the then Indian Foreign Minister, Jaswant Singh red-faced. The Indians also claimed that Mutawakkil was hostile during his mediation. When Jaswant Singh landed in Kandahar with Azhar, Sheikh and Zargar, the three freed prisoners, Mutawakkil assured him that the hijackers and the freed militants would be held in Afghan custody until the Indian delegation left Kandahar. However, as soon as the three Pakistani militants were handed over to the hijackers, they were provided with a vehicle which they drove away victoriously.

Some jihadi sources claim with certainty that one of the hijackers was killed during the American attack on Afghanistan, while two of them, disillusioned with the policies of Maulana Masood Azhar, joined a faction opposed to him. Now only one of his brothers is still with him.

As the scenario has changed so dramatically after 9/11, some new, and quite surprising, information may come out about this case. As of now, it is proved beyond doubt that these hijackers were associated with Pakistani jihadi organisations and they were supported by the Taliban, and possibly had the blessing of the ISI.

The Release of the Jihadis

In the crackdown on jihadi groups in Pakistan in January 2002, more than two thousand jihadis were arrested. Most of them were either low-ranking activists or were associated with sectarian groups like Sipah-e-Sahaba or Sipah-e-Mohammad but most of the more important (jihadi) leaders and mujahideen were not affected by this crackdown because they had either gone underground or had taken shelter in various jihadi centres and offices in Azad Kashmir. Among the major leaders, only Maulana Masood Azhar, of Jaish-e-Mohammad, and Hafiz Mohammad Saeed, of Lashkar-e-Taiba, were taken into custody. Only two months later, the process of releasing the jihadis started and it was confirmed that many of them were released on the basis of doubt regarding their association with jihadi groups. By June 2003, almost all of them had been released.

The Lahore High Court ordered the release of Maulana Azhar on 14 December 2002 but, regardless of the release order, he was kept under house arrest until

30 December 2002. He was released finally only when the court showed its displeasure at this defiance of the law by the authorities. Hafiz Saeed was also released on the orders of the Lahore High Court in 2002. He restarted his jihadi activities just after his release.

It is interesting to note that many jihadi leaders who fought alongside Taliban forces during the American attack on Afghanistan were not subjected to any legal action after they returned to Pakistan. The chief of Jamiat-ul-Ansar, also known as Harkat-ul-Mujahideen, Maulana Fazlur Rehman Khalil and his Executive Commander, Omar Farooq Kashmiri, along with the Supreme Commander of Tahreek-e-Khuddam-e-Islam, also known as Jaish-e-Mohammad, Haji Abdul Jabbar and Qari Zarar and Qari Saifullah Akhtar of Harkat-ul-Jihad-ul-Islami had commanded jihadi forces directly on various Afghan fronts. The secret services and the police, however, did not act against them. Rather, they were allowed to carry on their former jihadi activities as before. But their area of operation was not limited to Kashmir alone. They were also active in the affairs of Afghanistan and were helping in reorganising the Taliban. They were also sending human resources to Afghanistan. Confirmed reports about the continuing activities of these leaders have been coming to light from time to time.

Contractions and Expansions in Jihadi Organisations

While, on the one hand, jihadi leaders were still free in Pakistan, on the other hand, their jihadi organisations were undergoing internal feuding and dramatic changes. The biggest sufferers were the Deobandi organisations which split up into many different subgroups, but several other groups came together.

Before 9/11, as many as 104 different jihadi organisations were working in, and out of, Pakistan and Azad Kashmir but, since the clampdown when the game suddenly became personally risky for the leaders, they have now shrunk to about 35 in number. Readers of this writer's work, *Jihad – Gateway to Terrorism* published in 2003, will remember that many of the so-called Islamist mujahideen commanders who indoctrinated and trained so many religiously motivated young men and then launched them across the border to kill or be killed in fire fights with the Indian Army but who, themselves, invariably, operated from the safety of Pakistan and Azad Kashmir were, in fact, just playing at being jihadis for the money and prestige. Many of them melted away when their sponsors started viewing them as a problem and the easy money dried up. According to an Emir of al-Badr Mujahideen, Ameer Hamza, only sincere people and groups are now carrying on the jihad while the self-seekers and fund-collection organisers have vanished. Of all the organisations representing the Barelvi school, only Lashkar-e-Islam is still active. Several organisations devoted to recruiting and managing migrant Kashmiri youth, those who came over from Indian-held Kashmir, have either amalgamated with other organisations or have disappeared completely.

The Deobandi jihadi organisations have been the worst sufferers. While Jaish and Harkat were divided into subgroups, the terrorist organisation, Lashkar-e-

Jhangavi, that had splintered into factions, became reunited. The Deobandi groups were very closely associated with al-Qaida and the Taliban and that ultimately was the reason for their disintegration. Most of the rival groups accuse each other of being the tools or stooges of government agencies and some of them even go to the extent of charging each other with infidelity to Islam.

On the condition of anonymity, an officer of a security service told this writer that he had arrested several members of an important jihadi organisation accused of being Indian Army informers, many of whom face charges under the Anti-Terrorist Act in Pakistan. According to this officer, several of these paid jihadi informers had even double-crossed him. He gave one example. A senior member of Harkat-ul-Jihad-al-Islami of Lahore received two million rupees for informing on an Arab-born leader of al-Qaida. Before making the betrayal, the informer met Maulana Fazlur Rehman, the Chief of Jamiat Ulema-e-Islam, and confessed what he had agreed to do. The Maulana absolved him and provided him with protection but the 'blood money' was not returned to the secret service.

Lashkar-e-Taiba and Jamaat-ud-Daawa have become better organised over the past few years. Their internal differences have also minimised considerably. Jihadi sources claim that, in Kashmir, only Lashkar and al-Badr Mujahideen among the Pakistani jihadi organisations are now active on both sides of the border. Jaish, Harkat-ul-Mujahideen and Harkat-ul-Jihad-al-Islami are active only in Azad

Kashmir with their original names. They have devoted themselves to providing human resources for the Taliban. Some jihadi organisations have even eliminated their training and launching bases in Azad Kashmir. That is why little information is now received about their activities in Indian-held Kashmir. Some jihadi sources claim that their mujahideen are very disgruntled at the cutting-off of their support and communications and, as a consequence, they are joining other organisations like Lashkar, al-Badr, and Tahreek-ul-Mujahideen.

The ISI and Jihadi Organisations

On 16 June in Lahore, an important commander of Harkat-ul-Jihad-al-Islami revealed that the monthly briefing of the leaders of the jihadi organisations by the ISI is still going on but relations are now very cool, even frosty. Now, most of the talk is about limiting public activities and very few groups get permission to launch fighters into Indian-held Kashmir. There is so much secret service and establishment pressure on the militant leadership in Pakistan to stop the jihad that, as a result, their reorganisation is being carried out in secret in Afghanistan where no permission from the ISI is required. This commander also revealed that the previously plentiful supply of arms for the jihadis had largely dried up and future arms would be purchased in the open market of Dara Adamkhel and other tribal areas. With reference to interference in the internal affairs of the jihadi organisations by the ISI, he said that most of the jihadi organisations try to maintain secrecy about their affairs now because the ISI might try to create leadership rifts to weaken them.

This commander also admitted that there were many paid informers of the ISI in the jihadi organisations and that it was very difficult to identify them. Clearly then, not all of the 'in it for the money' militant commanders retired immediately after 9/11 when the going got tough in Pakistan. The ISI pays very well for accurate inside information and, as these types are much more motivated by materialism than by ideology, being an informer keeps the money coming in.

The New Face of the Jihadis

President Musharraf banned some jihad organisations in January 2002. However, as stated earlier, many assumed other names and started their activities under their new identities. A detailed account of the role of various organisations after 9/11 is presented below:

In November 2003, the Government of Pakistan announced again that it would keep an eye on Jamaat-ud-Daawa, formerly known as Lashkar-e-Taiba. This announcement was made along with a ban on seven communal organisations including Tahreek-e-Khuddam-e-Islam. Jamaat-ud-Daawa was, however, much more active than these other organisations and used to carry out jihadi conventions in which it openly highlighted its achievements in Kashmir, Afghanistan, Iraq, Chechnya, and Palestine. Hafiz Mohammad Saeed, head of Jamaat-ud-Daawa, gave an interesting speech at a convention held at the Yarmook Centre, Patoki, on

17 October 2003: "I confess it today that the mujahideen of Lashkar-e-Taiba and Jamaat-ud-Daawa are waging the jihad in Kashmir, inside India, and in all such places where Muslims are leading a miserable life. Jihad is obligatory on us. It is our prime aim and we shall sacrifice everything to save jihad. The mujahideen of Afghanistan, Chechnya, and Iraq listen! We are with you also but the rulers are putting chains on our feet and the Organisation of Islamic Conference (OIC) has become a centre of Jews and Christians. It should announce jihad to save Muslims, implement single currency, prepare a united army and face the non-believers in a united manner. I would also like to warn that the enemies of jihad are the disciples of Satan and they are also present among us." (Press release from the Lahore media office of Jamaat-ud-Daawa, 17 October 2003)

Hafiz Saeed was even more belligerent in his address of 14 August 2003 delivered at the Lahore conference of Jamaat-ud-Daawa in the Takmeel-e-Pakistan Conference. "We are not afraid of America, or of the Hindu baniways (cowards), for we may easily defeat them with the power of jihad but we have the enemies of jihad among ourselves in the garb of Muslims who are the real cause of danger. General Musharraf has become the biggest enemy of jihad. If this man gets out of our way, we shall deal with the non-believers. I would like to clarify today that a big wave of jihad shall surge from India. As a result of what the Hindu goondas (scourge) have done to the Muslims of Gujarat, one more Pakistan shall emerge from the map of India. With the blessings of jihad, the

Muslims will overpower once again and Islam shall have the sway." (*The Daily Times*, Lahore, 16 August 2003)

The special feature of the Yarmook Centre, Patoki, Annual Convention was that it also had camps for jihadi training and organisation where young men were registering themselves for participation in various jihadi fronts. In one of the camps, most of the young men were volunteering to go to Kashmir and Afghanistan and there were several volunteers for Iraq also.

According to the records of Jamaat-ud-Daawa, Hafiz Mohammad Saeed addressed as many as three thousand jihadi conventions after his release in December 2003. In spite of the government's clear ban on collecting funds in November 2003, the Jamaat continued collecting. They established camps at important roads in Lahore and Peshawar in the holy month of Ramadan and they had even greater freedom in small towns. In spite of their issue of advance notices through various newspapers for these fund-raisers, government agencies ignored these activities. A banner in one of the roadside camps read: Our Possessions are for Those Whose Blood is for the Ummah (Islamic world).

Jamaat-ud-Daawa spread its network in Pakistan very effectively and forcefully after 9/11. According to responsible sources inside Jamaat, it invested 20 million rupees in various of its subsidiary organisations which include; education, publishing, health, farming, and transportation. A further 20 million rupees has been spent purchasing land where training centres, madrasas and mosques are being established. The Jamaat plans to establish its centrés, madrasas and mosques in all the districts of Pakistan. In the first phase, attention is directed to Sindh where there are three districts. Three tracts of land have already been acquired there for this purpose and Jamaat intends to spend another twelve million rupees on land purchases in Pakistan over the next five years.

Apart from the money and land, the number of students in the model schools of the Jamaat has reached approximately ten thousand and in the madrasas it is about six thousand. In order to increase its area of influence with the people, it is also establishing health centres and dispensaries. According to one of its leaders, the Jamaat and Lashkar will become self-sufficient to such an extent that they will not need to collect contributions and they will then be in a position to train five thousand mujahideen annually.

The publishing wing of the Jamaat is working in a well-planned manner with two departments. One of these is responsible for publishing jihadi literature. The other department publishes eight magazines in various languages including, Urdu, English, Arabic, and Sindhi. It prints sixty thousand copies of its monthly magazine called, *Mujalla al-Daawa*.

It is quite significant that the government is reluctant to act against Jamaat and Lashkar in spite of this open defiance of the Anti-Terrorism Act. Some analysts are of the opinion that Lashkar and Hizb-ul-Mujahideen have networks in India itself as well as in Indian-held Kashmir and they are quite capable of damaging Indian interests.

The Jaish, Harkat, and other Deobandi jihadi organisations have devoted their attention to Afghanistan and security service sources claim that these organisations are no longer influenced by the ISI or the Pakistan Government because their relationship with the Taliban means they are vehemently opposed to Pakistan's new anti-terrorism policies.

A body of evidence has emerged regarding the terrorist activities of the worldwide network of the Lashkar-e-Taiba during the past year. There is little doubt now about its contacts with al-Qaida. Further, evidence is also available regarding terrorism by Lashkar and Jamaat in Pakistan.

Lashkar-e-Taiba and the Worldwide Network of Terrorism

Mohammad Rauf was arrested on account of his relationship with al-Qaida. Several other arrests were also made when he collaborated with the authorities and identified other people. In the US, a Virginia Federal Grand Jury heard their case. According to the details made available, these terrorists were planning to strike America on a big scale. There were two Pakistani nationals among those who were arrested and they had been associated with Lashkar-e-Taiba. About others also, it was said that they had contacts with the Lashkar and had received their jihadi training in its camps. This was the first proof of Lashkar's worldwide terrorist network. According to the reports of the American intelligence services, the Indian terrorist, Dawood Ibrahim, had links with Lashkar and al-Qaida. The

Karachi monthly, *The Herald*, in its issue of November 2003 reported that he was declared a terrorist on account of his links with these organisations. With reference to the fact sheet issued regarding Dawood Ibrahim, *The Herald* wrote: "'Dawood Ibrahim,' the son of a police constable, 'was guilty of financially supporting' Islamic militant groups working against India, such as Lashkar-e-Taiba. 'Citing information as recent as 2002, the fact sheet further claims that 'Ibrahim has been helping finance increasing attacks in Gujarat by LeT, the armed wing of Markaz-ud-Daawa-Wal Irshad – a Sunni anti-US missionary organisation formed in 1989.' The Lashkar, led by Professor Hafiz Mohammad, was last year placed on the State Department's list of officially designated terrorists outfits.

"Washington's decision is said to be largely motivated by the arrests in the US and Saudi Arabia of an Islamic paramilitary unit which is said to have received training in small arms, machine guns and grenade launchers at a Lashkar-e-Taiba camp in North-East Pakistan. The group, it is said, operated in the Washington DC area and nearby Virginia. Documents released by the FBI on 30 June 2003 state that some of those arrested even fought against Indian troops in occupied Kashmir and were funded by the Dawood syndicate to conduct terrorist activity in the Indian state of Gujarat."

Lashkar-e-Taiba and Al-Qaida

Dr Abdul Basit is a well-known legal luminary of

Lahore. A explanatory deposition that he filed in the Lahore High Court in 2003 revealed that al-Qaida wanted to establish a medical institute for its medical corp in Lahore. However, this plan had to be abandoned after 9/11.

Dr Basit was an unwitting party to this matter. Giving details of the plan, he said that M A Rauf, a former Registrar of Qaid-e-Azam University, along with an unnamed partner bought a plot of land from him to establish a medical college. They had a third partner with them, a man called Bahaziq, who was a Saudi Arabian national and who had made the major financial contribution to the project. When the construction of the medical college started, Bahaziq came on the scene and took over the entire project. Dr Basit's deposition said: "I had met him (Bahaziq) several times during that period. He was much interested in the registration of the college and he said that he would get together the best doctors from all over Pakistan who would educate the Arab students. He believed that individual ability was more important than the degree (in medicine)."

Dr Basit said that Bahaziq moved to lived in the college itself and he came to know that he used to stay in the Muridke centre of the Lashkar before that. Before coming to Pakistan, he had lived in Chechnya, Afghanistan, and Bosnia. Dr Basit said at that time he came to know that Bahaziq was one of the very close associates of Osama bin Laden. He came into contact with Rauf through his son who was an important member of the Lashkar and had come to Muridke with him.

According to Dr Basit, Bahaziq disappeared a few days before the attacks of 9/11 and was never seen after that. He said that he had filed the deposition about his involvement in order to save himself and that he had nothing to do with this network. This college is known today as Lahore Medical University. Security service sources say it has been raided several times and several Arab mujahideen and terrorists of Lashkar-e-Jhangavi have been captured. According to some security service sources, the Muridke centre of Jamaat and other centres are providing refuge to the al-Qaida mujahideen. It should also be noted that Lashkar-e-Taiba had taken part in the jihad in Bosnia with the help of Osama bin Laden and al-Qaida. They fought under the command of Abu Aziz and Abu Abdul Aziz in Bosnia. Lashkar sources say that Abu Abdul Aziz made financial contribution to the establishment of the Muridke centre. Security sources wonder whether Bahaziq was the same person known as Abu Aziz or Abu Abdul Aziz.

Terrorists in Pakistan and Attacks on President Musharraf

The Gujranwala District Police Officer conducted an anti-terrorist operation in the outskirts of Rasul Nagar City (Manger Chatta) and arrested an activist of the Lashkar on 31 December 2003. Associates of this activist from various other places were also arrested. According to law enforcement agencies, a phone call was made from a public call office in Manger Chatta saying; "Now the President should be pardoned." to which came a reply; "He will not be pardoned until his life is brought to an end." This was the biggest police action in the history of Rasul Nagar City. Even though the attackers on the life of President Musharraf in Rawalpindi had been identified and were said to be members of the Jaish, law enforcement agencies, nevertheless, broadened their area of inquiry to encompass other organisations and identify the entire network. The Rasul Nagar City operation was a part of this process and established that Lashkar-e-Taiba's involvement in terrorist activities in Pakistan could not be ruled out.

An important incident that was not reported in Pakistani newspapers with reference to the Lashkar and the terrorist network in Pakistan concerned the arrest of a man called Faisal Nasiruddin by the police for illegal dealing in vehicles. This man had been associated with Jamaat and Lashkar and he had also fought in Afghanistan. Some senior police officers were also involved in pro-jihad support activities with him. Although this case fell in the prerogative of the police, the secret services decided to investigate. Later, responsible security service sources said that an inquiry was conducted on him with reference to a terrorist network in Pakistan. He had, apparently, brought a truck full of arms from Kandahar to Pakistan during the time of the Taliban regime and this truck had reached Jhelum in Pakistani Punjab. Intelligence agencies continue their inquiries about this truck in an effort to discover how and where the arms were distributed. It was also suggested that he used to move about freely in a vehicle belonging to the Taliban

Ambassador to Pakistan, Mullah Zaeef.

Tahreek-e-Khuddam-e-Islam (Jaish-e-Mohammad)

The Pakistan government, on 12 January 2002, banned Jaish-e-Mohammad but even before this, its chief, Maulana Masood Azhar was taken into custody. The most important reason behind this ban was its acceptance of responsibility for the attack on the Indian parliament on 13 December 2001. Even though that responsibility was denied later by Jaish, there was a constant pressure from America and India to put a ban on it.

Jaish was established in March 2000 when Masood Azhar reached Pakistan after his release from India after the hijacking of the Indian Flight CI 814 en route to Katmandu. He was associated with Harkat-ul-Mujahideen before this but, when he established this organisation, it got the support of Deobandi organisations along with Harkat. It soon emerged as a big jihadi organisation in Pakistan and started its activities in Afghanistan and in Indian-held Kashmir. Before the ban, it was supposed to be the biggest anti-India organisation after Lashkar-e-Taiba. It should also be borne in mind here that the Kashmiri jihadi organisations kept Kashmir as the target of their activities and they did not promote jihad against India directly. The agenda of Lashkar and Jaish is, however, wider ranging than the Kashmiri mujahideen.

This may be seen in the following extract from an article by Maulana Masood Azhar which appeared in the fortnightly *Jaish-e-Mohammad* (15 September

2001): "This is a reality that when quite some time has passed after the demolition of the Babri Mosque and many Muslims have even forgotten speaking about it, but a section among them kept it alive in their hearts. They shed tears over this act of oppression and promised to God during the nights that they would take their revenge against the Hindus. This section of the Ummah calls itself mujahideen and they are called Jaish-e-Mohammad. How can the Babri Mosque remain uncared for in spite of them? How can the sons of the mosque not shed their blood for it. It would be an insult to the name of the Jaish if it happened. By the grace of God, Jaish did not allow this blot on the name of Mohammad (PBUH). It shared the pain with the Ummah. When millions of Muslims had shed their tears and got disappointed and forgotten about their great mosque, it was the Jaish that saved the Ummah from disgrace and held the heads high of the community. The three-four youth of the Jaish shed their lives for this and left behind an example others could not do.

"Jaish believes that the Babri Mosque shall be constructed on its original foundations and the Ram Temple shall be constructed only when blood and bodies will fall short of sacrifice. But the mothers of this Ummah have not yet turned infertile, and the mothers are nursing their children that they may take the revenge of the Babri Mosque. After those three, there are countless persons who are impatient to sacrifice their lives for this. Considering this high spirit, the Jaish announces that it will not allow the construction of the Ram Temple, and it will demolish its plan and the constructed areas."

Right from the very beginning, the destruction of the Babri Mosque has been on the main agenda of the Jaish and Maulana Masood Azhar has delivered more than 200 addresses and 25 booklets on the subject.

The Establishment of Tahreek-e-Khuddam-e-Islam

When the Jaish was banned on 12 January 2002, it was virtually paralysed. Following the arrest of Maulana Azhar, it broke into several factions. In order to save itself from internal differences and to counter the impact of the ban, it was renamed as Tahreek-e-Khuddam-e-Islam by keeping its organisational structure intact.

The camp of Jaish-e-Mohammad was active in Balakot before the ban but after the operations of the American FBI, it was closed down. It was shifted to the outskirts of Mensehra district to a place called Sangarbar in July 2003 and the camp is still active in preparing mujahideen. According to sources in Jaish, it had the assistance of certain government officials in the purchase of this site.

The Release of Maulana Masood Azhar

After his arrest during the clampdown, the family members of Maulana Azhar filed a writ in the Lahore High Court for his release. The court, considering his arrest illegal, gave orders for his release on 13 December 2001. Just a year later, the Indian Parliament was attacked.

Maulana Azhar was released after the decision but he was kept under house arrest in his Bahawalpur residence. This came to an end on 30 December 2002. Incidentally, this was the anniversary of his release from the Indian prison. He restarted his activities with fresh zeal after his release but the conditions were different this time because his organisation had faced division.

Division in Tahreek-e-Khuddam-e-Islam

In the beginning of May 2003, law enforcement agencies and Pakistani secret services, including the ISI, received a letter from Maulana Azhar saying that he had expelled twelve people from his organisation for their alleged involvement in sectarian incidents and the bombing of Christian churches and that they should be subjected to strict action. Details of this letter were later published on 21 June 2003 in a Lahore based English daily according to which these twelve people were; Abdul Jabbar, the chief commander of Jaish-e-Mohammad, his deputy, Emir Maulana Abdullah Shah Mazhar, Mohammad Tahir Hayat, Bait-ul-Maal Maulana Ghulam Murtuza, Ghulam Haider, Nasir Shirazi, Naved Farooqui, Qari Abdul Majeed, Ejaz Mehmood, Maqsood Ali Shah, Abdus Samad Sumroo and Shaukat Hayat.

Commander Abdul Jabbar was considered to be the backbone of the Jaish. He was a highly respected person in Afghanistan during the Taliban regime and had the privilege of enjoying the protocol of a minister. Maulana Abdullah Shah Mazhar had played a significant role in looking after the organisational aspect of the Jaish in the entire country. Others had also contributed their bit towards this end. This sudden 'ouster' publicly exposed the inner cracks of the Jaish. Those who were driven out came together under the banner of Tahreek-e-Khuddam-e-Islam. This led to encroachments upon each other's property and also to violence. This unrest within the organisation also made it clear that the al-Rasheed Trust which was declared a terrorist organisation by the US for supporting the Taliban and was also instrumental in strengthening the Jaish, had gone against Maulana Azhar.

The opponent groups and al-Rasheed maintained that Maulana Azhar had tried to forsake the path of jihad and passed on information to government agencies to facilitate the arrest of Taliban and Arab mujahideen. They claimed that this was how he bought his own release. With such 'dirty laundry' becoming public it is not surprising that armed violence between the factions became common. Mud-slinging allegations against each other also started at the same time. Most of the jihadi organisations believe the allegations contain elements of truth. The rift between these factions can be studied usefully in detail.

Allegations of Corruption and Disloyalty

Maulana Azhar was deeply involved in allegations of corruption and betrayal after these expulsions. An organ of the Jabbar group called *Tadbeer-e-Nau* (Lahore) and the weekly *Wajood* (Karachi) wrote in favour of the Jabbar group while *Shamsheer*

(Hyderabad) spoke for Maulana Azhar. Some of the important allegations against Azhar are as follows:

1. Undue favours to kith and kin: His opponents alleged that he gave all the key positions in the organisation to his brothers and brothers-in-law. Maulana Jabbar was ousted to accommodate his own brother, called Ibrahim. Similarly, the new head of the Balakot training camp was Yusuf Azhar, (a disciple of Azhar who had changed his surname in favour of his mentor and who later became his brother-in-law). Rasheed Kamran, another brother-in-law, is entrusted with responsibility for managing finances and Kashmiri affairs. The head of external affairs, Jahangir, alias Talha, is one of Azhar's brothers. Tahir, his older brother is the cashier of the Bahawalpur centre and the central offices. His younger brother, Abdul Rauf, is his special advisor and manager of finances.

Opponents also allege that after distributing positions among his relatives, the other five or six important positions remaining unfilled were given to his close friends. For example, he gave a bungalow worth three hundred thousand rupees to his close friend Tahir Hameed in Karachi. Similarly, he appointed Maulavi Masood as head of an important madrasa on a highway in Karachi. He also bought a plot of land in Bahawalpur Model Colony near his home. Earlier, it was used as a shelter for buffaloes but when objections were raised, he built a mosque and an office on that plot and gave it over to the charge of his father.

Strange revelations have been made by the opponents

regarding the distribution of vehicles. Maulana Azhar had two double cabin vehicles at his own disposal. One of them has been sold while the other has been gifted to a close relative. These days he uses a vehicle which bears Islamabad numbers. This apart, he has a Toyota and one other vehicle at his disposal. His brother, Abdul Rauf has two vehicles for himself. Younger brother Jahangir, alias Talha, has a grey colour Toyota Corrola vehicle for himself. His father and brother-in-law have a Suzuki each.

2. Azhar is accused of serious financial irregularities. In the weekly *Wajood* (Karachi) of 22 July 2003, his opponents have written: "This has not been ascertained so far as to how Maulana Masood Azhar moved to a posh bungalow from the government quarters of his father Master Allah Bukhsh. This is a truth, however, that he has been receiving huge funds from the al-Rasheed Trust from time to time. According to our sources, all contributions made to the Trust for the Taliban after 11 September (9/11) were transferred to Jaish and it was said that this was meant essentially for the mujahideen. According to reliable sources a bungalow spread over five hundred yards in Nazimabad, Number 4, was purchased from a medical chest specialist, Dr Mohammad Ayyub by the al-Rasheed Trust and given over to Maulana Azhar. Before and after 11 September, lots of gold and jewellery were collected from ladies all over which was, according to a reasonable estimate, about forty kilograms. This too was under the control of the organisation but it was taken over by him on the plea that this was also meant for mujahideen and he should take the responsibility of its

complete safety and security. Since then nothing has ever been mentioned about this huge collection in or outside the organisation."

According to other reliable sources, the al-Rasheed Trust has provided more than enough resources to Masood Azhar's organisation. After the establishment of the organisation, he was given a monthly amount of one hundred and seventy-five thousand rupees per month for his personal expenses. Apart from this, the trust used to pay the bills for six mobile phones in his use. In the very beginning, the trust had also provided millions of rupees to him to finance the running of the organisation. Over and above this, the trust also used to pay the salaries of sixty employees working for the organisation.

How is it that the administrators of the al-Rasheed Trust, who had initially provided such huge financial help, became angry with Masood Azhar? In the beginning it was ensured that he was following the principles of Sharia as insisted upon by Mufti Rasheed Ahmed (the trust's founder). It is certainly true that he was being gifted with all sorts of assets at first but he could not maintain the confidence of the trust's donors. The donated resources were utilised essentially for him and his organisation. Masood Azhar started a women's wing of the Jaish and put it under the control of his wife. Later, it proved to be a futile exercise. In fact, it became the cause of many other exposures, which would not otherwise have come to notice. When Mufti Rasheed came to know of these matters, he entrusted Mufti Abdur Raheem with the responsibility of sorting it out with Masood Azhar. Later, when he was taken by Mufti Raheem to meet with Mufti Rasheed Ahmed, another of the trust's administrators, he got extremely angry and returned without meeting him. It is strange that he did not like to meet some of the administrators yet continued receiving the trust's favours. He then started receiving his funds from Mufti Abdur Raheem, one of the new administrators, instead of Mufti Rasheed Ahmed.

Armed Confrontations Between the Factions

Maulana Azhar led one faction of Tahreek-e-Khuddam-e-Islam while Commander Abdul Jabbar led the other. Their first armed confrontation was fuelled by the controversy over the Karachi Centre. The weekly *Wajood*, in its issue of 8 July 2003, wrote about the background of this incident: "Masood Azhar's brother, Abdul Rauf and his brother-in-law, along with fifty others, came to Bataha Mosque on 22 June. They indulged in firing to gain control over the mosque. Cracks developed in several walls. Abdul Rauf and other attackers also targeted Maulana Omar Farooque, the leader of the other faction. In this clash and firing a young man called Asif received severe injuries. According to sources this was the second attack on this mosque. The first attack had taken place on 24 April. Abdul Rauf and his group insist that this mosque and the madrasa are the property of their organisation whereas Maulana Abdullah Shah Mazhar claims that he is the chairman of the mosque trust and has the right to its management."

Defence Against Allegations

Maulana Azhar has been offering his explanations

regarding these allegations in his public addresses and through his organ called *Shamsheer*. An important report in this connection entitled; "The Dangerous Conspiracy Against the Mujahideen and My Research" is spread over thirty-six pages and gives detailed explanations about every allegation. The researcher of this publication has been named as one Maulana Abdul Karim Peerzada and it has been published by Manshurat from Karachi. It is thought that the researcher is none else but Maulana Azhar himself. In the beginning of the report a detailed description of his services has been provided and all the allegations have been termed as malicious propaganda carried out at the instance of certain Pakistani institutions. Regarding the allegation concerning undue favours to his kith and kin, it is said that; "It is entirely misdirected because only one or two of the key positions are with his relatives. Further, the history of Islam bears out only too well that the leaders of community have always entrusted their relatives with responsibilities." Clarifying the position regarding financial irregularities, it poses a counter question: "How far is it justifiable in Sharia and in the matters of financial management to spend resources in newspapers, creating obstructions in jihadi activities, appropriating funds for personal purposes, and squandering lakhs (hundreds of thousands) of rupees in paying for air tickets to spoil the cause of jihad?" Regarding the attack on Karachi Centre it has been said: "The building of Khuddam-ul-Islam (Karachi centre) adjacent to Bataha Mosque was constructed out of a special fund created by some Muslims. This building has been used for jihadi activities for more than a year. When such centres were sealed all over the country in January 2002, this centre was also sealed. It was during this period that Abdullah Shah Mazhar, along with some of his friends, hatched a plan to take it over by him becoming the President of the Trust. Papers were prepared accordingly and these papers were asked for, alibis were offered. However, when Abdullah Shah was relieved of the responsibility, he took over the building in a very sly manner. Had the matter been limited only to the locking up of the building, it would not have been such a big issue but he encroached over the property by bribing the local police. He got the top floor occupied by a family to prevent its reoccupation by others. He also started a madrasa on the ground floor to establish that it was not an office. The two middle floors were turned into abodes for such people who were involved in disruptive activities. Under such circumstances the supporters of Maulana Azhar in Karachi took it upon themselves to counter this conspiracy."

Masood Azhar's Activities After His Release

The activities of the chief of Tahreek-e-Khuddam-e-Islam, which was a banned organisation, were looked upon with doubt by many people in Pakistan but law enforcement agencies did not take too much notice. The publications of Jaish-e-Mohammad, the previous name of Tahreek, which highlighted jihadi activities were available in general book stores and outside mosques after the prayers. In October 2003, Azhar went on a tour of Lahore and addressed gatherings in the posh areas and collected funds from the public in the name of jihad. He also toured industrial areas and collected huge contributions from industrialists. It is interesting to note that he collected a lot of these funds in large handkerchiefs and kept them with himself in bundles. He said that he would carry these funds to the mujahideen himself.

When the Pakistani and international media began to express anxiety about these activities, a ban was imposed on the Tahreek once again on 15 November 2003 and raids were conducted for the arrest of Maulana Azhar. However, by then he had disappeared from the scene and the police have not yet been able to find him.

Where is Masood Azhar?

Divergent opinions regarding his whereabouts have been coming. Some say that he is in the custody of some secret agency while others believe that he is a guest of Tahir Ashrafi, the advisor on religious affairs to the Punjab Government. *The Independent* (Lahore) in its issue of 12 February 2004 has written regarding their relationship: "Maulana Masood Azhar, chief of the defunct Jaish-e-Mohammad (JeM), escaped from his house in Bahawalpur over two months back by deceiving law-enforcement and secret agency personnel, sources in the interior ministry informed *The Independent*. The Maulana, notorious for his links with top international jihadi networks, had been placed under house arrest after the United States banned Jaish-e-Mohammad, terming it a terrorist outfit.

"Sources alleged that Maulana Masood (Azhar) escaped from his house in connivance with law-enforcement agencies and Hafiz Tahir Mahmood Ashrafi, advisor to the Punjab government on religious affairs, about two months back. 'The agencies are now thoroughly investigating covert relations between the two Maulanas to trace and arrest fugitive Masood Azhar,' a senior official in the Interior Ministry said.

"Hafiz Ashrafi confirmed to *The Independent* that Masood Azhar fled but showed ignorance about his whereabouts. 'I have no contacts with him and I don't know where he is hiding now,' Hafiz Ashrafi told this scribe.

"Maulana Masood had been under intensive investigation especially after the US launched its so-called war on terror in Afghanistan about two years back. A large number of Jaish-e-Mohammad activists were arrested on charges of attacks on churches and foreigners. Various agencies also blame JeM for the latest attempts on President Musharraf's life in Islamabad.

"Sources said that during house arrest Hafiz Ashrafi had been in contact with Maulana Masood Azhar and they used to discuss on the telephone matters relating to religious and jihadi parties and various other issues. That's why Hafiz Ashrafi is nowadays in troubled waters and finds it hard to satisfy the law enforcement and intelligence agencies about his relations with Maulana Masood Azhar. The probe was initiated when a Karachi based Urdu weekly published stories about contacts between the two leaders.

"According to these reports, these two Maulanas received huge sums and provided the Musharraf

Government with information about various sectarian and extremist religious leaders especially al-Qaida members to help the agencies arrest them. That's why they turned against them. According to a report of the weekly, the two Maulanas got millions of rupees in this 'operation'.

"Sources said Tahir Ashrafi had also formed an NGO (Non-Government Organisation), through which he got released a number of Pakistani prisoners from Afghan jails. These members of various jihadi groups were arrested during the US war on Afghanistan, and Hafiz Ashrafi made millions of rupees in the process.

"Sources said intelligence agencies were also investigating about foreign tours of Hafiz Ashrafi, because he made several trips to UK, France and Libya 'to discharge his official duties' during the past three years.

"Hafiz Ashrafi got into the limelight when some foreign tourists were kidnapped, allegedly by a jihadi group, al-Faran, in Kashmir and the British intelligence contacted him for their release. Sources said Ashrafi had close relationship with the leadership of al-Faran owing to Masood Azhar's influence in the valley.

"Sources in the Interior Ministry said Hafiz Ashrafi helped the agencies arrest dissidents of Masood Azhar's JeM and members of other sectarian groups opposed to his ideology. As a result, leaders of various religious parties including Jamiat-Ulamai-Islam the banned Sipah-e-Sahaba and Harkat-u-Mujahideen of Fazlur Rehman Khalil, wrote letters to Interior Ministry officials and condemned the activities of Hafiz Ashrafi and Maulana Masood.

"According to reports, Muttahida Majlis-e-Amal leader Maulana Fazlur Rehman met senior officials of the Interior Ministry some days back and demanded the removal of Hafiz Ashrafi from his official position because of his relations with Maulana Masood Azhar and his suspicious activities.

"The intelligence agencies were also investigating the financial affairs of Hafiz Ashrafi and Maulana Azhar because the latter had invested millions of rupees in the export of garments. He had many shops in the commercial areas of Lahore such as Karim Block, Allama Iqbal Town, Durand Road, Urdu Bazaar, etc."

Jamaat al-Furqan

This organisation was established on 25 September 2003 when the two warring factions of Tahreek-e-Khuddam-e-Islam came to terms suddenly in a surprising manner. Both of them agreed to work under different names. Commander Abdul Jabbar, Maulana Omar Farooq, and Maulana Abdullah Shah Mazhar named their new organisation, al-Furqan. Maulana Yusuf Shah, the General Secretary of Jamiat Ulema-e-Islam (Maulana Samiul Haq group) wrote while commenting on this; "Those who had brought them to fight, were instrumental in sorting out the matters."

The reconciliation took place under the auspices of the Provincial Advisor on Religious Affairs, Tahir Ashrafi, at his centre at Baitul Aman in Lahore. It is quite significant that the reconciliation occurred at the centre of a government official while he acted as referee. *Al-Hareer*, a monthly published under the patronage of Tahir Ashrafi wrote in October 2003: "The differences between the two groups of the defunct Jaish-e-Mohammad came to end on 25 September in Baitul Aman, Lahore. After holding talks continuously for sixteen hours, they decided to bring their differences to an end. While it was a news of jubilation for those concerned with jihad all over the world, there were certain other elements who could hardly digest the development. On 25 September itself they tried to ensure that those meeting for a reconciliation would not meet. A newspaper published a news item with reference to the host, Hafiz Tahir Mahmood Ashrafi, that Lashar and Jhangawi and Khuddam-ul-Islam workers are getting together. The intention was to alert the government so that it could put a check on the host, and in this manner the possibility of reconciliation would be doomed. When they could not succeed in this effort they called one of these group as encroachers and the other as mosque sellers in the newspapers of 27 September. They further went to the extent of seeking the help of such institutions that were looked at with doubt by the patriotic groups. They thus tried their best to block all possibilities and create an atmosphere of hatred and bitterness. The entire Islamic world was already tired of such allegations and counter allegations. This atmosphere surprised all those concerned from the jihad of Kashmir to Afghanistan. Differences may be there but can the differences be allowed to carry on to such an extent, they wondered. But the men of understanding and wisdom realised well that those defeated by Maulana Masood Azhar (a reference to the Indian plane hijacking) were now bent upon taking revenge. They are putting the blame for Maulana Abdul Jabbar's (may God release him soon) arrest on Maulana Azhar and they are sometimes taking him as an Indian agent."

All said and done, the two groups agreed to stop feuding and signed up to the following code of conduct: "Deliberations between the associates of respected brother Farooq and the delegation of Maulana Masood Azhar were held this day, 25 September 2003, at Baitul Aman in Lahore. There were four participants from the side of brother Farooq: Maulana Abdullah Shah Mazhar, Maulana Bhai Maqsood Ali Shah, Bhai Naved Farooq, Maulana Misbahullah. There was a delegation of five from Maulana Masood Azhar: Mufti Mohammad Asghar Khan, Bhai Sulaiman, Maulana Asif Qasmi, Mufti Mohammad Khalid and Mufti Abdul Rauf.

"The following was resolved: (1) The associates of respected brother Omar Farooq shall assume a new name to start their work. (2) The persons shall continue holding the capital of the organisation as they might be holding now. Only the group of Maulana Masood Azhar will pay to the group of Bhai Omar Farooq the debt of rupees five lakhs, apart from ten lakhs of rupees, that is, a total of fifteen lakhs. Apart from this, the white Corolla 88 model car will also be returned by 1 October. The Bataha centre shall be with Maulana Masood Azhar but the cost of new construction shall be borne by Bhai Farooq and the cost shall be decided in the presence of the parties concerned. Further, Maulana Abdullah Shah Mazhar shall relinquish the responsibilities of the mosque. (3) The associates of Bhai Farooq shall not use the name of Khuddam-ul-Islam, its flag, and the receipt books and the earlier receipt books shall be destroyed in the presence of the parties concerned. (4) A sum of ten lakhs of rupees as the first instalment of the above-mentioned sum shall be payable by 29 September. A week after this payment, the handing over of the Bataha Centre, disassociation with its name, and declaration of the receipts as null and void shall be done. After the completion of these formalities, the remaining amount of five lakhs shall be paid. (5) The parties shall not create any obstruction in the way of the life and property of the each other. (6) If any member wishes to change his affiliation, he shall make all the accounts clear before leaving. (7) The parties shall not indulge in negative propaganda against each other, nor shall they threaten each other. (8) The parties shall withdraw cases filed against each other within a week. (9) The associates working with the new name shall not express their association with the former Khuddam-ul-Islam. (10) In the case of any violation of the code of conduct, the matter shall be referred to Mufti Mohammad Asghar Khan and Maulana Abdullah Shah Mazhar. May God make the parties concerned follow this agreement Amen."

Hardly a week had passed since the finalization of this code of conduct when both the groups once again had their differences. On 20 October 2003 in the Sharafabad area of Karachi, Maulana Abdullah Shah

Mazhar was entering the mosque to say prayers when supporters of Maulana Masood Azhar fired at him. Maulana Mazhar was saved but the firing between both parties continued. The inner sources of Tahreek Khuddam-ul-Islam say that the reason for this difference was that Jamaat al-Furqan had not followed the code of conduct already agreed upon.

After this agreement/disagreement/agreement, the organisational structure of Jamaat al-Furqan came to be like this: Maulana Omar Farooq as Chief Commander, Haji Abdul Jabbar as Patron, Maulana Abdullah Shah Mazhar as Manager of General Affairs, Maulana Murtuza as Chief of Punjab Province and Osama Rizwan as Chief of the Frontier Province.

The Support of the al-Rasheed Trust

Jamaat al-Furqan got complete co-operation from Jamia Banauria and the al-Rasheed Trust. The trust stopped all financial assistance to Maulana Masood Azhar. It was claimed that he had played an important role in the arrest of important leaders of al-Qaida in Pakistan, but the al-Rasheed Trust still helps al-Furqan to this day.

Commander Abdul Jabbar was arrested in July 2003 on a charge of attacking Christian missionaries and churches in Pakistan. This arrest occurred a few weeks after the denunciatory letters written to law enforcement agencies by Maulana Masood Azhar in which he demanded action against Maulana Abdullah Mazhar and nine others who had allegedly been involved in sectarian attacks.

Even though Commander Jabbar is in detention, he is still the head of al-Furqan, a group opposed to Masood Azhar. He has asserted that he was removed by Masood Azhar because he criticised the ambivalent policies of the Jaish regarding its support for the Taliban government. The Masood Azhar group, however, claimed Abdul Jabbar and his companions left the organisation under protest. A new report of Tahreek-e-Khuddam-e-Islam *Recent Conspiracies Against Mujahideen and My Research* has it on record: "The following responsible persons from Khuddam-e-Islam have parted ways with the organisation under protest: Bahi Omar Farooque, (former member of the Advisory body), Maulavi Ghulam Murtuza, (former member, Advisory body), Shaukat Hayat (former deputy for the affairs of the detainees), Maqsood Ali Shah (former circulation manager, *Shamsheer*), Maulavi Aijaz (former assistant for the affairs of the detainees) and Maulavi Obaidullah Anwar (Deputy Manager, Sindh province).

"The following persons were suspended on the charge of violating jihadi rules and regulations and for going against the Sharia, and also for creating rifts in the organisation: Commander Abdul Jabbar (former manager of the affairs of war and former officiating Emir), Maulana Abdullah Shah Mazhar (former manager of Sindh province).

"It is interesting to note here that all the above mentioned persons have been insisting that they left the organisation because Maulana Abdul Jabbar has been thrown out of the organisation without any justification but the reality is that the said members have been present in all meetings where the question of his expulsion was discussed.

"The biggest blame on Commander Abdul Jabbar is that he reacted against the American attack on the Taliban Government by attacking the churches and the Christian missionaries in Pakistan so that the Pakistan Government could be taught a lesson for pursuing a wrong policy. At the time of these attacks, he was the commander of Jaish-e-Mohammad. Maulana Masood Azhar denied having given any such orders for attacking the churches."

Another extract from this report puts this dispute about attacks on Christian establishments into context: "Some time later when attacks on churches increased and those involved in it started coming out openly, the Maulana asked Commander Jabbar to take leave from organisational responsibilities for some time so that other matters related to jihad did not go unattended. During this time, a seven member advisory body that was looking after the organisational matters removed Abdul Jabbar from his position as officiating Emir. The committee asked Commander Jabbar to sit back for some time, which he accepted happily. The period of his withdrawal was fixed for three months. But several members of the said committee are protesting against the expulsion of Commander Jabbar today.

"This step gave some satisfaction to Maulana Masood Azhar and his companions and they thought that things would get better and those activities that caused danger to the mujahideen would come to an end. The release of Maulana Masood Azhar was postponed again and again because of these activities.

This reached such an extent that, after the attacks on the churches, the police transferred the Maulana from his residence to jail and no one knew for a month and five days where he was and in what condition. The Pakistan police behaved with utmost cruelty to him during those days. The police wanted him to say that he had given the order for attacking the churches but the Maulana denied this.

"The withdrawal of Commander Jabbar was, however, fixed for three months and he had promised to abide by this. However, this did not happen because he toured various parts of the country during this period. He also attended a convention and met about five hundred people there. Even this was not so bad but he crossed all limits when he kept on making propaganda that he was expelled from the organisation and that charges had been levelled against him without any justification. These were the charges he had accepted before the advisory body. By giving this description to his followers, he was only extracting a promise that if Maulana did not take this back, they would stop protesting.

"When Maulana Masood Azhar came to know of this, he was extremely pained because he had advised Commander Jabbar only for the reason that he would be under protection and, until the facts came out, he should stay out of controversy. No one knows why and how he fell prey to doubts and went against the position of the Emir and opened the way to group politics which the Maulana had sealed with great efforts on his part."

Jamaat al-Furqan and the Taliban

After its establishment, Jamaat al-Furqan concentrated on its efforts to help the Taliban and to provide human and other resources to them from Pakistan. The al-Rasheed Trust played an important role in this area. According to sources in Jamaat al-Furqan, more than a hundred Pakistani mujahideen joined Taliban forces in 2003.

A ban was imposed on Jamaat al-Furqan in November 2003. It is surprising, therefore, that its patron, Commander Jabbar was released in January 2004 in spite of all the serious allegations made against him. According to *The Daily Times* (23 January 2004), even jihadi circles were surprised by this sudden release.

Jamiat-ul-Ansar

The biggest Deobandi militant group, Harkat-ul-Mujahideen, was declared a foreign terrorist organisation by the US State Department in 1998 and was banned in Pakistan in November 2001. It had renamed itself Jamiat-ul-Ansar. At that time the government froze all of its assets. Jamiat-ul-Ansar also comprises a breakaway faction of another jihadi group Harkat-ul Jihad-e-Islami. Before the formation of Jamiat-ul-Ansar, there was some pressure initially on Harkat-ul-Mujahideen to merge with Jamiat-ul-Mujahideen, another Deobandi jihadi group. However, this plan could not be executed because of resistance within Harkat-ul-Mujahideen. In fact, the dissent led to a group breaking way from Harkat-ul-Mujahideen and calling itself Harkat-ul Mujahid-al-Alemi. This is the group responsible for the suicide bombings in Karachi and also for two abortive attempts on the life of President Musharraf. Most of its activists and its top leaders are under arrest at the time of writing. It also had links with the sectarian Deobandi terrorist organisation, Lashkar-e-Jhangavi.

So, the Harkat-ul-Mujahideen, instead of merging with Jamiat-ul-Mujahideen, decided to reincarnate itself as Jamiat-ul-Ansar. When Pakistani authorities moved in November 2001 to ban the group and freeze its assets, it suffered a major setback. It got a second shock when some of its activists and leaders broke away from Harkat-ul Mujahid-al-Alemi. The organisation still retains links, like other groups, with Taliban remnants and al-Qaida terrorists. Sources close to the Jamiat-ul-Ansar told *The Friday Times* that the new organisation has come into existence after six-month-long negotiations between Harkat-ul Mujahid-al-Alemi and the breakaway Harkat-ul Jihad-e-Islami. Meanwhile, reports say some clerics and intermediaries are trying to get the rest of the Harkat-ul Jihad-e-Islami also to merge with Harkat-ul Mujahid-al-Alemi in its new incarnation, the Jamiat-ul-Ansar. The leaders of the Harkat-ul Jihad-e-Islami who had joined the Jamiat-ul-Ansar are Maulana Abdul Samad Sayal (Patron), Commander Ilyas Kashmiri (Commander-in-Chief), Dr Badar Niyazi and others. Qari Saifullah Akhtar and Maulana Ahmad Omar of Harkat-ul Jihad-e-Islami have still not joined the new organisation and continue to keep their independent identity. According to Jamiat-ul-Ansar sources, Dr Sher Ali Shah of Jamia Akora Khatak has played a major role in the unification of both organisations. He is still actively trying to get the Harkat-ul Jihad-e-Islami to join up with Jamiat-ul-Ansar. Interestingly, when Harkat leaders approached Jaish-e-Mohammad to convince its leader, Maulana Masood Azhar, to join up with them, he refused to do so. It is earlier recorded that Azhar, after being sprung from an Indian prison by the aircraft hijack, broke away from Harkat-ul-Mujahideen to form his own group, Jaish-e-Mohammad. However, Jamiat-ul-Ansar sources say; "Our doors are still open for him and other activists of Jaish."

Harkat-ul-Mujahideen, now called Jamiat-ul-Ansar, had gone through many incarnations over the years. It was formed in 1987. In 1993, Harkat-ul-Mujahideen merged with Harkat-ul-Jihad-al-Islami to form what came to be known as Harkat-ul-Ansar. In 1995, an organisation called al-Faran kidnapped some foreign tourists in Indian-held Kashmir. The two commanders in question, Abdul Hameed Turkey and Commander Sikander, who set-up al-Faran, both belonged to Harkat-ul-Mujahideen. Subsequently, the US declared al-Faran as a foreign terrorist organisation. Meanwhile, Harkat-ul-Ansar had split into two factions over the al-Faran issue. The Harkat-ul-Jihad-al-Islami faction blamed Maulana Khalil of Harkat-ul-Mujahideen for allowing this to happen since the two commanders who set-up al-Faran belonged to his group. Maulana Khalil came under pressure and denounced al-Faran. Both commanders were killed later, which made it easy for Khalil to detach himself from al-Faran. But the issue kept hanging and finally in 1996 the Harkat-ul-Jihad-al-Islami split formally. Both groups reverted to their previous identities.

Harkat-ul-Mujahideen leaders claimed that their cadres participated in the 1999 Kargil War (between India and Pakistan in the Kargil region of Kashmir). Maulana Mohammad Farooq Kashmiri, head of Harkat-ul-Mujahideen, stated in Muzaffarabad on 15 July 1999, that his militants would not vacate the Kargil Heights unless the Indian army left Kashmir. He also criticised the peace proposals made in the Lahore Declaration and the Washington announcement by President Clinton (that Pakistan would seek to withdraw mujahideen from the Kargil area) as a betrayal of the jihad for the liberation of Kashmir. He announced that Harkat-ul-Mujahideen would wage a jihad in support of the oppressed all over the world. Maulana Fazlur Rehman Khalil revealed (Rawalpindi, 19 July 1999) that 2000 militants belonging to the Harkat-ul-Mujahideen, Lashkar-e-Taiba, al-Badr and Hizb had participated in Kargil and 50 of their activists were killed in the fighting.

Harkat-ul-Mujahideen suffered a major setback when Maulana Masood Azhar defected to form Jaish-e-Mohammad in February 2000. A large number of Harkat activists joined Azhar's Jaish and his new organisation also captured Harkat assets in the Punjab. The feuding also cost Harkat the lives of some of its activists. Sources say that, later, Osama bin Laden compensated Harkat for the losses sustained by it after the Jaish breakaway group captured its assets and deprived it of its funds. In 1998, when the United

States launched cruise missile attacks against mujahideen bases in Afghanistan, two Harkat training camps were destroyed and twenty-one of its activists were killed. Later, at a news conference in Islamabad, Harkat-ul-Mujahideen vowed to avenge the attack. That prompted Washington to declare it as a foreign terrorist organisation. When the US attacked Afghanistan in 2002, Harkat's mujahideen fought on the side of al-Qaida and the Taliban against the Americans.

In November 2003, the Pakistan Government banned Jamiat-ul-Ansar on charges of recruiting mujahideen and collecting fund. But it is still active in the jihad, especially in Afghanistan, and is fighting against American troops along with the Taliban and al-Qaida. Its camps are still training new cadres in Mensehra, a North-West Frontier district.

Hizb-ul-Mujahideen

Hizb-ul-Mujahideen was suffering from multiple internal crises before 9/11, but the atrocity in US made these crises more serious because the US also included this group on its list of suspected terrorists organisations.

Differences between Salahuddin, Majid Dar, and Commander Masood Sarfaz groups were considered as major setbacks for Hizb-ul-Mujahideen in its history but after 9/11, Jamaat-e-Islami also limited its cooperation.

New Adjustments with Jamaat-e-Islami

The Kashmir freedom struggle began with the

partitioning of the subcontinent in 1947 but only became a serious conflict between India and Pakistan in 1989 after the Americans collaborated with the ISI in creating, financing and arming the modern mujahideen for the war against the Soviets in Afghanistan. The Hizb-ul-Mujahideen emerged as the biggest Pakistani based militant organisation. It came into existence in 1990 when twelve small jihadi groups merged to form a formidable organisation.

Many of its founding cadres were veterans of the Afghan struggle who had fought under the Hizb-e-Islami of Gulbaden Hikmetyar. It depended on the experience and the training of the Afghan war veterans. The Jamaat-e-Islami adopted it in 1991 when insurgency in Indian-held Kashmir peaked. Hizb was working under the direct patronage of Jamaat-e-Islami and its offices were in the offices of Jamaat around the country. Qazi Hussain Ahmad was the head of Jamaat-e-Islami and he was also the chief patron of Hizb-ul-Mujahideen and, according to the constitution of Hizb-ul-Mujahideen, had the authority to remove or assign any person as the head of organisation. However, while talking to a reporter at a seminar in May 2003, Qazi Hussain Ahmad categorically stated that his party had no links with Hizb-ul-Mujahideen and added that the jihad outfit was based in Indian-held Kashmir and was fighting for the right of self-determination of the Kashmiris. When a reported tried to pin him down on reports that most of the Hizb offices in Pakistan were being run by Jamaat workers, he said these offices were set-up by Hizb-ul-Mujahideen sympathizers in the party and not by the Jamaat itself.

The same month, Jamaat-e-Islami asked Hizb-ul-Mujahideen to shift its offices from Jamaat premises in Pakistan. The Hizb had been operating from Jamaat premises since 1990. The Jamaat leadership also asked the Hizb to remove all of its hoardings and signboards from Jamaat offices across the country.

However, these were just cosmetic steps and Hizb-ul-Mujahideen is still working as a Jamaat-e-Islami subsidiary organisation. In Pakistan, it is working under the Shabab-e-Milli, the youth wing of the Jamaat. According to inside sources, Jamaat ordered its officials to ensure that Hizb-ul-Mujahideen in Pakistan was worked as a wing of Shabab-e-Milli and it should stay that way. "The decision was taken in March 2003 to show that the Hizb is an indigenous movement in occupied Kashmir, that it is a Kashmiri organisation which had no links with the Jamaat and all its activists are Kashmiri," inside sources said. When this decision was taken, the Hizb-ul-Mujahideen based in Kashmir was also separated from the Jamaat and the Hizb in Pakistan was told that its role in the Kashmir jihad was only to collect donations and recruit volunteers. "It was decided that the Hizb in Pakistan would recruit mujahideen from the Kashmiri community in Pakistan." These sources say. According to another Hizb insider, Jamaat-e-Islami had taken these steps because it was under pressure to renounce all jihadi groups so as to improve the image of Muttahida Majlis-e-Amal (a powerful new alliance of six religio/political parties). "There has been pressure from outside the Jamaat since some al-Qaida operators were arrested in Jamaat workers' homes," the insider disclosed.

The Deaths of Dar, Saiful Islam and Other Commanders

Hizb-ul-Mujahideen lost its chief operational commander, Saiful Islam in the jihad. It was considered a huge loss for the organisation. Before this, Hizb-ul-Mujahideen had lost another seven of its chief commanders since 1989. Commander Ahsan Dar, Ashraf Dar, Maqbool Allai, Commander Bagro, Commander Naseerul Islam, Commander Masood Nattiary, and Commander Abdul Majeed Dar were martyred (killed in the jihad). One important aspect of their martyrdom is that most of these commanders lost their lives they separated from HM.

Commander Naseerul Islam was killed in 1993 by Indian forces. At that time he was the head of Jamiat-ul-Mujahideen, which he had formed after differences with the leadership of Jamaat-e-Islami and its organisational head, Ahsan Dar. It is interesting to note that, later, Ahsan Dar also left Jamaat-e-Islami for the same reasons as Naseerul Islam, because Jamaat-e-Islami's involvement in Hizb-ul-Mujahideen organisational matters was causing disputes within the mujahideen. Abdul Majeed Dar was the last commander to be killed before Saiful Islam. Majeed Dar had also formed his own group after differences with Syed Salahuddin, the supreme commander of the organisation.

Some reports suggested that there might be some relation between the killings of the last two commanders because disputes between these two groups had sharpened considerably. Abdul Majeed Dar was the man who created ripples among the mujahideen by calling a unilateral ceasefire with the Indian security forces in Kashmir in August 2000. After the Hizb commanders had conducted initial talks with the Indian government in Srinagar, the Pakistan based Hizb Supreme Commander, Syed Salahuddin, called for a fortnightly ceasefire. This became the main cause of the rift between the Indian and Pakistan based Hizb leaders who were once very close.

Syed Salahuddin replaced Dar with Saiful Islam in November 2000 and finally dismissed Dar and his loyal commanders in May 2001. Saiful Islam belonged to Shopaiwan, a village near Srinagar. At the time of his appointment as the Chief Operational Commander, he was in the base camp of Azad Kashmir. His new duties were very hard as he had not done any organisational work earlier although he later earned his name as a guerrilla commander. At that time Hizb-ul-Mujahideen was faced with a lot of internal problems due to the rebellious attitude of Dar-supporting commanders in the organisation. When Salahuddin launched what was called, Operation Take Care of Terrorists, in Indian-held Kashmir against Dar and his supporters, it was Saiful Islam who led the operation. This operation led to violence between the two groups that went on until May 2002. After that bitter internal conflict, many commanders including, Zafar Fateh, Dr Asad Yazdani, and Zubair were expelled from the Hizb-ul-Mujahideen organisation.

The differences between these groups emerged again in 2003 when Syed Salahuddin expelled three more of his commanders for supporting Dar in November 2002. These commanders put their cause before the Kashmir Committee, the supreme council of Hizb-ul-Mujahideen, which consists of the chiefs of Jamaat-e-Islami, in Pakistan, Azad Kashmir and Indian-held Kashmir. The Kashmir Committee gave them a probationary period of six months to prove their loyalty to Hizb before they could rejoin the organisation. Among these commanders, Tufail Altaf, Nadeem Usmani and Almas Khan were prominent. According to some Hizb men, the leadership of Hizb was not happy with this decision and they put this matter before Qazi Hussain Ahmad, the head of Jamaat-e-Islami in January 2003. He asked both groups to make efforts to reunite Hizb-ul-Mujahideen. This decision was also against the wishes of Syed Salahuddin and his allies in the central command of the Hizb. These developments were still taking place when Majeed Dar was shot and killed on 23 March in his native town, Sopore, in Indian-held Kashmir. He had been a senior Kashmiri guerrilla leader who spent around 23 years of his life in the jihad.

Some reports suggested that the internal dispute might have led to his assassination but Jamaat-e-Islami denied these allegations and expressed condolences for his death. A Hizb-ul-Mujahideen leader, on condition of anonymity, told *The Daily Times* that both groups were very aggressive towards each other and are blaming each other for the assassination of their leaders. This tension has spread on both the sides of the LoC (Line of Control) in Kashmir. To prevent clashes in Azad Kashmir, the police took seven members of each group into preventive detention. This situation in Hizb-ul-Mujahideen is not just proving harmful for the organisation itself but also for the freedom movement in Kashmir, according to this anonymous Hizb source. He also said that the leadership of the Jamaat-e-Islami was taking careful notice of the situation and has held all the matters in hand. He hoped the Hizb would resolve the situation very soon.

According to press reports, a little known militant group calling itself the Save Kashmir Movement, had claimed responsibility for shooting down Abdul Majeed Dar for being 'an informer for Indian agencies,' and weakening the Kashmir movement.

In January 2003, Dr Mufakker Ahmed, a former General Secretary of Hizb-ul-Mujahideen and a prominent jihadi leader, told the *The Friday Times* that; "Dar has lost his ground, and is now busy in propaganda and conspiracies against Hizb-ul-Mujahideen and the Kashmir Liberation movement." He also denied Dar's claim that there was a long list of commanders sympathetic to his views. Dr Ahmed said: "If this was true, then why are his men trying to join Hizb-ul-Mujahideen again?" He further added that Dar's chapter was now closed. About the ceasefire decision, Dr Ahmed said: "It is a fact that such a plan was under consideration and through this decision we had the plan to expose India before the world but he (Dar) was not sincere to solve the Kashmir issue, the plan was immature and its terms and conditions were not yet finalised but Dar had announced prematurely in his capacity. Hizb-ul-Mujahideen did not deny it because we knew that it would cause a great crisis in the organisation." Dr Ahmed, apparently, also said there are some reports that Majeed Dar had links with the Indian intelligence agency, the RAW (Research and Analysis Wing) If actually said, it represented a final nail in the coffin of a rival.

However, Abdul Majeed Dar was always opposed to certain tactics used by other groups, such as suicide attacks. In Pakistani jihadi circles, this reflected an image that he had turned into an Indian agent but, in his last interview, he said: "We can be bitter about or unhappy with a few personalities. Pakistan is the state. The people of Pakistan helped us a lot. Some of those who could have helped us did not in spite of having full knowledge of the situation. For us Pakistan is the centre of our hopes."

The death of these two commanders widened the gulf between the two factions of Hizb-ul-Mujahideen and hopes of a reconciliation died with them. Later, the Dar faction in Indian-held Kashmir formed the Jammu Kashmir Salvation Front to save young men from the use of guns and they started a political struggle instead. On the other hand, Syed Salahuddin emerged as the single and only leader of Hizb-ul-Mujahideen. He resolved the disputes, one way or another, and saved his own faction. Jamaat-e-Islami also gave its approval to Hizb-ul-Mujahideen for the following five years. The Muttahida Jihad Council also extended Salahuddin's chairmanship for five more years.

The Alternative Non-violent Islamic Movement

There are as many as 247 religious organisations at work

in Pakistan today. All of them have almost the same aim of establishing an Islamic system of governance in the country. Some of the groups are working for the re-establishment of the Khilafat-e-Rashida (from the Arabic – Caliphate – traditional Islamic governance) such as Dr Asrar Ahmad's Tanzeem-e-Islami, Ahl-e-Hadis's Jamaat-ul-Muslimeen, Jamaat Ahl-e-Hadis, and Ikhwan-ul-Muslimeen. These organisations have not been able to achieve very much except for minor expansions of their areas of influence, nor are they capable of bringing about a big movement. During the last five years, however, several Khilafat organisations from abroad have been successful in establishing networks in Pakistan, among which Hizb-ul-Tahrir and al-Mahajiroon are prominent. These organisations have an agenda to establish Khilafat universally. They are looking for a land where they can establish Khilafat with the consent of the people before moving on to other places. They have been unsuccessful in finding such a place in Arab or African countries during the past forty years and have shifted their centres mainly to Europe, especially Britain. They now have Pakistan in mind for the fulfilment of their vision of creating a model Islamic state.

Hizb-ul-Tahrir

In 1999 some Kashmir-born young members of Hizb-ul-Tahrir living in Britain decided to initiate the organisations program in Pakistan. Hizb-ul-Tahrir considers Pakistan, and states such as Tajikistan and Uzbekistan, suitable for the implementing of their program. Their British headquarters provides them with assistance. The well-known Islamic scholar, Khalid Ahmad, wrote in *The Friday Times* (August 2002) with reference to the background and the aims of this organisation: "Let us take a look at how the Pakistani community reacted to integration inside the United Kingdom. The Pakistanis living in the UK are 700,000, the third largest minority community. (There are a million Indians in the UK). The majority of these British Pakistanis are Kashmiris, including those displaced by the building of the Mangla Dam in Azad Kashmir. They are concentrated in four regions: 30 per cent in and around London, 22 per cent in Birmingham, 20 per cent in Bradford, 4 per cent in Manchester and 3 per cent in Glasgow. The figure of 700,000 has grown from 5000 in 1951. Today, because of their high birth rate, 47 per cent of them are under the age of 16, as compared to 17 per cent for whites. They have the highest unemployment rate, five times more than the British average; and the crime rate is higher among them than in any other community. 2 per cent of the prisoners rotting in British jails are Pakistanis, the highest for any one community.

"Unemployment is the cause of alienation and crime among them. Aggressive organisations (sic) like Hizb-ul-Tahrir and al-Muhajiroon have come up by exploiting the unrest among the unemployed British Pakistanis. There is discrimination in the UK against them and, as always, it is based on how 'different' the Pakistanis are from other citizens. Muslims are less easily employed because of their namaz (prayer) timings, fasting times and conflicting Eid (festival) days, so requiring employers to make special arrangements. In the case of Muslim women, the hijab (head scarf) becomes an obstacle to employment. Employers simply refuse to employ a Muslim or a Pakistani applicant even without confirming whether he would insist on namaz exemptions or not. (This is also true of the private sector in Pakistan where Muslim employees usually put forward a plea of namaz for general absenteeism). Pakistani Christians are, however, more readily accepted in the market. According to one study, in the next ten years the Pakistani community in the UK will suffer further decline in integration and prosperity. The community's Islamic and Pakistani identity will become stronger, which clearly means that there would be less integration. This will lead to more discrimination against them by a society coming under the influence of Islamophobia.

"The rise of Hizb-ul-Tahrir in Pakistan can be understood in the light of the above figures. The 1997 Islamic constitution announced by Hizb, decrees total segregation of the sexes while awarding 'equal rights' to women. The constitution also does not allow a woman to be appointed to a position of authority in government. This again is close to the Salafi (Ahl-e-Hadis) position in Pakistan that a woman cannot rule the country, a position on the basis of which Jamiat Ahl-e-Hadis has been a loyal ally of the PML (N). It is interesting to note that the founder of Hizb-ul-Tahrir in 1953 was of the view that women could be given the job of a judge but, in 1979, the same constitution was issued with a clause clearly banning women from it."

Regardless of the opinion of Khalid Ahmad, Hizb-ul-Tahrir advocates claim they are opposed to sectarian thinking, neither are they concerned with propagating the Salafi message of Ahl-e-Hadis. They claim that the Islamic concept of Khilafat is a complete alternative to the capitalist system and the organisation has done its 'intellectual homework' in an effort to implement it. This homework has been done on the basis of a review of the economic, political, judicial, social and administrative concepts of Khilafat and the practical possibilities of implementing it as an alternative system. A special slogan that caught the imagination of the people in Pakistan is that, in the Khilafat, there would no utility billing such as those used for the supply of electricity, gas, telephone and suchlike, as these would be the responsibility of the government. The Hizb has also declared taxes as being contrary to Islam and it has indicated the sources that would make finances available for the government.

Hizb-ul-Tahrir does not regard itself as an aggressive organisation and it is against all kinds of violence. It considers that the destructive activities going on in Kashmir, Afghanistan and other places are improper. It believes that Muslims should first establish Khilafat after which it would be for the Khilafat to take care of all concerns and complaints.

Wherever Hizb-ul-Tahrir became popular in any country in central Asia, it came under obstructive, very hostile, government pressure, not surprisingly as it is essentially a form of Islamic socialism, not popular with the rulers of any capitalist country. In Pakistan also, it is faced with the same situation. A ban was put on it in November 2002 but, regardless of the ban, it continues to work as usual. Now running second in popularity to the jihadi organisations, Hizb-ul-Tahrir and al-Muhajiroon are still, nevertheless, attracting large numbers of Pakistani youth into their Islamic movements. One of the reasons for this shift in popularity is that these organisations have youth who were educated in foreign countries and, therefore, cannot be so easily persuaded that the jihad is justified in any and every circumstance. They would also be more sceptical about the alleged miracles which would protect them from Indian bullets as professed by some jihadi recruitment leaders in Pakistan.

Organisational Network

After bitter experiences in Arab and central Asian states, Hizb-ul-Tahrir made its organisational network quite complicated to avoid a breakdown in case of bans or persecution. In Pakistan, it has its office in the Siyokas district of Lahore, known as Naved Butt. Naved Butt releases statements issued by the centre in London and is responsible for keeping contacts with the media. Its members are also active among advocates, army personnel, traders, trades unions, unions of professors and teachers who they try to convince of the righteousness their agenda. It is interesting to note that Hizb-ul-Tahrir activists working in different departments generally do not know anything about each other. For example, those working with the army have no contacts with those working with advocates or traders. There are only a few occasions where they may possibly get to know each other. All of them take their instructions from London and send their general reports to Siyokas and special reports to the centre direct.

The Method of Revolution

The Naved Butt office revealed details of the method of revolution of Hizb-ul-Tahrir in Pakistan. It states that it has adopted two operational policies. First, the media and the army is to be influenced to encourage favourable conditions so that powerful institutions and people might become sympathetic to its viewpoint. Considering the special conditions in Pakistan, Naved Butt said that creating an area of influence in the army would mean gaining influence over the nation and; "we are concerned about reaching out to four or five such persons who might establish Khilafat in the country." The second policy course is more traditional and amounts to creating influence and popular support for their program among the public and, thereby, to pressurize the government to establish Khilafat. This program for the creation of Khilafat applies in other countries also where Hizb-ul-Tahrir is active.

According to Naved Butt, both of these policies are to run simultaneously but one method may be more used depending on the special condition of a particular country. For example, the public influence and pressure on the government method is being more widely used in Uzbekistan. Because of the subtlety of this methodology and its low profile network, Hizb-ul-Tahrir has been described as 'non-existent' (illegal) in some countries but, according to some reports, it has already gained ground among army circles in Pakistan.

Al-Muhajiroon

Al-Muhajiroon is also working, more or less, along the same lines but it has not been able to establish a big network anywhere and its activities are limited to holding seminars only.

New Targets

Because of the fall of the Taliban in Afghanistan and the change in the Pakistan Government's policy regarding the jihad in Kashmir, the jihadi organisations have turned to new targets. Some sources claim that secret institutions of the Pakistan state have helped the jihadis to find these new targets so that their power may be used more 'effectively'. These new targets concern Sindh and northern areas.

The Thar region is located in a part of Sindh in Pakistan and in the state of Rajasthan in India. In this desert region, there is a border three hundred kilometres long between India and Pakistan. The Thar desert in Pakistan is spread over 21,000 square kilometres. Its total population of one million is mainly composed of about 550,000 Muslims and 400,000 Hindus. Qadianis (an Islamic sect believing in a second prophet) represent around five per cent and there is a much smaller minority of Christians. Politically, it is the centre of the Mohajir group called the Muttahida Qaumi Movement. The secret agencies say that since it is not possible to properly guard the border, people frequently cross from one side to the other. In this way, it is claimed, agents of the Indian secret services, the RAW, also enter Pakistan without much difficulty. This area has also been the centre of RAW activities and, according to reports, those receiving training in sabotage and violent activities in Pakistan also keep sneaking into India.

As mentioned earlier, Jamaat-ud-Daawa purchased tracts of land in this region and they have been given permission to establish their welfare, organisational, and military networks there. The al-Rasheed Trust is also active in supporting the Jamaat in this new drive. These organisations have, therefore, established dozens of madrasas, mosques, dispensaries, and other welfare centres. Their first target is to 'reform' the Hindu population of the area. In view of its aims and objectives, Jamaat-ud-Daawa has already launched a Sindhi language magazine while the area also gets special attention in its other publications as well. Several editorials and travelogues regularly appear in the publications of the Jamaat and al-Rasheed Trust. *Mujalla al-Daawa* published one such travelogue from which the following extract is taken: "Most of the Hindus have decorated their doorways in the town of Mithi with pictures of Hanuman (a Hindu deity – the monkey/ape who helped Rama). Walking through this town, one gets the impression that it is a Hindustani village where Hindus perform their rites against Islam and Muslims. They also make a dent on their faith. This group came back after two days of moving around in the desert and saw so many things during this time that exhibit how artfully their faith has been defiled and it is difficult for an ordinary Muslim to even mark that defilement. The Hindus are spreading their culture by mixing their ways into the Muslim lives. The ulema and propagators of faith should try their best to stop this wave and if every Muslim plays his role, the increasing influence of the Hindus on religious and political life in Sindh may be stopped. If no attention is paid to these, not only the people and the country will be affected crucially but they shall be liable to answer on the day of judgment. May God give us senses."

In the October issue of the Jamaat-ud-Daawa magazine *Mujalla al-Daawa*, an editorial described the Jamaat's services: "Muslims and Hindus live together in this area. Most of the people here are poor who live in non-solid structures. The last two months had torrential rains and waves of the sea hit the shores. The area that craved for a drop of water was submerged in water. The flood was so heavy that most of the houses along with their inhabitants were washed away. When Sindh Government civil servants were squabbling over the distribution of relief items, the members of Jamaat-ud-Daawa arrived to help them. Its public welfare department distributed 3,500 kilograms of flour, 4,200 kilograms of rice, 1,600 sets of clothes and other consumables to thirty families in Shakoorabad, seventeen families in Gharibabad, seven in Rahmanabad, ten in Goth Saton Wire, fifteen in Peer Jogoth Mutthi, twenty in Lokot and fifteen in Koloi Farm.

"The al-Daawa Medical Mission also did not lag behind. Ten persons under the leadership of Dr Jawed Iqbal from Faisalabad reached Thar with three ambulances and medicine worth four lakhs (400,000) of rupees. They treated people in various areas and walked several hundred metres to bring medical relief to people surrounded by water from all sides."

The editorial went on to describe the success derived from this operation: "Being influenced by this spirit of service rendered by Jamaat-ud-Daawa, 49 persons belonging to 20 families embraced Islam in Markaz Bab-ul-Islam. Hafiz Mohammad Ayub helped them recite the Kalimah (learning about the five pillars of Islam and the method of saying prayers, etc.). Those who embraced Islam mostly belonged to Badin, Lokot, Omarkot, and Mithi and its neighbourhood where Hindus live in a majority."

Jihadi sources claim that, with the establishment of these networks of jihadi and religious organisations, the influence of India in the region will decline, illiteracy will be removed and divisive forces will be side-lined. Tahreek-e-Khuddam-e-Islam, al-Badr Mujahideen, and other jihadi and religious organisations also started establishing their networks in the region following the example of Jamaat-ud-Daawa and the al-Rasheed Trust. It appears they have found a new front for their activities.

Tensions in Northern Areas

Pakistan share borders with China and Afghanistan in its northern areas but a narrow appendix of land in Afghanistan, called the Wakhan, reaches to the Chinese border and separates Pakistan from Tajikistan, the former Soviet republic. Most of the people in the

Wakhan are Shias of the Ismaili or Asna Ashari sects, whereas the Ahl-e-Sunnat, a Sunni sect, makes up only five per cent of the population. The Jamaat Ahl-e-Sunnat represents the Sunni minority and it is based in Baltistan. They have a good number of their madrasas and mosques there.

The Agha Khan Foundation is quite prominent in the Wakhan and it runs a number of welfare projects. However, Jamaat Ahl-e-Sunnat claim that the Agha Khan Foundation is working only for the Ismaili population because it wants to establish a separate state. Perceiving this as a threat from the Ismailis, Jamaat Ahl-e-Sunnat provides hideouts to jihadi organisations in these areas and maintain very close links with them. Conditions arising out of 9/11 and the fall of the Taliban attracted the attention of jihadi organisations to the Wakhan and opposition activities against the idea of an Ismaili state also increased.

The Ismaili religious leader, Prince, the Agha Khan, met President Musharraf in December 2003. The flag of the Ismaili state was flapping at this meeting. A report in *The Daily Islam* (an al-Rasheed Trust publication) claims that Prince Karim Agha Khan had got the agreement of Ziaul Haq (General Zia) to make the northern areas into a separate state but this conspiracy failed on account of Ismaili opposition to the political leadership in Kashmir. This claim must be questioned in view of General Zia's belief in an enlarged Pakistan. However, *The Daily Islam* also claims that people belonging to Ismaili organisations receive their training in Israel, that they have close links with Israel and want to concentrate on the northern areas in order to create an Ismaili state.

Apart from Jamaat Ahl-e-Sunnat, Tanzeem-ul-Ikhwan was also running some welfare organisations in Wakhan but now, as well as the al-Rasheed Trust, Jamiat-ul-Ansar, Jamaat-ud-Daawa, and Tahreek-e-Khuddam-e-Islam have also started setting up their networks. Their aim is to minimize the impact of the Agha Khan Foundation in these areas and to find safe training camps for their mujahideen so that they may reach into Afghanistan and central Asia more easily.

Chapter 4
MEDIA WAR FOR HEARTS AND MINDS

As with all conflicts, there are two sides to the story. To put it in a nutshell, western propagandists claim that Muslim extremists are a threat to the peace of the world while Muslim jihadis claim themselves to be the liberators of Muslim people from western, particularly American, imperialism and moral corruption. The discerning reader may well conclude that there is an element of truth to be found in every philosophy and getting the balance right is never easy.

What follows is an examination of the dissemination of anti-western pro-militancy propaganda by the jihadi movement to maintain the sympathy of their supporters and to persuade the 'floating voters' of the righteousness of their cause. Without popular support from Muslim people in the streets, the jihadi movement would be non-existent. They need volunteers, manpower, because money alone cannot do much except attract criminals whose loyalty is always dubious. Popular support is essential and that is true for any political, religious or nationalist movement in the world. Concerning this propaganda war, the reader should always bear in mind that the common citizen in Pakistan is not that well educated and is, therefore, more susceptible to even the most ridiculous conspiracy theories or claims made by propagandists.

On 6 March 2002, the federal government asked the Sindh, the Punjab and Azad Kashmir governments to ban the publication of as many as 22 magazines, the propaganda organs of different religious and jihadi organisations being issued from Karachi, Lahore and Muzaffarabad. Putting this ban on 17 monthly magazines and 5 weekly and quarterly magazines was an extension of the measures set by the UN Security Council Sanction Committee and the US Government against terrorist individuals and entities.

The monthly magazines, which had been selected to be banned included: *al-Irshad International* (Islamabad), *Banat-e-Aisha* (Karachi), *al-Daawa* (Lahore), *Kashmir Action* (Lahore), *al-Rihat* (in Arabic, Lahore), *al-Masood* (Muzaffarabad/Karachi), *Sada-i-Kashmir* (Muzaffarabad), *Sada-i-Mujahid* (Islamabad/ Karachi), *Voice of Islam* (in English, Lahore), *Shahadat* (Srinagar/Muzaffarabad/Islamabad), *Jihad-e-Kashmir* (Muzaffarabad), *Zarb-e-Taiyyaba* (Lahore), the monthly digest *Badar* (Lahore), *Mahaz-e-Kashmir* (Muzaffarabada), *Dawaat-e-Tanzeemul Islam* (Lahore/Sialkot/Gujranwala) and *Weekly Asia* (Lahore), the weekly *Zarb-e-Momin* (Karachi), the weekly *Jihad Times* (in Urdu, Lahore) the fortnightly *Jaish-e-Mohammad* (Karachi) and the quarterly *Taiba* (Lahore). The Jaish-e-Mohammad, al-Badr Mujahideen, Jamaat-e-Islami, Lashkar-e-Taiba, al-Rasheed Trust, Hizb-ul-Mujahideen, Sunni Jihad Council, and Hizb-e-Jihad-e-Islami were managing and issuing these publications. Within just two months of the new restrictions coming into effect all of these publications reappeared in the market, mostly under the same names though some also reappeared with alternative names. In recent years, jihadi publications have played a major role in promoting jihadi culture in Pakistan. A new genre of jihadi journalism with its wide range of outlets has arrived on the Pakistani media-scene. Their printing systems reflects the use of modern technology and, in terms of layout, the use of colour imaging and multimedia techniques, they are no different from any other printed media product available in the market. Their marketing strategy resembles mainstream newspaper publishing and they are sold at most newsstands around the country as well as having special distribution networks run by local jihadi organisations and madrasas. The publishers of these papers and magazines often make claims for their sales/circulation which compare well with the largest circulation newspapers and magazines in the country.

The prices of these jihadi publications are amazingly low and are affordable to low-income groups. Along with their hard copy issues, these publications are also available on interactive websites run by the jihadi groups. In terms of their general content, these publications fall into the category of an alternative media wherein they forcefully propagate jihadi views of life. According to authoritative data, of the known 3000 religious publications, more than five hundred are being published on a regular basis, more than half appear only irregularly and some only sporadically. Out of 1500 of these publications 300 of them propagate the ideas of Islamic jihad. Many different jihadi groups manage 120 publications between them.

Most of the religious seminaries are also promoting jihad and their publications support different jihadi groups (see appendix I).

Six major jihadi organisations; Jamaat-ud-Daawa (Lashkar-e-Taiba), Tahreek Khuddam-ul-Islam, al-Rasheed Trust, Jamaat-ul-Mujahideen, Hizb-ul-Mujahideen and Harkat-ul-Jihad-e-Islami bring out a range of publications to target children, adolescents, youth, women, and general readers separately. Of these, Jamaat-ud-Daawa also runs a web-based radio station, *Radio al-Jihad*, as well and it broadcasts in four languages; Urdu, English, Arabic and Sindhi, to disseminate their message at home and abroad.

The publishers themselves claim that their publications have over five hundred professional journalists employed on the express condition that they must subscribe to the jihadi worldview.

The emergence of this new genre of journalists and publications coincides with the Afghan jihad against the Soviets in the 1980s when wire services like the Afghan Islamic Press emerged. Later on, in the 1990s, the Kashmir Media Service and Kashmir Press International were established in Pakistan. With the rise to power of the Taliban in Afghanistan, it got a tremendous boost and became quite vocal and proactive in favour of what could be described as 'the Talibanisation of hearts, minds and souls' in Pakistan. In legal terms, many of these publications have legitimate Declarations (charters/licences) issued by the appropriate authorities. The Audit Bureau of Circulation which entitles them to receive government public advertising has certified a few of them and has favoured them with placements. However, most of them prefer to print jihadi advertisements such as those offering training opportunities, appeals for donations, notices of congregations, et cetera.

At the time of writing, the following publications were making their regular appearances on the newsstands: the monthly, *Mahaz-e-Kashmir* (Jamaat-ul-Mujahideen, Jammu and Kashmir), the monthly, *Shahadat* (in Urdu), *The Message* (in English) and an Arabic monthly, *Tahreek-ul-Mujahideen* (Jammu and Kashmir). The fortnightlies *Jihad-e-Kashmir* and *Jamaat-e-Islami* (Jammu and Kashmir). *Shamsheer, Binatul Aisha* and *al-Aslah* (Tahreek Khadimul Islam), *Islam* and *Zarb-e-Momin* (al-Rasheed Trust) *Mujalla al-Daawa, Tiayabat,* and *Ghazwa Times* (Jamat-ud-Daawa).

Leading Propagandists

Four leading jihadi groups offer the following publications:

1. Jamaat-ud-Daawa publish the monthly *Voice of Islam* in English, the monthly *al-Ribat* in Arabic, the monthly *Mujalla al-Daawa* in Urdu, the monthly *Tiayabat* in Urdu for women, the monthly *Zarb-e-Taiba* in Urdu for youth and students. They also publish the weekly *Ghazwa Times* in Urdu and Sindhi and they run *Radio al-Jihad* broadcasting in Urdu and Arabic. Their website – www.markazdawa.org – is very popular.

2. Jamaat-ul-Ansar publish the monthly *al-Hilal* in Urdu, English and Arabic. Complimentary copies of this are sent to the families of the martyrs.

3. Tahreek-e-Khuddam-ul-Islam brings out the fortnightly *Shamsheer* in Urdu and English, and the monthly *Binat-e-Aisha* in Urdu for women.

4. Al-Rasheed, ostensibly a charity organisation, advocates a jihadi view of life through *The Daily Islam* in Urdu and the weekly *Zarb-e-Momin* in Urdu and English.

The editorial content of these papers show support for the Taliban, Jamaat-ul-Furqan, Sipah-e-Sahaba. Occasionally, the activities of Lashkar-e-Taiba are also supported.

Unlike Deobandi and Ahl-e-Hadis, which are Wahabi sects, the Shia and Barelvis are not visible in the jihad business. However, two publications, *Zarb-e-Islam* (in Urdu) and the monthly *Dawat-e-Islam* (in Urdu) are printed by Barelvis and they eulogise the jihad in Afghanistan and Kashmir but they are not publicly associated with any jihadi organisation.

About the readership of these publications, the monthly *Mujalla al-Daawa* (in Urdu) claims the highest circulation of 400,000 copies per month. Next comes the weekly *Zarb-e-Momin* with a claim of 250,000 copies sold every week. The weekly *Ghazwa Times* recently announced that its print order is 200,000 copies. *The Daily Islam* (al-Rasheed Trust, Karachi/Islamabad), launched after the 9/11 attacks in New York and Washington, claims that it sells 60,000 copies every day throughout the country. The visitor count on the websites of Jamaat-ud-Daawa and Tahreek Khuddam-ul-Islam reveal that their sites are browsed daily by approximately 500 and 150 visitors respectively.

Traditionally, the clergy has been a repository of religious knowledge and information and shared it with their followers mainly by means of oral communication. However, Guttenberg's invention of the printing press radically changed the transmission of knowledge from oral communication to mass produced print communications in Christendom. Historically, Lutheranism was the product of the printed book. Within Islam, the Koran was revealed upon the prophet Mohammad (peace be upon him) and his companions learnt it by heart. Even today, memorising the holy Koran is regarded as a prized scholarship. In the context of the subcontinent, in the 1820s, Muslim religious clerics were among the early users of the printing press when they realised the power of this technological advancement. By the 1830s, the first Muslim newspapers were being printed. In the 1870s, editions of the holy Koran and other religious books were selling popularly. Many ulema (Islamic scholars) used print technology to compensate for the gradual loss of political power in the subcontinent.

The trend started with the magazines of religious seminaries such as *al-Haq*, run by Darul Uloom Haqqnia and *al-Jamia*, run by Jamia Mohammad Sharif. Later, right wing religious parties such as Jamaat-e-Islami and Jamiat Ulema-e-Islam launched religious publishing houses with a variety of newspapers and magazines. Besides regular newspaper and magazine production, wall-size posters, handbills and, later, audio cassettes also served as tools of communication among the clergy. They have not been slow to exploit the new medium of the Internet to propagate their jihadi message. Today, most jihadi groups print magazines or newsletters on the web and offer services in Arabic on their websites as well as Pushto, Dari, and the regional languages of Afghanistan and Kashmir (their main theatres of operations). Another testimony to their pan-Islamic approach is a series of glorified stories about mujahideen from all over the world in Afghanistan and non-Kashmiri Pakistanis in Indian-held Kashmir, though many Urdu language newspapers accord massive coverage to jihadi organisations in the country. The mastheads of almost all these newspapers carry one of the Islamic verses to assert their distinct Islamic identity. The trend has been so inspiring that the Christian daily *Aftab*, published in Quetta, carries text from *The Bible* on its masthead now.

The common man reads vernacular newspapers which are, by and large, conservative in their approach, whereas elite English publications are quite progressive but have a smaller readership. At the time of independence in 1947, Pakistan inherited a nationalistic and progressive press in the shape of the Progressive Papers company but the state's takeover of this publishing house eventually brought it to an end. Meanwhile, a series of media guidelines issued by the state-run Islamic Ideology Council along with unrelenting pressure from a coterie of ideologues squeezed out liberal ideas and killed-off the democratic will to dissent. Consequently, there are many people with a jihadi mind-set now working in the country's newsrooms who are pushing their own narrow agenda.

If one examines the political economy of the jihad movement, it reads like a profitable industry's balance sheet. They have a huge turnover of revenue and their media products are forcefully marketed in a very effective way. For example, pictures of women donating their jewellery and ornaments for the cause, accompanied by highly emotive captions, frequently appear in jihad publications. Further, these publishing houses can act conveniently to launder the black money which pours into their coffers along with other regular donations for the cause. The decision to issue separate publications in Arabic by these groups hints at this aspect of jihadi finances but further investigation is required to substantiate the matter.

The All Pakistan Newspapers Society and the Council for Pakistani Newspaper Editors, albeit under government pressure, stated that they would not publish sectarian statements in mainstream newspapers. Fear of a complete blackout in the mainstream media has encouraged the trend towards an alternative, underground, jihadi press. The editorials of these jihadi publications often criticize the mainstream media in Pakistan for being hostage to secular-minded journalists who they describe as the "advocates of obscenity". They also complain of half-hearted coverage of the jihadi point of view. Therefore, the growing alternative jihadi press and media offers ample space to these organisations to construct, propagate and magnify their version of reality.

In the South Asian context, the effective publishing network of the hawkish Hindu, the RSS (Hindi) – Rashtria Savak Sangh – the nationalist religious wing of the BJP), has been an inspiration to Islamic jihadis. It is worth mentioning here that the RSS – the mentor of the extremist Hindu political party, the BJP, floated the Bharat Prakashan Trust in 1946 and launched *The Organiser* in July 1947. Later, the Sangh Parivar (Urdu – united Hindu family) started its weekly, monthly and daily publications for children, youth, women, and the general public in various Indian languages. The jihadi groups have imitated the same methods and this trend continues. One can draw many interesting inferences from the amazing religious/political discourses conducted in these publications. Following is a brief outline of these discourses.

Immediately after the 9/11 attacks in New York and Washington, the jihadi press elevated the Taliban leader, Mullah Omar, from Amireeul Momineen (supreme leader) of Afghanistan to that of Supreme Leader of the entire Ummah (the Muslim world). They termed the Islamic Emirates of Afghanistan as being the only complete Islamic state in the world and opined that Jews, Hindus and Christians were all out to demolish this castle of puritan faith with the sword of dollars. They described the global war against terrorism as the 'crusades'. They criticize the Pakistan Government's policy of 'putting Pakistan first' and emphasize the creed that all believers are obliged to die for Islam and everything else comes later. They glorify the cult of death and regard human development indicators and the preservation of human life as an infidel move to sap the spirit of jihad. According to the dominant message of these jihadi publications, the real lives of believers begin after their martyrdom.

They often talk of different deaths. For example, they repeatedly say that thousands of Muslims killed in Palestine, Kashmir, Chechnya, or Bosnia cannot move the world or the UN conscience so much as the death of a single American or Israeli. Using this same logic, they motivate believers to embrace martyrdom through jihad to reach Heaven instead of being killed by Jewish or Hindu bullets.

These jihadi publications criticize Pakistan for joining the global coalition against terrorism and for surrendering despite its possession of nuclear weapons and its spending of billions of rupees on its armed forces. In a way, they have started criticising Pakistan's massive defence spending for the first time. They claim that the Jews, Christians and Hindus have laid the entire Afghan nation to waste to penalize Pakistan because of its development of nuclear weapons. Regarding the 9/11 attacks on America, the jihadi press claim that it was a Jewish conspiracy and that Osama bin Laden and his al-Qaida network do not have the technological capability to execute such a sophisticated operation.

In many jihadi publications there are usually articles giving details such as the last will of the latest martyr, letters from mothers, sisters or wives of martyrs eulogising the sacrifices of their loved ones. However, the lists of martyrs published in these newspapers and magazines also indicate the fact that many foreign operators are busy in the jihad inside Pakistan.

The jihadi publications regard the American freeze on their organisational assets as an honour and maintain that they care not for material assets but instead boast that the US cannot freeze their faith. These publications make fun of democracy and capitalism as the instruments of obscene civilization and urge Muslim youth not to study in Europe or America because they will end up losing faith in the glitter of what they call the 'nude civilization' of the west. The jihadi press urges Muslim children to immerse themselves in the spirit of jihad as early a possible. They should play with guns as toys and eventually should learn to use them against the infidels. They criticize the Musharraf regime's policies of reforming religious seminaries and restricting jihadi donation boxes.

This analysis of jihadi propaganda is necessarily brief but one interesting aspect needs to be pointed out and that is that most of these publications do not carry any sort of material that is critical of the various Arab monarchies and emirates in the Middle East, despite the fact that one of the reasons behind Osama bin Laden's anger was the presence, with the consent of the Saudi monarchy, of American infidel troops in the holy land of Saudi Arabia. This failure to criticize Arab regimes provides a clue to the identity of the foreign operators, and the sources of finance, but it also exposes the double standards and hypocrisy of the jihadi press. A later chapter deals with the extent of Saudi and other oil rich Arab states' investments in western capitalist corporations and enterprises but this information is never made available to the readers of the jihadi propaganda machine's press.

The jihadi groups still collect donations from the Pakistani public and almost every paper and magazine regularly carries appeals for funds, Below are two examples showing the style and tactics these organisations use to attract donations.

Jamiat-ul-Ansar's *al-Hilal* published the following jihadi advertisement on the last page of every recent issue:

The Bleeding World of Islam

Iraq – The land of prophets
Where hungry, American oppressed,
orphan children are crying for help

Afghanistan – The land of martyrs
Where the war between the infidels and Islam goes on

Indian Kashmir – The heavenly land
Where prestige is unprotected and women disparaged

Palestine – The holy land
Where dear ones of the mothers are being sacrificed

Chechnya
Where lively marketplaces and towns
are turning into derelict places

Bharat
Where the lives of Muslims are under attack

Is it not incumbent upon you to help these Muslims?

Are they not your brothers in the Islamic brotherhood and human concern?

Can this not be your fate too?

Be aware of your duties

A regular advertisement of Jamaat al-Furqan published
in *Tadbeer-e-Nau* is as follows:

Have You Ever Thought?

Crores (millions) of Muslims are living in a state of
helplessness from Kashmir to Palestine.

Who will help them? Who will put balm on the
wounds
of the innocent children injured by the bombs?

Who will secure the release of the great
Generals of Islam imprisoned in the jails of the kafirs?
Who will save the faith of the Muslims trapped by the
NGOs?

The Cola War

Even before the American attack on Afghanistan,
religious and jihadi organisations had been appealing
for people to boycott Pepsi Cola, Coca Cola, and other
European and American consumer products. They
claim that the profits earned from the sale of these
products is being used against Muslims. PEPSI was
turned into an acronym reading; Pay Each Penny, Save
Israel. This slogan was given a lot of space in the
Islamic media.

The boycott campaign gathered momentum after
the American attack on Afghanistan. The Pak/Afghan
Defence Council, which later gave birth to Muttahida
Majlis-e-Amal, issued a list of 224 American, European
and Israeli consumer items, products and companies to
be boycotted. It was believed that they were
transferring Pakistani capital outside Pakistan to be

used against Muslims. Later, when America and its allies invaded and occupied Iraq, Muttahida Majlis-e-Amal organised marches and protest movements all over Pakistan and gave a strident call to the people to boycott the products of multinational companies.

During this time, more than twenty new soft-drink products appeared in the market; Mecca Cola, Zam Zam Cola, Pak Cola and Makki Cola are a few of the new brand names. It seemed as if a 'cola war' had started in Pakistan. Religious organisations gave a good marketing boost to these new drinks and this resulted in a marked fall in sales of both Pepsi and Coca Cola in Pakistan and the Muslim world. The reality, however, is that no products like Mecca Soap, Pak Tyres or Zam Zam Windows 2000 appeared to compete with foreign consumables, nor are they likely to appear. The instigators of these campaigns, having done their jihadi boycotting service for the day will, most likely, climb into their Mercedes cars to drive home to watch their Sony television sets while their wives prepare meals on their GEC electric cookers and, if they have to organise another boycott campaign in another Pakistani city, may well travel on a Boeing 727 to their destination.

The jihadis will learn, if they do not already understand, that boycotts can be effective against individual companies but capitalism cannot be boycotted and it is a competitive market that determines consumer spending. In Pakistan, and throughout the Muslim world, most of the people still buy and use the products of the multinational companies.

Nevertheless, organisers of boycotts and protest campaigns get publicity and, therefore, many jihadi organisations took a very active part in the boycott of foreign products. The publications of Jamiat-ul-Ansar, Jamat al-Furqan, and Tahreek-e-Khuddam-e-Islam repeatedly brought out comparative statements of domestic and multinational products, favouring indigenously produced goods by providing detailed information about them. They consider it to be a part of jihadi activity now. This boycott campaign is also used to fuel anti-semitism with Nazi style propaganda.

In its June 2003 issue of Jamat al-Furqan's *Tadbeer-e-Nau*, the following was published: "International Jewish organisations have made the Islamic and the third world their slaves economically with the help of later conspiracies. The Americans are oppressing Afghanistan and Iraq with the help of Britain and other European countries in order to realize the dream of a Greater Israel. Israeli forces have continuously crushed innocent Palestinians under their tanks. It must be remembered that money is the biggest tool in the hands of the Jews, as it is their biggest weakness.

"If we have a look around today, we would find that all that we have is in the hands of the Jews. All our household items, whether big or small, are either Jewish or Christian products. We are virtually throttling ourselves. We do not know how badly we are damaging ourselves, how our mothers and sisters are outraged. We do not need to make complaints but to examine ourselves. Have we grown so insensitive that we are paying for the killing of our own people? Has our Sharia gone so far down that we have agreed to eat the prohibited items? Do we have a face to show to our prophet on the day of judgment?

"We may mend ourselves even now. We may still direct our money to reach our own pockets rather than the pockets of the Christians and the Jews. If each one of us decides to boycott their products, we may make our contribution to jihad against the Jewish forces. There are examples to show that wherever efforts to boycott their products have been made, these multinational companies have come to terms immediately because their entire economy is based on earning interest and spreading lies.

"Let us get together and make our contribution to this jihad and damage the Jewish interests. Let us boycott the Jewish drinks such as Pepsi Cola and Coca Cola that damage health and save ourselves from the wrong effects of these on our health, and more importantly, let us save our faith.

"We would like to make use of this opportunity to tell all the national producing units, along with you, that we should move forward and standardize our own products and make them available to our people at competitive rates to help get out of their clutches. We may save our freedom in this way and save ourselves from being slaves to others. We shall have the grace of God and surely successful are those who have their consciousness alive."

The tone of this article speaks for itself but reason requires that some perspective is applied, something these highly prejudiced Islamists seldom do. They confuse Zionism and Zionists with Jews generally, ignoring the fact that there are many Jewish critics of Zionism among the population, and in the major political movements, of Europe and America. They, presumably, would say all Germans were Nazis if

Hitler had persecuted Muslims instead of Jews. No doubt, there are Jewish members among the rulers of America and Europe but they are a minority and, apart from Israel, certainly do not decide the destiny of their nations, regardless of any inordinate influence they may enjoy. Saudi royals, and other wealthy Muslim families from Africa to Asia, are major stakeholders of economic interests in America and Europe. Alas, as said earlier, fanaticism, political or religious, creates its own logic, self-deceptions and self-perpetuating mythologies which are then used to self-justify any actions which appeal to the self-elected. The failure of the jihadi propagandists to mention the influence of the Japanese (non-Jewish and non-Christian) products which dominate the domestic market simply underlines their bias as does their failure to take account of the fact that 'the west' is not a homogenous mass of single-minded people conspiring against the Muslim world. They ignore the fact that there are many people, including Jews, in the west; politicians, writers, intellectuals and ordinary citizens, who oppose Zionism, the persecution of the Palestinian people, the invasion of Afghanistan and Iraq and the occupation of those countries by their own forces. Prime Minister Tony Blair and, to a lesser extent, President George Bush, are themselves being severely criticised and could lose their offices because of the massive ground-swell of anti-war public opinion which they ignored when they made their decision to invade Iraq.

The monthly *al-Halal* published a story headed: WAIT, ARE YOU EATING HARAM BY ANY CHANCE? (haram – unclean – forbidden food – pork) in its September

2003 issue. The article went on; "A research centre in Beirut has published a report which contains a list of items that have pork fat and other ingredients of that dirty animal in them. The list is long but a few of them are being mentioned here that are generally used in Pakistan. (1) Lata soap (2) Camay soap (3) Prince biscuit – only in chocolate flavour (4) Rite biscuit (5) Colgate toothpaste (6) Lux soap (7) Palmolive toothpaste (8) Liscap cream (9) Brylcreme (10) Pepsi Cola, which contains a chemical called pepsin made out of hog's blood (11) lipsticks of all kinds which contain pork fat that melts with human body heat (thereby to enter the body through the skin).

"Laws in all countries make it incumbent upon companies to name the ingredients of the product on the packing, but several companies provide only codes instead of the real names. Some of these codes are completely prohibited for Muslims. We are producing hereunder a table of the codes that you my keep as a photocopy."

The article continued: "It is difficult to remember all the codes. It would be easy to check if the ingredient of any product has the capital letter E, and if it is there, you will know that the product has something prohibited in it. In the summer season, Tang is used as a drink in most of our houses. If you care to look, you would find code E110 on the packet, which is a prohibited ingredient. It is, therefore, important for us to stop drinking it immediately. If we have been drinking it unknowingly, God will forgive us for that. We should now take care in future and abstain from using such products. If we take a little precaution and pray to God, our prayers will surely be answered."

Needless to say, this calls for a boycott of almost every foreign consumable product in the market. It does not give any verifiable details of the source of the claim that pork fat is actually in the listed E-numbers. The Beirut 'centre' is not identified. Yet, most western producers of consumables have indigenous Muslim, and Jewish consumers as well as Christian and they export to Muslim countries all over the world. One must be sceptical, therefore, in believing these producers are so insensitive to their markets that they deliberately use pork extracts in consumables they know will be consumed by Muslims and Jews. No doubt, most of them would know the story of the Indian Mutiny when an earlier Muslim/Hindu independence movement started a rumour, a lie, amongst Muslim troops loyal to the Raj that the British were using pork-fat in their cartridge cases (which had to be bitten open). Nevertheless, the lie was effective and led to mutiny by those troops who believed the rumour and the British had a more difficult job in reasserting their rule over the subcontinent as a consequence.

Propaganda does not have to be true, it just wants people to believe the slogans. The jihadi propaganda machine does not bother to explain how we must accept that the very same Jews who, according to the very same propagandists, are running the world from America and Europe and whose religion also forbids the consumption of pork, are deliberately making all other Jews eat haram because the same products are in the shops in Tel Aviv. Clearly then, reason and logic play no part in this propaganda war.

Another Ban

In November 2003, Tahreek-e-Khuddam-e-Islam, Millat-e-Islamia Pakistan, and Tahreek-e-Islami were declared illegal once again. Jamaat-ud-Daawa was kept on the watch list. In the next phase, Jamiat-ul-Ansar, Hizb-al-Tahreer, and Jamat al-Furqan were also banned. After imposing this ban, a nationwide crackdown on the jihadis was carried out all over Pakistan and seven hundred activists were arrested. The central leadership of the organisations was, however, spared in these arrests except for Allama Sajid Naqvi, the Chief of Tahreek-e-Islami who was named in the killing of the Maulana Azam Tariq. Raids were also carried out to arrest Maulana Masood Azhar, the leader of Jaish-e-Mohammad, but he was in hiding. Some sources suggest that the ISI provided him with a secure refuge.

Later, the process of releasing the arrested activists started as it had done previously and, in spite of all the bans, most of the organisations started working openly in the same manner as before. One of the reasons for the ban being ineffective is said to be the fact that it was done only to establish the belief abroad, especially in America, that Pakistan was quite serious about acting against the jihadis. The English weekly, *The Friday Times*, wrote in its 21 November 2003 issue: "The report by the American 'Task Force on New Priorities in South Asia' clearly indicates that the US $1.5 billion package is linked with Pakistan's progress in implementing political, economic and social reforms and its co-operation in the war on terrorism.

America has a major stake in friendly and long term ties with Pakistan. A positive relationship, however, will be difficult to sustain unless Islamabad firmly turns its back on terrorist groups and plays a non-proliferation role,' the report says.

"Insiders, however, say the ban may not be effective since the groups have a way of morphing. 'The government has not done much more than seal the offices of these groups and post some policemen there,' says an observer. Even after last year's action in January the government did not press charges against any of the arrested leaders and was forced to release all those who were detained after the ban. They included Masood Azhar of Jaish-e-Mohammad who was put under house arrest later and Hafiz Mohammad Saeed of Jamaat-ud-Daawa. 'We could not initiate any case except against those involved in sectarian violence,' DIG (Deputy Inspector General) Karachi, Asad Ashraf Malik told *TFT*; 'Hundreds of activists of these outfits went underground and police could not recover any weapons caches. The day the government announced the ban, on 15 November, thousands of followers of Masood Azhar were gathering to listen to him address jihad rallies in Karachi later that day. Most of them immediately went underground. Azhar himself dropped plans to make speeches and left for some unknown destination. He remains at large despite police efforts to track him down.' 'The government remains undecided on how to handle thousand of followers of these groups,' says another police officer, adding, 'They are armed and motivated and I am not sure if official bans can get them to stop doing what they are hell-bent on doing.'

"Azhar was last arrested following the ban on Jaish-e-Mohammad but was later put under house arrest. 'We did not have any orders to arrest him until the recent ban,' said police chief, Tariq Jamil. 'The resistance to American forces in Iraq has given new hope to thousands of Islamists here. They are spoiling to engage in jihad.' Abu Mustafa, a student of an Islamic seminary in Karachi told *TFT*. Most observers say the ban will test the government severely.

"President Musharraf banned Lashkar-e-Taiba and Jaish-e-Mohammad last year after they were listed as terrorist organisations by the United States. *TFT* investigations show that membership of these groups has increased despite the ban. What is worse from the government's viewpoint is the fact that their policies have become more radical.

"The most organised of the groups is Jamaat-ud-Daawa. Daawa's outspoken chief, Hafiz Mohammad Saeed, continues to be strident in his condemnation of the United States, India and the Musharraf Government's policies. The group received a setback last month when one of its main madrasas was raided and police arrested a few Malaysian students for alleged linkage with Hanbali's Jema-ah-Islamiyah. But it has escaped a ban this time and the government has merely put it on the watch list.

"An intelligence official with long experience of interrogating jihadi and sectarian activists says the ban will hardly help the government. 'It's true that it (the ban) may restrict their activities in public but how can the government change their minds? Those in custody are not scared of arrest or even death,' he said. Jihadis often put interrogators in an awkward position. 'We are fighting for Islam and you put us in prison, is the usual line,' he said."

In spite of this ban, these jihadi and sectarian organisations are still active. Hizb Tahreer and Tahreek-e-Islami maintain they have not received any government banning notice in this regard and that militant organisations cannot be banned without public announcements. Millat-e-Islamia is now active under the name of Sunni Action Forum.

The journals of jihadi organisations are still being published as usual, and they carry threats as they did before. Jamiat-ul-Ansar's *al-Hilal* carried a piece by Maulana Fazlur Rehman Khalil in its December 2003 issue: "Great warriors of Jamiat-ul-Ansar! It is our aim to establish Khilafat-e-Rashida all over the world. We have to overpower all the oppressors proud and overbearing forces. We have to pay the debt of the blood of our martyrs. The blood shed in the valleys of Afghanistan, Kashmir, Iraq and Palestine calls you. Each part of the earth is eagerly awaiting a revolution. You know all this and yet you have chosen to go slow.

"You have stopped to rest on the way even before reaching the destination. You too have been enamored of the scenes by the wayside. Who will then transform the autumn of this garden into a spring. Why have dark clouds cast over the heart's horizon? The caravan of the right moves ahead in spite of all obstacles. The obstructions on the way only test one's fortitude. The hard winds may blow out the candles but the embers get enlivened further. Similarly my friends, people with little courage give way with little opposition but those with high conviction do not yield.

"Dear workers of Jamiat-ul-Ansar! Get united – join your soldiers – hold your hands – get up with a new spirit and tell the world that you are the soldiers of those who have defeated the most powerful in the past. Be friends with jails, chains and bullets. You will have to wade the sea of blood, face the tough test of time while moving on the path of jihad. And remember that blood shed in this way is never wasted. The death of a martyr is the life of the community and his blood its zakat (charity). The pains borne for any ideological reason bring the goal closer. The lamps lit with the blood of the martyrs cannot ever be quenched with the hard winds of the times. These are the sources of light for the future generations.

"Great warriors! Come and stand like a boulder before the waves. Come and face the enemies like the brave ones. If you die, you will be treated as a martyr and people will sing songs in your praise. Life is to face and fare forward. Making efforts is better than lying low. If we are cowed down by fear, we shall be laughed at but if we reach the destination, we shall sing the songs of victory. Get rid of dark thoughts, wipe your tears, and take a vow that you will sacrifice your lives for the great mission. (Maulana Fazlur Rehman Khalil, Emir – Jamiat-ul-Ansar)."

A New Law

In order to keep the jihadi activists in complete check, the government made some amendments to Schedule

4 of the Anti-Terrorist Act of 1997. It was added that the jihadi activists would have to keep their area police chief informed of their movements and they would also have to submit a guarantee bond.

This amendment was severely criticised in jihadi circles. On 25 January 2004 *The Daily Islam* (Lahore) wrote; "During the last few days, some ulema of Rawalpindi were called to the police station through the organizers and deputy organizers of the respective areas and they were asked to fill up a form. (Is it a part of the organiser's duties to keep an eye on the ulema and ensure their presence in the police stations?). This form was sent to the police stations by the Punjab Government where the chief minister hails from a religious family and who has reached this position after making great efforts. The concern of this family with religion can only be gauged by the wedding ceremony of his son. The form was clearly indicative of the attitude that the Punjab Government had towards the ulema and how sincerely it was trying to follow the American agenda. The first part of the form has Annex-B which has a personal undertaking under IT-EE Schedule 4 of the Anti-Terrorist Act of 1997. In case of one's failure in following the undertaking, a fine will have to be paid to the treasury of the Punjab government. It says at one place 'if I go out of the city of my residence, I will inform the local SHO (Chief of Police station) in writing and will also inform him of my return.'

"The other part of the form is a guarantee as Annex-B in which the guarantor has to agree that he has been appointed to stand a guarantee regarding the activities of the said person as per the provision of IT-EE under Schedule 4, and make him follow the conditions. The

British (during the Raj) had included the imams of the mosques in their papers in the category of the low ranking people but the slaves of the British ideology and mentality have included the imams and the ulema in the tenth category of criminals. By doing this, they have given an example of their enlightenment, reasonableness, and love for their religion."

The activities of the jihadi activists continued in spite of the new law and along with the wave of criticism that accompanied it. After the latest attack on the life of President Musharraf in December 2003, the security services felt that the law was still inadequate.

Why was Jamaat-ud-Daawa Exempted from the Ban?

Jamaat-ud-Daawa is the most prominent of the jihadi organisations in Pakistan. Its activities are still going on. Even though there are several grounds available for putting a ban on it, this organisation is still only on the watch list. A knowledgeable source from a law-enforcement agency said that Lashkar-e-Taiba was the only organisation left now that is playing a role in the Kashmir jihad and it has thousands of its activists in Kashmir even today. A ban on them here would mean spreading disappointment among the mujahideen there. He said that no ban on Jamaat-ud-Daawa can be imposed while the mujahideen are there.

Chapter 5

MUTTAHIDA MAJLIS-E-AMAL: THE POLITICAL FACE OF THE JIHADIS

After the 2002 election in Pakistan suddenly, Pakistan's political map has been painted the colour of the Muttahida Majlis-e-Amal (MMA – United Action Forum) that combines the six major parties of the religious right mentioned earlier. They already form the governments in the Frontier Province and Baluchistan. Their latest victory comes 55 years after the Muslim League's Direct Action Day that precipitated the partition of the subcontinent and 32 years after the country's first general election swept a professed socialist PPP to power. While Direct Action Day gave birth to a modern Muslim state with no coherent political agenda, the recent election of so many MMA members to the National Assembly created conditions for a reactionary backlash that catapulted the state's intelligence apparatus to the top of the power hierarchy. The MMA's victory comes amid circumstances shaped by this power structure.

In November 2002 *The Herald* produced the following interview with Liaqat Baloch, Deputy Secretary of the MMA who had been present as a key member in the discussions held between the government and the MMA "Things were moving in the right direction and it was quite possible to achieve a rapprochement with the government on the issue of the legal framework order when President General Pervez Musharraf met some members of our National Assembly belonging to Jamiat Ulema-e-Islam (Fazl group)) at the residence of Tauqeer Zia and instigated them to work towards an Islamic system of governance and talk of the manifesto that might bring them to the assembly. He wanted the demands brought to him with this reference and assured them of positive action. Our men believed General Musharraf and so Jamiat Ulema-e-Islam (F) started pressurising other groups that if the General was sincere about the implementation of Islamic rule, we must co-operate with him. Yielding under this pressure, we put forward seventeen points along with the solution to the LFO problem (Legal Framework Orders – amendments to the constitution introduced by President Musharraf) and demanded that action on these must also be ensured. When we presented these points, the government, especially President Musharraf, reacted very sharply."

According to Liaqat Baloch and some other leaders of MMA, President Musharraf's meeting with the Jamiat Ulema-e-Islam (F) delegation also influenced his future political course. The Frontier Province Government of the MMA passed the Sharia Bill and this was supported by members of the Musharraf endorsed Muslim League (Qaid-e-Azam). The Sharia Bill and the Seventeen Point Program changed the national political scenario quite suddenly. Now, President Musharraf, who had encouraged such a movement, emerged as its biggest opponent. He said several times that these actions of the MMA were adversely affecting the image of Pakistan at international level. MMA passed the Sharia Bill before President Musharraf was due to visit the United States on 22 June 2003.

Before President Musharraf's trip to America, in order to strengthen the case against the MMA, all the district level managers (elected representatives) of the Frontier Province sent their resignations to the President in the second week of June saying that the state government (the MMA) was not allowing them to work. The Chief Minister of the province, Akram Durrani, responded by saying that the matter was blown up deliberately. The resigning elected representatives met Aziz Danial, Chairman of the National Reconstruction Bureau, in Islamabad. This is the body that created the system for running the district level administrations. Akram Durrani claimed that he had been continuously receiving complaints of corruption against certain officials. He abstained from any action because he thought it fit to report the matter to President Musharraf who had said that such officials should be dealt with immediately.

The MMA claimed that the efforts to create favourable conditions before President Musharraf's visit to America were being made for a special purpose. The MMA leaders claim that he was doing this only to please America and to create an impression that religious forces in Pakistan were against his reformative programs. He wanted to show that he had received threats from them. How real were the threats can be gauged from the way democracy has worked during the past year and a half. In fact, the Sharia Bill is the only issue that was opposed by the central government and the interesting point is that this bill was supported by state members of the Muslim League.

The Seventeen Points of the MMA included a call for the ending of the usurious interest earning system, the restoration of Friday as a holiday, the ending of the FBI network in Pakistan, the implementation of the Islamic Ideology Council's recommendations, and the withholding of the Pakistani contingent to Iraq. The MMA, however, did not adopt an aggressive posture to press these points.

On the issue of sending Pakistani forces to Iraq, the MMA issued a fatwah (decree) saying that if Pakistani soldiers were killed in Iraq they would not be regarded as martyrs, rather as those who died a haram (unholy) death and the janaza (funeral) prayers could not properly be said for them. However, some other sources claim that the national government is behind this because it did not really want to send a contingent to Iraq, rather, they wanted a fatwah issued and a million strong march to be organised by the MMA and others in order to create the impression that there was a very strong internal pressure on them over this issue.

While the government has been using the MMA for its own ends, it had also been keeping it under legal pressure. MMA then decided they were being taken for a ride when, out of the blue, an obscure Maulavi, Haider Khaki, made a challenge in the Supreme Court against the National Assembly membership of those people with religious degrees. The MMA leaders saw this as a political act of the government and decided against becoming a party to the litigation in court. They decided instead to face this challenge to their political legitimacy by producing a list of Assembly members of the ruling party with religious degrees. The list was interesting as it had the names of the Muslim League (Qaid-e-Azam) Chief Minister from Sindh, Ghulam Mohammad Mehar, Minister for Agriculture, and Sardar Yar Mohammad Rind, apart from the members from the politically liberal Peoples Party. According to this list, the Muslim League Finance Minister from Baluchistan, Syed Ehsan Shah, Senator Akram Wali Mohammad Badani, Senator Pari Gul Agha, Begum Mehnaz Rafi, the wife of the former Chief Minister of Baluchistan, Nadir Magasi MNA (member of national assembly) Parveen Magasi MNA, Rashid Akbar Nawali MNA, and his brother, Sayeed Akbar Nawali MNA, and Peoples Party Amjad Warraich MNA. Apart from 40 members from the National Assembly, 99 from the Frontier Assembly, 17 from Baluchistan, and 14 from the Sindh Assembly who had taken part in the election on the basis of their madrasa degrees. The MMA also claimed that Assembly members from the ruling and other parties have got fake religious degrees and said that they would file cases against them in retaliation. The issue died its death with the same speed as it had come up and MMA also changed its political course of action.

The MMA ultimately decided that it would concentrate first on solving the LFO crisis. It should be noted that in the first phase of talks about President Musharraf's LFO, the Alliance for the Restoration of

Democracy (ARD) was also involved. The ARD along with the Muslim League (Nawaz division) had won the highest number of votes in the election and submitted its reservations and recommendations on the LFO to the Speaker of the National Assembly. It was decided that the Prime Minister, Mir Zafrullah Jamali, would convene a combined session of the ruling party and all of the opposition parties in order to make final recommendations about the issues. In August 2003, however, the government suddenly made an announcement that it would be holding discussions only with the MMA. Thus, the largest opposition party in Pakistan, the ARD, was relegated to third place and MMA emerged as the 'real opposition' on this issue because only they were involved in negotiations with the government.

President General Musharraf appeared to be successful in his designs and the MMA, which had a close proximity to the army anyway, was on the political board allegedly as a counter to the army. The Minister for Information, Sheikh Rashid, in a meeting with journalists said, jokingly, "It is easy to play with (Muttahida) Majlis-e-Amal."

And Musharraf Won the Game

President Musharraf won the round and on 24 December 2003, ignoring the parliament, his government struck a deal with MMA. According to the agreement, the LFO became a part of the constitution with a few changes. Liaqat Baloch, the leader of the MMA, commented; "We made several compromises because we had no other way." Before their acceptance of the LFO, the MMA had maintained that it was illegal, but now, after its incorporation into the constitution, it had acquired legal status, even though the two big opposition parties do not agree. Earlier, MMA had insisted that Musharraf could not have the dual charge of the Presidency and also be the Chief of Army Staff. They said he would have to resign from his position in the army to become the president and, according to the law, he could not take part in political activities. Now, he is accepted both as the President and also as military commander for a certain period. Other previous MMA objections to clauses and details in the LFO concerning the constitutional status of the National Security Council and the retirement age of judges were also abandoned or compromised.

How Did the MMA Come Into Power?

President Musharraf is playing the MMA card to get his way. He has successfully led the international community to believe that these 'extremists', by being in the government, could become a danger to European and American interests. But this alliance of religious groups is also not ready to accept him as the country's true leader even though they have accepted him as a President in Uniform and the LFO has become a part of the constitution. The main advantage for them is that MMA has also acquired national status as the most powerful opposition in the country.

The religious organisations, which had never previously put up much of a show in the election politics of Pakistan, have suddenly risen to prominence in just a few years. Is it only because of the new conditions that developed after the 9/11 atrocities? Many analysts think that this development is not solely attributable to the reversal of the pro-Taliban policy in Pakistan but that the exile of the big party leaders from the country has caused a disintegration within those parties as well. The government's support for the new alliance of the six religious parties which created the MMA and its favouring of them in the election process could also be among the major causes of this political disaster.

The military government played a prominent role in the success of MMA candidates in Baluchistan and it issued several administrative orders in this connection. To take an example, the Law Department issued orders to four Anti-Terrorist Activities Courts in Quetta that cases against accused persons participating in the elections should be withdrawn. This administrative order helped a large number of MMA candidates to avoid prosecution or internment and many of them became members of the State and National Assemblies. To date, no information of any such assistance given to MMA members in the Frontier Province has come to light.

Regarding the benefits brought to MMA in Baluchistan, *The Daily Times* published the following editorial on 8 November 2002: "According to the revised election schedule by the Election Commission of Pakistan, the nomination papers were to be filed from 19 August to 26 August whereas the scrutiny of nomination papers by the Returning Officers was to be completed from 27 August to 2 September 2002. But on the last day of the filing of these nomination papers and just a day before the beginning of their scrutiny period by the Returning Officers (26 August 2002), the Law Department of the Government of Baluchistan issued a letter to the Public Prosecutors in the four Anti-Terrorist Courts located at Quetta, Khuzdar and Sibi, withdrawing cases against over 100 activists of religious parties in Baluchistan. The document reveals that five MNA-elects (members of national assembly) and some MPAs-elect (members of provincial assembly) are included among those religious leaders against whom cases were consciously withdrawn just one day before the elections. 'The purpose of withdrawing these cases, many of which were of a criminal nature, was to ensure the eligibility of these people for contesting the elections so that they might not be disqualified at any stage of the scrutiny of their nomination papers,' a highly placed source in the Provincial Government of Baluchistan told *The Daily Times*.

"Those who benefited from this particular administrative order and subsequently won the elections to the National Assembly include the MMA nominee for the office of the Prime Minister, Maulana Fazlur Rehman, the Central Secretary General of the MMA, Maulana Abdul Ghafoor Haideri, and Hafiz Hussain Ahmad, Maulavi Mohammad Khan Shirani and Maulavi Noor Mohammad.

"Sources informed *The Daily Times* that the Home and Tribal Affairs Department of the Government of Baluchistan forwarded a letter dated 26 August 2002 entitled 'Withdrawal of Cases Registered Against Leaders/Activists of Religious Parties in Baluchistan' requesting immediate action.

"The Law Department took prompt action and forwarded the 'request' of the Home Department to the Public Prosecutors of the Anti-Terrorist Courts at Quetta, Khuzdar and Subi saying: 'You are requested to kindly move an application in the respective courts for the withdrawal of the cases under references with their consent under intimation to this Department as well as the Home Department.' A two-page list of the religious leaders against whom cases were ordered to be withdrawn was also sent to the Public Prosecutors.

"Sources told *The Daily Times* that the MMA leaders duly accorded their 'consent' for the withdrawal of cases against them so that they could contest the 10 October elections and 'feel obligated towards the government for this gesture of kindness.'

"According to the letter there were six cases pending against Maulana Ghafoor Haideri in Anti-Terrorist Courts I & II at Quetta. The cases were registered in Police Station Sadar, Police Station Airport and Police Station Civil Lines, Quetta.

"There were four cases pending against Hafiz Hussain Ahmad in Quetta which were registered by Police Station, Sadar, Quetta.

"There was one case pending against Maulana Mohammad Khan Shirani in Quetta which was registered by police station Airport Quetta.

"Similarly, Maulavi Noor Mohammad was facing one case in Quetta registered by City Police Station."

Later, on 24 October, a Deputy Secretary of MMA,

Hafiz Hussain Ahmad, revealed in Lahore that the Quetta army authorities had made an offer of 25 million rupees to him not to contest the election. Another candidate, Shujaul Mulk, claimed an offer of 50 million rupees was made to him not to stand (*The Daily Islam*, 25 October 2003). It was said that by giving this statement he wished to deny that the government had played any role in sending them (MMA candidates) to the Assemblies. His statement definitely underlines the fact that the army has been interfering in the election process rather directly. It is not yet clear how many people were given such offers and how many accepted or rejected it. The Deputy President of MMA, Maulana Samiul Haq, says that several leaders of various parties of the alliance maintain relations with secret services institutions and they spend much of their time together.

Osama bin Laden in the Success of Muttahida Majlis-e-Amal

The jihadi organisations played a prominent role in the success of Muttahida Majlis-e-Amal in the Frontier Province and Baluchistan. A letter from Osama bin Laden is important in this context. The weekly *Nidai Millat* (Lahore) wrote in this regard in its issue of 17 October 2002: "Osama bin Laden had also put in a word to help this anti-government alliance. This help had come in the form of a letter which was written in Arabic but had its translation in Urdu. The letter written over a full page had his name at the end, although it did not have his signature like his other letters. The letter said that General Pervez Musharraf is an American agent and the Pakistani voters should use their votes to send him out of the corridors of power. He has shown his surprise over the Islamic identity of this state and asked as to what kind of Islamic state is this that allows the enemies of Islam to kill the Muslims. Osama appealed to the people of Pakistan to help the mujahideen and they should not be handed over to the Christians. This letter condemned the ISI operations in a camp on the outskirts of Peshawar. The last sentence of the letter said that copies of this letter may be distributed among Muslims. As such, the letter was distributed in Peshawar on 19 October. Who wrote this letter actually and who distributed it among the people, is still a mystery. However, there is no difference between this letter and the ones that have been coming from time to time under his signature. In the light of this, it is estimated that this letter must have been issued by some spokesperson of Osama. Whatever be the case, the letter filled religious militants with great courage in favour of Muttahida Majlis-e-Amal."

A leader of MMA believes that it is no less than magic that such divergent forces within the alliance have remained united. "This magic is because of our friends who do not want the alliance to break," he said. By friends, he meant the heads of some military establishments. However, the parliamentary leader of the Majlis, Qazi Hussain Ahmad says that the parties have no other option but to stay together because Majlis-e-Amal had become such a force that their very existence without it would be in danger. He also says;

"The biggest cause of our success is our unity and had all the religious parties joined together on one platform in 1970, success would have been ours."

The religious parties have not come together on the platform of Majlis-e-Amal for the first time. In fact efforts to bring them together have been going on since 1995. The religious parties had established a unity council to bring communal terrorism to an end but it could not work well owing to rifts in Sipah-e-Mohammad and Sipah-e-Sahaba, and over the distribution of positions between the two factions of Jamiat Ulema-e-Islam. In 2000, Jamiat Ulema-e-Islam (Fazl group) created an alliance with 29 religious groups and the new organisation was called Islami Muttahida Inquilabi Mahaz. Its main aim was to stop the increasing impact of western culture in the Frontier Province and Baluchistan. The NGOs (non-government organisations) working for the rights of women were its special target. Its workers started a 'remove cable' movement to cut the power cables supplying NGO offices in Peshawar's Char Sada and other districts at night.

When America used cruise missiles to target Osama bin Laden in the Khost area of Afghanistan, Maulana Samiul Haq called an important meeting of all religious and political organisations in Jamia Akora Khatak. As many as forty jihadi, religious and political organisations attended this meeting and they created a council called the Pak-Afghan Defence Council which later became the vehicle for the establishment of the MMA. On the eve of this meeting, firearms were openly exhibited in spite of bans. When the police came to Maulana Samiul

Haq to investigate the matter of illegal firearms, boldly, he instructed them to go to the secret services in Peshawar to look for those who wielded arms. That was the beginning and the end of the investigation.

The events of 9/11 and the world's response provided an opportunity for the religious organisations to come together even though important moves had already been made in this direction, the first manifestation of which was the establishment of the MMA. According to Qazi Hussain Ahmad, Muttahida Majlis-e-Amal was established at a meeting of six religious organisations at his residence in June 2001. This was the time when America had formulated its new Pakistan-Afghanistan policy and which also had direct effects on relations with the Pakistani secret services agencies and their links with the Taliban, jihadi organisations and the al-Qaida network. The visit to Pakistan of the American Under Secretary of State had already been planned for 14 September 2001 when she was due to make an announcement regarding the new American policy.

The Protest of the Pak-Afghan Defence Council

After the atrocities of 9/11, when Pakistan made a U-turn on its own Afghan policy under American pressure and when America started its attack on Afghanistan, the Pak-Afghan Defence Council engaged in street protests in Pakistan. However, their demonstrations did not get a very warm response anywhere in the country and no demonstration exceeded about five thousand people. Maulana Fazlur

Rehman, Qazi Hussain Ahmad and selected other leaders of the Council were put under house arrest and their release was conditional upon President Musharraf announcing general elections.

Did America Keep MMA Out of Power?

In the National Assembly elections held on 10 October 2002, Muttahida Majlis-e-Amal emerged as the third largest party by winning 57 seats. As such, Maulana Fazlur Rehman was nominated as the Prime Ministerial candidate. After holding discussions with various political parties for about a month, the MMA came to believe that it would be in a position to acquire power. There was all the more reason for this as the ARD leader, Nawabzada Nasrullah Khan, also came out in support of Maulana Fazlur Rehman. However, the PPP leader, Makhdoom Amin Faheem, vetoed this decision after consulting Benazir Bhutto in the matter.

The *English Daily Nation* published a report on 12 November 2002 which said that the Policy Director of the American State Department, Richard Haas, was going to Islamabad with an important message. It was said that the message was intended to advise President Musharraf to keep the religious groups out of power. Another message of the same nature was also brought to Benazir Bhutto. The position, at that time, was such that the Pakistan Muslim League (Qaid-e-Azam faction) was not in a position to form the government in spite of the support of the Muttahida Qaumi Movement. On the other hand, the Peoples Party was also unable to form a government in spite of the support of all the members of ARD. In such a situation, whosoever wanted to form a government could do so only by seeking the support of the MMA but it, in turn, imposed a condition that the Prime Minister must be from their party. Suddenly, 14 members of the Peoples Party moved away to form a patriot group and supported the Muslim League (Qaid-e-Azam) thereby depriving Muttahida Majlis-e-Amal of its strength.

Later, the parliamentary leader of the MMA, Qazi Hussain Ahmad, commenting on the situation later, said that he was kept from power at the instance of America. Some analysts also claim that President Musharraf himself was not in favour of the MMA acquiring power at the centre. Its success was to be utilised only to maintain pressure on the government at the centre and to give a message to the world that religious and extremists forces still wielded strong influence in Pakistan.

The Jihadi Face of MMA

On 26 June 2003, the secret services of Pakistan arrested Haris bin Asim from Kucch Gadhi, Peshawar who was the leader of al-Qaida and the Taliban information network. Three current CDs made by Osama bin Laden were recovered from him which showed that the al-Qaida leader was alive and well. According to some sources, President Musharraf presented these three CDs to President Bush when he visited the US. It came to light after the arrest of Haris that he had also been in touch with the Chief of Jamat Islami, Qazi Hussain Ahmad, the Chief of Jamiat Ulema-e-Islam, Maulana Fazlur Rehman and with Gulbaden Hikmetyar, the Chief of Hizb-e-Islami of Afghanistan. None of the two chiefs of the religious organisations of Pakistan denied their links with Haris and a complete silence was maintained over the matter.

There is no secret about the relationship that the constituents of MMA had with Pakistani jihadi organisations, the Taliban and al-Qaida. The leaders of the MMA themselves acknowledge this even though they have grown a little more cautious after 9/11. A few examples about this relationship follow.

Osama's Masters and Disciples in the Assemblies

There are at least fifteen members in the Senate, National and State Assemblies of Pakistan who have not only met Osama bin Laden but had a close relationship with him. Maulana Samiul Haq is on the top of the list and it is claimed that he had sworn allegiance on the hands of Osama. This relationship is confirmed by the fact that he named one of his sons Osama. It is also interesting to note that his son Hamidul Haq Haqqani, who is a member of the National Assembly, and Osama bin Sami, both sons of Maulana Haq, have also vowed allegiance on the hands of Osama bin Laden. It is also said that one of his sons-in-law holds an important position in the al-Qaida network.

Very few people know that during the Taliban regime's period of power, only Maulana Samiul Haq and Maulana Fazlur Rehman had authority to issue passes to Arab and other foreign mujahideen to join the Taliban forces. It was essential to have a card signed by Maulana Samiul Haq for entering Afghanistan from the Frontier Province and a card signed by Maulana Fazlur Rehman for entering Afghanistan from Baluchistan. The intelligence and security system of the Taliban was so strong that anyone who did not have this card could easily be traced in Afghanistan. Only those with a card could receive training in the camps. The foreigners were supposed to have these cards for security purposes but this condition did not apply to Pakistanis and the Pushtons who could join any jihadi organisation to go to Afghanistan to receive their training.

Apart from Maulana Samiul Haq and Maulana Fazlur Rehman, several other members of the Senate and the National Assembly have met Osama bin Laden and they had their contacts with the Taliban and other jihadi organisations. These include the MNA's Maulana Khalil Ahmad, Mufti Abrar Sultan, Shah Abdul Aziz, Maulana Naseeb Ali Shah, Maulana Amanullah Khan, Qari Abdul Baas Siddiqui and Maulana Rahmatullah.

Six elected Assembly members of Jamat Islami have also been the standard bearers of Kashmiri jihadi organisations while several other members have been associated with the Hizb-e-Islami of Hikmetyar. The direct relationship of Qazi Hussain Ahmad, Senator Professor Abdul Ghafoor, Senator Khurshid Ahmad, the MNA's Liaqat Baloch and Maulana Asadullah with jihadi groups is undeniable. The Assembly Members of Jamat Islami having links with Hizb-ul-Mujahideen include, Sabir Hussain Awan, Maulana Inayatur Rahman, Mohamad Usman and Dr Ataur Rahman.

Jamiat Ulema-e-Islam and Jihadi Groups

Statements made by Maulana Fazlur Rehman, the Chief of Jamiat Ulema-e-Islam, during his visit to India in May 2003 attracted severe criticism back at home. When he reached Lahore after completing his tour of India on 24 May, he had to put up with persistently awkward questioning by journalists and, according to one report, he claimed that "Neither he nor his organisation had any contacts with any jihadi organisation and that the mujahideen of Kashmir should now stop using arms and begin discussions to solve the problem."

His statement was looked at with scepticism by the MMA but the Deobandi jihadi organisations had a different perspective on his tour of India. For example, *al-Hilal* of Jamiat-ul-Ansar wrote in its editorial in August 2003 that Maulana Fazlur Rehman was the main force behind a very important religious organisation of Pakistan. Because of his association with the Deobandi school of Islamic thought, he is supposed to be an informal patron of some Kashmiri jihadi organisations. However, the kind of 'ulema diplomacy' he displayed during his tour of India was enough to leave the other big players in amazement. He talked on all the issues and said that the Simla agreement was the solution to all the problems. He did not have any objection to acceptance of the LoC (line of control) as the border between the two countries. He even went to the extent of proposing a round-table conference to bring both the countries together once again. The editorial said that these proposals emerged out of the fact that the main aim of his tour was to acquaint the Indian public with the American neo-colonial design, to counter the stereotyped impression about Muslims and Pakistan and, in that, he was quite successful in achieving this aim.

In spite of Maulana Fazlur Rahman's clear declaration that he had nothing to do with any jihadi organisation, for their part, the jihadi organisations are not ready to end their relationship with him. As it appears from an *al-Hilal* editorial, it is all part of his 'diplomacy'. Certain changes seem to have occurred in his attitudes and statements with the passage of time. While giving an interview to *The News* (3 August 2003), he said: "I knew that the Indian media had picked this up from the Western media. I think I managed to overcome this image during my 10-day visit to India. By the end of the visit, the media was saying that I was more of a politician than a Maulana. They were also writing that I was a soft-liner rather than a hard-liner. I must say that the Indians and their media are largely unaware of our party's stance on various issues and the role of our elders in the struggle for freedom in the pre-partition days. They don't know that Jamiat Ulema-e-Islam has been a part of every democratic movement in Pakistan and has always struggled for human rights and the rule of law. They are unaware that our party wants a negotiated solution of Kashmir, that it backed Vajpayee's (India's current Prime Minister) visit on the 'bus for peace'. I kept telling the Indians that we surely did back the Taliban because they were a continuation of the Afghan mujahideen who fought against the Soviet occupation troops in Afghanistan. We considered the Taliban freedom fighters in the same way as the Palestinians and Chechens but at the end of the day they were Afghans and we are Pakistanis and we operate in different situations."

According to an important Jamaat-e-Islami leader, the Maulana's Indian visit established that the Kashmir jihad was only secondary to him. He further said that even before September he had been issuing instructions to the Deobandi jihadi organisations to pay attention to Afghanistan. He himself gave the reason in the interview for paying attention to Afghanistan with reference to the Taliban being Deobandis and Pushton. He had been rendering important services with the ISI of Pakistan.

A report published in the weekly *Nidai Millat* (Lahore: 19 August 1999) about the Maulana's visit to Afghanistan is important in this context because, later, his party distributed thousands of photocopies about it in the country: "From the first week of July to the first week of August, preparations for an attack on the Taliban were completed by the forces of Ahmad Shah Masood. According to the plan they had to march towards Kandhar. Dozens of teams were watching all these along the borders of Pakistan, Afghanistan, and Iran. The secret service agencies in Pakistan, however, could procure the blueprint regarding the proposed operation on the Taliban and Osama bin Laden. As soon as the operation plan was accepted in the meeting held in the Indian embassy in Britain on 7 June 1999, the Taliban were given a red alert on the one hand, and Maulana Fazlur Rehman was made aware of all the hideouts of Ahmad Shah Masood where Indian relief material, Russian tanks and other modern war vehicles were stored. Along with this, he was also told about the presence of the American commandos available with Ahmad Shah Masood, and in the tribal areas of Pakistan. He was also informed about the plan to chase out the foreign teams and turn over the plan regarding a major operation against Osama to a great extent. When Maulana Fazlur Rehman reached Chaman along with his companions on 21 June, foreign teams, American representatives and the CIA network got an alert. The next day's morning prayers were said in Chaman and as soon as Maulana Fazlur Rehman moved towards the Afghanistan border, the entire American machinery working against Osama bin Laden suddenly got activated. The Americans saw their plans going to ruins when they saw that the Pakistani officials and those from the secret services bid him farewell with all protocol on the Pak-Afghan border before entering Afghanistan. Preparations to receive him in Kandhar with the protocol of a visiting head of state had already been completed.

"According to sources, the Pakistani guest met the Taliban Emir, Mullah Mohammad Omar Mujahid after the luncheon in which the Governor of Kandahar, important commanders of the Taliban and senior intelligence officials were present. After this meeting, he met three important Afghan leaders separately for two hours. According to reliable sources, the Maulana informed the Afghan officials regarding the activities of Ahmad Shah Masood's brother in Britain and his cousin's activities in India. The details of the imminent American attack in July-August were also discussed after giving all information regarding the plans of Ahmad Shah Masood. The participants were made to believe that it was inevitable to attack Ahmad Shah in order to procure Russian and Indian arms and machinery from his secret stockpiles and also because this act would make the American and Indian commandos, and the officials of the secret services, leave via Russia. It was also intended to get the rebels in a defensive position and help Osama shift to a safer destination for some time.

"Maulana Fazlur Rehman gave a practical shape to the first part of his plans in the very first meeting he had with Mullah Omar. The second part of the program consisted of the threats and fatwahs that had to be given against America. A big convention was held to do this in a place called Arghandab which the Maulana addressed. Important personalities of Afghanistan, Taliban commanders, and members of the personal force of the Taliban and Osama bin Laden attended this meeting. The rebel commandos were also present there who were informing masters on all the details. The Maulana made an announcement of jihad in a proper way for the first time there. After his address, the Taliban and Afghan nationals decided together that if someone was found preparing for an attack on Afghanistan, he would be killed. A speaker was supported with applause after saying that if any damage was done to Osama, one lakh (ten-thousand) Americans would be killed in lieu of that. This was the message that shook the American officials. Even before Maulana Fazlur Rahman's return to Pakistan, America issued orders to its forces on the borders to be on alert and shift to safe places until the receipt of fresh orders."

The concluding part of the report said: "According to sources, any dangers America had before, it now had with Pakistan. Now it was important to keep an eye on Maulana Fazlur Rehman also. In view of this, the American ambassador was sent to Maulana Fazlur Rehman after the failure of the third operation (the third cruise missile attack) and the launching of the fourth so that he might be contained with threats and not become an obstacle in the American operation against Osama."

There is a persistent allegation against Maulana Fazlur Rahman's Jamiat Ulema-e-Islam that it is still helping to get the Taliban reorganised in Chaman and Quetta and the madrasas are providing a safe haven for them in the frontier areas. The JUI leadership, however, denies this allegation. One Jamiat Ulema-e-Islam leader, Hafiz Hussain Ahmad, said that the JUI was not a properly organised political entity. He said that it had its own individual policies, madrasas and mosques in the cities and it was not mandatory that these policies conformed with any central policy.

Another group of Jamiat Ulema-e-Islam runs under the leadership of Maulana Samiul Haq which clearly professes its support for and association with jihadi organisations. Maulana Samiul Haq's madrasas at

Akora Khatak and Naushehra were a nursery for the Taliban and he is proud of this fact. Sixty per cent of the Taliban Government's ministers and other important government official were graduates of his madrasas. Jamia Haqqania, head of the Akora Khatak madrasa, had awarded an honorary degree to Mullah Omar because he did not have a formal degree from any other institution.

It is well known that Jamia Haqqania and the madrasa at Akora Khatak and had been in contact with the Taliban and al-Qaida even though Maulana Samiul Haq denies this. He said (25 May 2003) that he has been receiving information regarding the Taliban and that Mullah Omar and Osama bin Laden are not only well but are also guiding their mujahideen in the jihad against America. There is information regarding some other members of Maulana Samiul Haq's group that establishes their links with the Taliban and al-Qaida. When Maulana Yusuf Shah, the General Secretary of JUI (S) was asked whether some al-Qaida mujahideen were, according to some reports, taking refuge in the madrasa of Maulana Abdul Aziz Hashmi, he openly wondered if there was anything wrong in that. He said: "It is not a crime for us to provide refuge or to help mujahideen."

Jamaat-e-Islami and Al-Qaida

The ISI, for the first time in its history, called a press conference on 12 March 2003 and categorically denied reports regarding links between Jamaat-e-Islami and al-Qaida. News regarding these links were published when an important al-Qaida member, Khalid Sheikh Mohammad, was arrested in the house of a member of Jamaat-e-Islami in Rawalpindi earlier in March that year. A similar incident had taken place earlier in Karachi also. According to other secret service sources, at least twelve members of al-Qaida were arrested either in the houses of Jamat members or else they had close links with them. The ISI official said in the press conference that Jamat did not have any links with al-Qaida even though some al-Qaida members might have had sympathies with them. He went on to argue that the whole organisation and its leadership could not be blamed on those grounds.

It is certainly true that guilt cannot be inferred by association alone. Nevertheless, the way Jamaat-e-Islami maintains its contacts with Islamic movements all over the world and the way it organizes its network creates doubts about the issue.

Jamaat-e-Islami operates more than five hundred religious seminaries in Pakistan wherein significant numbers of foreign students also receive their education. There are several institutions wholly given to the education of foreigners of which the Maulana Maududi Institute in Lahore is the most important. There, selected students from all over the world are admitted. An important point with regard to this institution is that when tension was at its peak in Bosnia, Bosnian students were receiving their education in this madrasa and, when the military movement started in Chechnya, fifty per cent of the students there were from Chechnya. One of the teachers from this madrasa said that apart from Arabs and Africans, the institution had students from the Philippines, Burma, and Bangladesh in significant numbers. They stay there for a period ranging from two to four years but, according to this teacher, most of them leave before completing their academic year because they go to jihadi training camps in Afghanistan and Kashmir during their vacations. However, all of them do not return from their vacations because they go on to destinations around the world. Some of these students join the al-Qaida network later. Those students who do return to the institution after their vacations in the training camps maintain relations with the jihadi network and its members.

Clearly, it can be argued that since these students have already developed contacts and friendship with members of Jamaat-e-Islami during their education, those who did become jihadis later might have sought refuge with their Jamat friends during the period of the American attack on Afghanistan. Nevertheless, it is certainly no secret that the Jamat has links with jihadi and Islamic movements all over the world and the external affairs department of Jamaat-e-Islami plays an important part in building up this relationship. The Emir of Jamaat-e-Islami, Qazi Hussain Ahmad, talking to reporters on 21 March 2003 said: "We do not even know if any organisation called al-Qaida exits anywhere, not to talk of maintaining links with the organisation." Most analysts do not give too much importance to this denial by Qazi Hussain Ahmad because two religious organisations, Jamaat-e-Islami and Jamaat-ud-Daawa, both with big networks, are operating freely in Pakistan today and they have many well-educated people among them. Since al-Qaida was not the name of any particular individual organisation before 9/11, and since it is now assigned exclusively to Osama bin Laden with members from all over the world, especially from Arab countries, it is not at all surprising that these organisations have had contacts with al-Qaida. Whether or not they have contacts with al-Qaida today is the moot point.

Another important indicator of relative strengths and power is the fact that this issue faded out of Pakistani politics as quickly as it had arisen. These two major organisations have a good deal of influence in Pakistan. The last statement about the issue was from Pakistan's Home Minister, Faisal Saleh Hayat, on 12 April 2003 when he said: "Jamaat-e-Islami shall have to explain its links with the terrorist network called al-Qaida." But this was the last pebble in the water and it did not create much of a splash. On 15 April, an important member of the External Affairs Department of Jamaat-e-Islami revealed that he had only been able to bury this matter with great difficulty and that he would abstain from making any statement on this issue. No response would be made in future regardless of reaction from any quarter.

Markazi Jamiat Ahl-e-Hadis

Markazi Jamiat Ahl-e-Hadis represents the Ahl-e-Hadis school of Muttahida Majlis-e-Amal (MMA). Even though it does not have a radical view regarding jihad as does Jamaat-ud-Daawa, it has always patronised the Kashmiri jihadi organisation Tahreek-ul-Mujahideen. In 1999, Tahreek-ul-Mujahideen was declared to be the jihadi wing of Markazi Jamiat Ahl-e-Hadis and the Jamiat Chairman, Sajid Mir, was appointed its patron. In most districts of Pakistan and Azad Kashmir both organisations have shared common offices. However, Markazi Jamiat Ahl-e-Hadis has not been under any kind of pressure with respect to its relationship with Tahreek-ul-Mujahideen. The basic reason behind this is that in spite of being a part of Majlis-e-Amal, the Jamiat is an ally of the Muslim League (Nawaz group) and maintains a liberal political image to a certain extent. Also, it does not make too much of its relationship with the Tahreek and, from an external pressure point of view, the Tahreek's Kashmiri jihad dedication does not much concern America.

Jamat Ulema-i-Pakistan (JUP)

The former President of Muttahida Majlis-e-Amal and the Chief of Jamiat Ulema-i-Pakistan, Maulana Shah Ahmad Noorani is considered to be one of those few leaders who has not only supported the jihad of Kashmir and Afghanistan but also patronised the Barelvi jihadi organisations in this connection. According to one member of the Jamiat, Qari Zawar Bahadur, the Maulana has always been sad about the fact that the Barelvi jihadi organisations always lagged behind in jihad. Therefore, he kept making efforts to spur them on in this direction. He played an important role in the making of Lashkar-e-Islam and he had great hopes with this group. On the whole, Jamiat Ulema-i-

Pakistan is a supporter of the Barelvi organisations but it did not play a major role.

Islami Tahreek Pakistan

Islami Tahreek (the new name of Tahreek-e-Jafaria) is no different from Jamiat Ulamai Pakistan in the area of jihadi activities. Islami Tahreek has been patronising the Shia jihadi organisation Hizb-ul-Momineen but this organisation has not played any significant part in the Kashmir jihad. This jihadi background of Majlis-e-Amal is playing an important role in strengthening the al-Qaida and other jihadi organisations' networks in Pakistan.

The Administration of the North-West Frontier Province: Patrons of the Jihadis

The Muttahida Majlis-e-Amal administration of the Frontier Province has provided protection for jihadi organisations operating in and from the region. Most of the training camps of the jihadi groups have shifted from Azad Kashmir to the district of Mansahra in the Frontier Province. Reliable sources claim that they are patronised by the provincial administration and they have complete freedom to pursue their training and operations there.

Apart from this, the Majlis-e-Amal set free more than a thousand jihadi activists held under arrest in the province soon after coming to power, and it has continued helping the organisations generally. An extract from *Nidai Millat* (13 February 2003) is indicative of the administration's policy: "Dera Ismail

Khan police raided the Jamiat-ul-Ansar office situated on Circular Road in the presence of a good number of people and arrested twenty-one persons from there. Of the arrested persons, eleven belong to Dera Ismail Khan, two to Malakund, and two to Azad Kashmir. An FIR was registered against them under 16 MPO in the Cantt. Police Station. The articles recovered during the raid included an unlicensed Kalashnikov and a pistol. An FIR was also registered against two persons for possessing arms without license. Subsequently, they were presented in the court of the civil judge who remanded them to judicial custody. A sharp reaction that was expressed by the public over this raid was only natural. The MMA leaders especially were more critical of the raid and called it an interference in the working of the government. Before their arrest these persons told the police that they had gone to Karachi for saying prayers for their departed martyrs and as soon as they reached here, the police conducted a raid and arrested them.

"When the Chief Minister, Akram Khan Durrani got news of this raid, he issued orders for their instant release. On his instructions, nineteen workers were released on the night between Wednesday and Thursday at 1. Two others, on whom the charge of possessing weapons without license had been registered, were released next morning by the court on bail. According to extremely reliable sources, the Home Ministry, on the report of the secret services had issued instructions to the Home Secretary to take action against the office of Jamiat-ul-Ansar. The Home Secretary kept the Chief Minister in dark and informed IGP, Frontier, who gave instructions to SSP, Dera Ismail Khan, Usman Zakaria to take action. This led to the arrest of twenty-one persons. The Chief Minister expressed his extreme anger over this move and instructed that his permission must be sought before handling such a matter in future. Further, he gave orders to act against the officers involved in the matter."

On the one hand, the Frontier Province Government is protecting Pakistani jihadi groups but, on the other, it is unable to control or halt FBI operations against al-Qaida in the province. The Chief Minister, Akram Durrani, has said several times that these (FBI) operations are being conducted without his permission. Some groups of Majlis-e-Amal, especially Jamiat Ulema-e-Islam, maintain that Akram Durrani has actually granted permission to the FBI to carry out their operations. It must also be borne in mind that Jamiat Ulema-e-Islam has claimed non-involvement in the Frontier Province Government.

A Peshawar member of Jamaat-e-Islami said that Akram Durrani is helpless with regard to FBI activity in the Frontier Province because of pressure from the Musharraf Government but, in spite of this, he has been trying to help the mujahideen. Further, he has promised to provide his full support to the Assembly Members in case of any action against the mujahideen taken by the police or the secret services, including making arrangements for their bail.

Chapter 6

THE REORGANISATION OF THE TALIBAN AND AL-QAIDA

According to a report published in *Zarb-e-Momin* (11 December 2003), the Taliban have retaken control of more than forty districts of Afghanistan. Some western media sources have suggested that this Taliban success has been achieved with the assistance of Pakistan. America has also expressed reservations in this regard.

However, the suggestion of official Pakistani collaboration is based upon the fact that mujahideen are crossing regularly from Pakistan into Afghanistan. Colonel Roger King, a senior officer of the Allied Forces in Afghanistan told *The Daily Times* (Lahore: 20 July 2002) that al-Qaida and the Taliban are continuing to enter Afghanistan through the border areas of Pakistan and that this infiltration is not just a few people but groups of twenty to thirty persons at a time. Asked how this infiltration was possible when Pakistan had already stationed some seventy thousand men on the border, Colonel King replied that it was poor tactics to post them in the sort of units in which they were deployed and, if that continued, even greater numbers of troops would not stop the infiltrations.

Colonel King was right of course. If one looks at the

seven hundred kilometre-long border, it is clear that a stationary army in fixed posts cannot control infiltration. Realising the problem, Pakistani military chiefs took several steps to tighten the controls. 186 regular army posts have been established on the Pak-Afghan border where trained American military personnel have been posted. In addition, fencing of the border is also being implemented. However, most military tacticians, and the Americans in particular from their Vietnam experiences, know that stopping an enemy from infiltrating across a long border is never easy. It should always be borne in mind that the indigenous people in the tribal areas along the border sympathise with and help the Taliban and they do not distinguish between al-Qaida and other jihadi groups. Madrasas situated near the border also sympathise with the jihadi groups. Their is very little sympathy for the coalition of Pakistani and western military units in the region. The advantage in the campaign for 'hearts and minds' in the Frontier Provinces is with the jihad and stopping al-Qaida and Taliban mujahideen crossing in either direction is a tall order.

The Washington Post (20 October 2003) published an interview with a Pakistani citizen, Abdul Zahir, who is waging jihad along with the Taliban. This report shows that the Taliban have been able to establish a strong network on the Pak-Afghan border and they also receive human and financial resources from Pakistan. An extract from the report reads: "Abdul Zahir and 14 other Pakistanis set out by bus for Afghanistan last summer, determined to join Taliban forces waging a renewed jihad against US and Afghan

Government troops. It was almost too easy. Stopped by border guards in the town of Chaman, they said they were Afghan refugees returning home on various personal or business errands. Zahir said: 'I said I sold a buffalo to someone in Afghanistan and I needed to collect my money.' The guards waved them through.

"A few days later, he and his comrades joined a Taliban unit in the mountains of Zabol province. They were issued weapons and spent the next 40 days engaged in sporadic combat – including the ambush of an Afghan Army patrol – before he and several others returned to Pakistan by taxi in late July. Their commander gave them each 250 Pakistani rupees – about $4.50 – to cover the fare. 'It's no problem to cross back and forth,' said Zahir, a 33-year-old apple grower and self-described Taliban recruiter from the remote tribal district of Qila Abdullah along the Afghan border in northern Baluchistan Province. 'The Americans have robbed us of the right to live, but still we have the right to die, and we are using that right.'

"That is more or less the picture sketched by Zahir, a father of six with a 10th grade education who makes his living off the 30-acre apple orchard he owns with relatives just a few miles from Afghanistan in Qila Abdullah. A Pushton tribesman, he said he identifies more closely with Afghans than with Pakistanis and first offered his services to the Taliban soon after the United States launched its campaign against the movement in the fall of 2001. He joined a Taliban unit in the Afghan provincial capital of Kandahar, he said, and was promptly dispatched to the city of Mazar-e-Sharif as part of a mission to deliver money and winter clothing to Taliban forces there. But he saw no action, he said, and as the Taliban resistance collapsed he returned to Pakistan four days before Kandahar fell to US-allied Afghan fighters. 'After I came back I was continuously trying to go back, but the jihad had not yet resumed,' he said. In February, Zahir said, he succeeded in meeting a Taliban military commander who 'realised I was a genuine person' with ties to the movement and urged him to 'go back and convince other people' to join the jihad.

"Over the next few moths, Zahir said, he rounded up 14 other men from his village and surrounding areas while he waited for further instructions. Finally the summons came in the form of a visit from an old Taliban comrade, an Afghan named Abdul Hadi, who approached him in his orchard one day last May, Zahir recalled. 'He said: We are ready to take you. There are different jobs. You can fight at the same front line. You can cook. You can be a male nurse. You can give money. Everything is welcome because jihad has started.' At their own expense, Zahir said, he and the 14 others boarded the bus for Afghanistan, where at one point they were stopped and searched by a US-Afghan patrol. But they repeated the same stories they had told at the border crossing and were allowed to continue to the town of Qalat in the border province of Zabol. After hiking into the mountains, he said, they hooked up with a unit of 120 fighters and were supplied with Kalashnikov assault rifles, hand grenades, rocket launchers and ammunition.

"As he described it, the group saw little combat, except for one occasion when it ambushed two Afghan

Army vehicles about a mile and a half outside the town of Maruf, wounding one soldier and capturing one of the vehicles. Zahir said he fired his weapon but missed his target because he was too far away. After that battle, he said, the Taliban fighters took refuge in nearby tunnels while US helicopters patrolled the area for two days. Zahir said he eventually had to return to Pakistan for the simple reason that he was hungry after more than a month of living on flat bread and occasional cups of yoghurt milk. 'You don't really have enough to eat, so you become weak,' he said.

"Once he got home, Zahir said, he resumed his recruitment drive and soon lined up six more Pakistanis – four madrasa students, one farm worker and an English-speaking computer expert – between the ages of 22 and 30. He said jihad is an easy sell where he lives. 'We are basically anti-American,' he said. So what I do is I go and tell these boys, 'The door for jihad is open and let us go fight Americans.' In August, he said, a Taliban commander named Aminullah gave the recruits 1000 rupees – about $17 each, to cover their travel costs to Afghanistan. Four have already left, Zahir said, and he plans to join them soon. 'I am waiting for their call,' he said matter-of-factly. 'Where I'm needed I'll go. I'm all set.'"

This report demonstrates where lie the sympathies of the regional population in the Frontier Province and the tribal areas near the borders. But it is not just in these areas that the Taliban and jihadi groups have support. They have sympathisers all over Pakistan and in other Muslim countries, at least among the general population if not certainly in government circles.

It should also be noted that arms and narcotics smugglers are also active on the Pak-Afghan border and they have been providing assistance to the Taliban and al-Qaida on a commercial basis, for money and gold. This smuggling network has not only been providing the Taliban and al-Qaida people with shelters but they also help them reach various destinations in Pakistan; Karachi, Quetta, Peshawar, and Lahore. According to some reports, this criminal network has also been helpful in sending al-Qaida people and their family members abroad.

It should also be mentioned that Ahmad Wali Karzai, the brother of the Afghan President, Hamid Karzai, is also said to be active in the smugglers' network operating on the Pak-Afghan border. According to secret service reports in Pakistan, the Governor General of Kandahar, Gul Agha Shirazi, is also involved in smuggling arms and narcotics and his network is spread from Chaman in Pakistan to Kandahar in Afghanistan, although some jihadi sources say that he procures his arms from the same network of the smugglers. This network is also reported to assist in sending al-Qaida mujahideen from Arab and other countries to various towns in Pakistan and from there to foreign destinations. They send them easily to Quetta, Karachi, and Lahore on a fixed payment. Sending the families home in safety was a big issue for al-Qaida earlier. The smugglers network provides a valuable service in this connection and the Taliban seem not to care that the smugglers are only in it for the money.

Further, Libya has also been helping Arab families

in this connection. *Nidai Millat* (6 June 2002) wrote: "The Gadafi International Foundation for Charity Association (GIFCA) works under the patronage of Saiful Islam, the son of President Gadafi. In the recent past, a special Libyan plane carried 16 women and children of the families of al-Qaida members from Lahore to Libya who were arrested during the Faisalabad and Lahore operations. Some of them who are foreigners are still under custody in the Chauhang investigation centre. When an effort was made to find out details regarding their handing over to Libya, it came to light that the Gadafi Foundation had carried hundreds of the families of al-Qaida members to Libya in special aircraft earlier also. According to the sources in the Foundation, 200 family members of 45 Arab families were taken to Libya. These families hailed from Saudi Arabia, Morocco, Kuwait, United Arab Emirates, Yemen, and Algeria. These people were brought to Islamabad after detailed discussion with the Afghan government and from there they were sent to Libya in special planes. These were the families who were in the custody of the Afghan government since 15 November or who were arrested while crossing the Pakistan border. The Foundation sources have said that when America killed a big number of Arab mujahideen in Afghanistan or arrested them to send to Cuba, the Libyan President Colonel Gadafi announced that, 'We will not allow the Arab women and their children to live in such harness, and we shall bring them back from Afghanistan and Pakistan in spite of all opposition.' Libya was successful in the effort. When Colonel Gadafi's son, Saiful Islam came to Pakistan some time ago, he assured the Pakistan government that he would look after the families of the Arab mujahideen until such time as they are accepted by their respective countries. Many families of al-Qaida members had been kept in detention by the warlords in Afghanistan but who were rescued by representatives of the Gadafi Foundation, after they made heavy payments, and were brought to Islamabad."

This action by Libya occurred shortly after images of mujahideen prisoners from Afghanistan were seen being herded, blindfolded and manacled, on to US aircraft for transportation to cages in Guantanamo Bay. But the Gadafi Foundation has now largely ceased this activity. Jihadi sources say in this connection that the foundation was only established at the behest of some Arab countries so that family members of arrested or transported mujahideen, especially women and children related to a royal family, could be sent back to their respective homes. When this task was accomplished, the foundation also chose to wind-up its activities.

There are also people working for the release of mujahideen belonging to Arab and other countries from government prisons and detention centres in the Frontier Province. Leading members of Muttahida Majlis-e-Amal are active in the province in this regard. The Muslim League leader, Jawed Ibrahim Paracha, is also struggling on the legal front for these releases. He has not only been successful in securing the release of more than sixty mujahideen from various courts of law up to December 2003, but also paid their passage back to their respective homes.

Counter-Offensive and New Alignments in the Taliban

An audio cassette of Mullah Omar was released on the Pushto service of the BBC in August 2003. In it, he exhorted the Taliban to make a concerted effort to throw foreign forces out of the country. He also announced a ten-member advisory body which included Maulana Jalaluddin Haqqani, Abdul Razzaq Akhund, Mullah Biradar, Akhtar Mohammad Usmani, Maulana Abdullah, Mullah Mohammad Rasool, Mullah Akhtar Mohammad Mansoor, Saifur Rahman Mansoor and Mullah Abdul Samad. Most of these men are former Afghan army commanders and governors. After this announcement, jihadi circles in Pakistan revealed that a major operation against foreign forces is due to take place soon, after which time, they say, foreign forces will have no option but to leave the country. After the release of the audio cassette, a report was received that the Taliban and Hizb-e-Islami have established radio stations in Afghanistan from where jihadi news and messages are broadcast.

Night posters are now well-used tools of the mujahideen and these are pasted during the night. They contain information on current military advances, recruitment and messages for mujahideen fighters. These night posters and radio broadcasts are playing an important role in the reorganisation of the Taliban because they keep 'hearts and minds' on their side. Pamphlets from Muttahida Majlis-e-Amal supporting the jihadi cause and other jihadi organisations' leaflets and publications are regularly distributed at public meetings in various parts of the Frontier Province and in Baluchistan. These pamphlets have content material similar to that in the night posters. They also show how effective the Taliban are in these areas. Further, about 2000 ulema have issued their fatwahs of jihad against American forces and the Karzai government, according to a report in *Zarb-e-Momin* (5 February 2004).

The Taliban get most of their volunteers from Afghanistan itself, but they also have a very good support base among the general public in both Pakistan and Afghanistan. The new Karzai regime is really only in control in Kabul and the previous Northern Alliance areas of the country. Other areas are just temporarily occupied by their forces only with American military support and the Taliban move in as soon as they move out. According to some reports, the Taliban have several warlords and even some Karzai government officials among their supporters. Therefore, it is not surprising to find the Taliban reorganising themselves very well and gaining areas of control. The American and Allied Forces still depend on Pakistan to operate against the Taliban and al-Qaida in Afghanistan. In spite of the initial rout of the Taliban, American forces now face a guerilla army that has a broad popular base of support in the Pushton areas of Afghanistan and in the tribal areas of Pakistan. They are reluctant to mount major offensives into the mountains on their own.

This is evident from a reading of the following report from *The Washington Times*: "US commanders have turned down as too risky plans for special operations missions to attack Taliban and al-Qaida fighters in Afghanistan, according to soldiers and Bush administration officials. Military sources said that on several occasions, Army Green Beret A-Teams received good intelligence on the whereabouts of former Taliban leader Mullah Mohammad Omar, one of the United States' most sought after fugitives. In each case, soldiers said, commanders turned down the missions as too dangerous or because they believed the intelligence was shaky.

"The military sources said that in recent months, Green Berets, also called Special Forces, have written detailed plans, or what are called, 'concepts for operations' (conops), to find and attack Taliban leaders. In virtually all the cases, the officials said, the conops were turned down by Task Force 180, the overall Afghanistan command at Bagram air base north of Kabul. Colonel Roger King, chief spokesman for Task Force 180, issued a statement yesterday rebutting these accounts from Special Forces soldiers. The statement said 580 conops had been conducted by Green Berets during the past three months.

"Special Forces sources, however, said the vast majority of missions involved reconnaissance or searches for weapons caches – not a specific plan to attack a Taliban leader. 'We had a good plan,' said one Special Forces soldier, who, like others interviewed for this story, asked not be identified for fear of retribution from superiors. 'We came in hard in November, December, January, February and we won,' the soldier said. 'Since then, we've been floundering.'

"Said another soldier with knowledge of operations

in Afghanistan: 'If you put in a conop, if it said 'raid', 'ambush', 'kill', 'sniper' or anything like that, the conop would be disapproved based on the vocabulary used. If you said my team has intelligence that a Taliban corps commander was going to be at such a place, set-up an ambush and engage and try to kill or capture him, that would be out of hand rejected.'

"Defence Secretary Donald H. Rumsfield has ordered all senior US commanders to 'lean forward' or be aggressive in the war against Osama bin Laden's al-Qaida fighters and other terrorists. A senior defence official said the lack of what are called 'direct action' special operations missions comes at a critical time. The military sources said that based on intelligence collected by A-Teams and US agencies, there are likely only 50 to 100 devoted Taliban leaders left in Afghanistan. Some are trying to form new guerilla groups by merging with Pakistani and Arab militants.

"Special Forces soldiers on the ground say that if the United States misses its chance now to kill or capture them, the hard-core Taliban leaders may be successful in reorganising their units and other militants and destabilising the regime of Afghan President Hamid Karzai. An administration official said the issue approving conops has been discussed at high levels in the Pentagon.

"Soldiers traced the operational slowdown in Afghanistan to an incident last June at Deh Road called Operation Full Throttle, a major direct action by coalition commandos in Afghanistan. As groups moved toward Taliban targets in areas north of Kandahar, an AC-130 gunship fired rounds into a village where anti-aircraft fire was spotted. When the smoke cleared, 34 civilians had been killed, according to an investigation by US Central Command, which runs the war in Afghanistan. Some Special Forces soldiers contend that the casualty total was much lower.

"Still, Special Operations troops considered Full Throttle a success because it flushed out some Taliban leaders and sent them scurrying to Pakistan, where they remain today, soldiers said. Soldiers also said that since Deh Rawod, the process of winning approval for conops became more bureaucratic when they called for missions involving ambushes. Military lawyers started playing a larger role in reviewing and recommending against direct missions.

"Some commandos viewed the disapproval as a sign of timidity by commanders at the Bagram Air Base, who did not want to see their careers damaged by missions that might go bad.

"Task Force 180 is led by Lt. Gen. Dan McNeill, an army corps commander whose units include the 82nd Airborne Division. Commandos say there is an attitude at the Task Force that Special Operations Forces have been in Afghanistan too long.

"Historically, conventional warfare commanders have harboured a distrust of Special Operations units, believing some of their missions' risks outweigh the benefits. 'The fear of getting prosecuted for anything there is real. There is a paranoia,' said the soldier. 'There are so many lawyers.' Said another Special Forces soldier: 'There is nothing worth dying for in Afghanistan. None of us want to take an unnecessary risk, but we did want to catch terrorists.' General

McNeill was in Washington last week briefing Mr Rumsfield and President Bush on the pace of operations in Afghanistan.

"The Task Force 180 statement from Col. King to *The Washington Times* said: 'Without knowing who you talked to, I can't comment on either their motives or familiarity with operations in Afghanistan. However, Special Forces here executed 580 conops during September, October and November. These operations were not all offensive in nature, as some were reconnaissance, but it is a good indicator of the pace of operations in Afghanistan. Additionally, conventional forces here conducted approximately twenty larger operations during the same time frame. All those operations were offensive in nature. The primary mission of (Task Force) 180 remains to 'kill or capture' terrorists in Afghanistan. To that end, coalition forces have apprehended more than 550 persons since May.'

"In early November, Gen. Richard B Myers, Chairman of the Joint Chiefs of Staff, expressed some unhappiness with the pace of intelligence collection and anti-terrorist operations in Afghanistan. 'They've adapted their tactics, and we've got to adapt ours,' he told a gathering at the Brookings Institution. He spoke of, 'an intelligence flow that has to be more exquisite, if you will, than it's been in the past,' and of, 'the ability of our forces to strike very quickly on intelligence that may not be 100 per cent perfect or sure, but to take that kind of risk because the payoff is so important.' He added: 'In general, I think that's where we need to improve. And I think in a sense we've lost a little momentum there, to be frank.'

"A Pentagon official, speaking on the condition of anonymity, said on Friday that Gen. Myers was referring to the lack of success in capturing key al-Qaida fighters. He said that since the general made his remark to the Brooklyn Institution there have been improvements. A soldier told of an incident within one A-Team this summer. An Afghan soldier repeatedly followed and watched the team as it moved around eastern Afghanistan, one of the last strongholds of Taliban and al-Qaida fighters in that country. One day, the Afghan approached and pointed his rifle. An A-Team member responded by shooting and killing him. The incident would have ended there, except that support personnel attached to the team filed a complaints at the headquarters. 'The word got out. Anyone can be prosecuted,' said the soldier."

Pakistani Help for the Taliban: Duplicity or Helplessness?

The Friday Times (Lahore: 10 December 2002) published the story of a Pakistani soldier who had entered Afghanistan with the help of the ISI after the 9/11 attacks on America. According to this report, this soldier, given the cover name of Nazir, met well-known religious/jihadi leader Mufti Nizamuddin Shamzai in Karachi who introduced him to an ISI officer, Colonel Sultan Amir Imam. Nazir said that, after this meeting in Karachi, he entered Afghanistan via Chaman on 23 September 2001 and he was surprised to find Pakistan Army personnel present there in large numbers along with mujahideen from

Jaish-e-Mohammad, Lashkar-e-Taiba, and Harkat-ul-Mujahideen. He saw about 80 Pakistan Army officers along with officials of the ISI. Nazir stated; "All these men (the mujahideen) had reached there with the help of the Sakhi Ehsan Mosque which is run in Karachi with assistance from the al-Rasheed Trust. In all, there were 2000 Pakistanis and 400 Arabs there."

Since Nazir had engineering and technical expertise, he was assigned to duties concerning his trade. When America started bombing Afghanistan, an order for the return of the Pakistan's military personnel was given. He came back to Pakistan and tried to rejoin the army but he was not accepted. While narrating his experiences he said, "I am ashamed that those who sold the blood of their brethren showed their backs when Afghanistan was attacked."

Pakistan withdrew its support for the Taliban when the American attacks began but reports have been coming in after the fall of the Taliban that Pakistan still helps them directly. Such reports were published in October 2002 and claimed that the Military Intelligence Agency of Pakistan had opened a 'Taliban Desk' in Peshawar to reorganize the Taliban. These reports were strongly refuted by Pakistan Government officials. Ministers of the new government in Kabul have continuously claimed that the Pakistan Army and secret service agencies are busy reorganising the Taliban. The interim Afghan President, Hamid Karzai, while giving an interview to *The Daily Times* on 8 December 2003, admitted that more than three members of Pakistan's army and police who were arrested in Kandahar had been returned to Pakistani authorities. An expert on Afghan affairs, journalist Ahmed Rashid, wrote in the same paper on 25 July 2003: "Afghanistan suspects the Pakistani leadership has resumed providing covert support to the radical Islamic movement. Some diplomats contend that President Musharraf, his army and the powerful security agency known as Inter-Services Intelligence (ISI), are directly supporting the Taliban as a matter of state policy.

"Musharraf's personal denials of such claims now carry little weight with Kabul's diplomatic corps. Even a boost from President Bush, who Musharraf met with in June, has been unable to dispel diplomatic scepticism.

"American officials are among those calling on Musharraf to step up anti-terrorist efforts. 'Every effort has to be made by Pakistan not to allow its territory to be used by Taliban elements,' said Zalmay Khalilzad, the American special envoy to Afghanistan at a press conference on 15 July. 'We need 100 per cent assurances on this from Pakistan, not 50 per cent assurances,' Khalilzad added, 'We know the Taliban are planning and organising in Quetta.'"

In spite of the denials of such reports by government circles, nevertheless, Pakistan has concerns about the India-friendly policies of Karzai and the Northern Alliance. Indian consulates are being bitterly criticised for their alleged involvement in anti-Pakistan activities and for planning terrorist activities in Pakistan. Some analysts suggest that, because of this, Pakistan may be involved in reorganising the Taliban on a limited scale just to keep the Karzai government under pressure.

Suspicions about Pakistan's possible duplicity in its implementation of the anti-Taliban/anti-jihad program are not confined to Afghan government critics. As said earlier, it is well known that there are still a lot of Taliban sympathisers among the Pakistani military and secret service agencies as well as among the population and it may simply be a case of the left hand not always knowing what the right hand is doing at any one time.

The Character of the Tribals

Many tribals on the Pak-Afghan border are, undoubtedly, also helping with the reorganisation of the Taliban and much evidence is available to substantiate this. *Al-Hilal* of Jamiat-ul-Ansar wrote in its September 2003 issue: "It is not easy to have access within a difficult area like Waziristan. According to President Musharraf, we won this area where (previously) the army could not enter for a hundred and fifty years. But why couldn't this army stay on after crossing over Kargil? He may not like to answer this question because it was done on the orders of an 'ally'. It is not easy for Pakistani officials to stand by the promises made. Posts were established to stop the Taliban but the area of operations remained rather limited. The doorway into Afghanistan cannot be stopped even by America, not to talk of Pakistan. On the one hand, the long stretch of this border is a cause for the impossibility to stop infiltration, while on the other, there are fighting tribals on both sides who also happen to be relatives of each other. They have a tradition of being warm to the guests and remain united against the aliens. The strength of the states of Khost and Paktia in Afghanistan is also because of their physical proximity with Waziristan. Famous Taliban commanders, Jalaluddin Haqqani and Saifulla are popular in countless households. They are not strangers for the Taliban; in fact they happen to be their kith and kin. They have a history of their own. They did not allow the British to enter their areas by waging guerilla war. The story of Russia is too fresh in memory. An army may stand in the battleground only when they have the support of the people."

The Pushton tribes on the Pak-Afghan border were hostile to the Soviet Union ever since the Afghan jihad. The increasing number of madrasas in this area has given a considerable boost to the jihadi culture. According to Abdul Mannan, a journalist from Meeranshah in southern Waziristan, these madrasas have given birth to the Taliban and the entire area has been eminently suitable for the nurturing of Pakistani jihadi organisations. This fact is confirmed by the above extract from *al-Hilal*.

Since these tribes are situated on both the sides of the Pak-Afghan border, they help in providing shelter to both Taliban and al-Qaida elements and bring them closer to each other. According to reliable tribal sources, more than four hundred members of both of these organisations were provided shelter in various places there. The mountain villages and jungles of the area are an important refuge for them and they have enough arms to defend these enclaves.

The seven thousand volunteers of the Sufi

Mohammad movement, called Nifaz-e-Shariat-e-Mohammadi, who entered Afghanistan in October 2001 to help the Taliban, mostly belonged to these tribes. When they returned home, many members of al-Qaida and the Taliban returned with them to the tribal areas. In fact, some reports claim that Osama bin Laden, disguised in tribal garb, had also arrived with them in mid-November 2001.

Chaman: A Taliban Centre

There has been a constant inflow of news that the Pakistani cities of Quetta and Chaman have become new centres for the Taliban. There have been rumours of Mullah Omar being in Quetta. The Afghan External Affairs Minister and President Hamid Karzai have been continuously claiming that these two places have turned into new centres of the Taliban. Syed Salim Shahzad, a Karachi based journalist and researcher wrote in *Asia Times* after his tour of Chaman: "Immediately after entering the centre of Chaman city, located in Pakistan's Baluchistan province in southwest Pakistan right on the border with Afghanistan, a road curves left into the dusty distance. It leads to a chain of villages scattered along the border, some in Pakistan, some in Afghanistan, some spread across both countries, and all staunchly Pushton – and tribal – before anything else. Chaman, although not a particularly pretty city especially at this time of the year when the dust swirls down its streets from the surrounding barren mountains and plains, is a busy one. Its large markets are full of cheap, mostly smuggled, electronic goods, ranging from laptop computers to satellite and mobile phones. The city has several markets just for stolen cars, while the local 'mafia types' ride around in style as if Chaman were the Las Vegas of the east.

"But the curve from the heart of Chaman takes one to a different world, the world of dozens of tiny villages along the border which, according to one Akram of the Edhi Welfare Trust Centre in Chaman, are too numerous to be counted. The Edhi Welfare Trust is one of Pakistan's largest non-government organisations (NGOs). 'I have been posted here for several years. I roam all around the villages looking for charities and such things. I would simply say that there may be hundreds of villages, but I cannot give you the exact number as there are no records available. Sometimes the villages are situated in the mountains, and sometimes in the plains, half in Afghanistan, half in Pakistan,' says Akram.

"Village life is extremely traditional. However, the people of these areas have a reputation for being clever operators in trade and business, although their cultural life is completely guided by what they are taught by their mullahs. Says Akram, 'My experience with the Edhi Centre in Chaman have been very bad It is a completely mullah-dominated society. If you live in Karachi (from where Akram hails) you know that people trust our (Edhi) services all over Pakistan, we give most of the donations we receive to our trust. Here, our experience is different. You will know that the fitrana (a fee that all Muslims pay to a needy person before saying their Eid, a major Muslim festival of prayers) for example, comes to 300 rupees (US $5). Similarly, the number of sacrificial animal skins – cows or goats – comes to seven. Here in Chaman, even these seven skins and 300 rupees are donated by army officers posted in Chaman, not by the local people. And then these entire donations go to the Islamic seminaries. Here the people say that their lives are with the mullahs, not with you people.'

"In this tribal society there is of course both prosperity and poverty. The more children a family has, the more the economic burden on the breadwinner, usually just the head of the house. In this environment, Islamic seminaries (madrasas) provide an ideal way out for providing education, especially when the ideology, food, facilities and education are all free, and in some cases they even pay their students a stipend for pocket money. No wonder that they are popular. Commented a local leader of the Pushtonka Awami Party, who is a doctor by profession, on condition of anonymity. 'Before the Taliban emerged there used to be a few Islamic seminaries and they were unable to meet their day-to-day expenditure. The mullahs used to send the students from door to door to collect meals twice a day for both the mullahs and the students. But after the emergence of the Taliban the situation changed upside down. The Taliban heavily influenced the politics of the area and the people were influenced by their Islamic ideologies. As a result, donations were showered on the Jamiat Ulema-e-Islam (a Pakistani organisation ideologically associated with the Taliban movement) which then established a network of Islamic schools and which had funds to operate them. Now, sometimes in a single village, there are two Islamic seminaries, and I think the total number in Chaman and the villages around it comes to 200, with at least 50 students in each seminary.'

"This is the real fuel for the Taliban (resistance) movement in Afghanistan and for the fighters of the Taliban. Maulana Noor Mohammad, the chief of Jamiat Ulema-e-Islam in Quetta and a member of the National Assembly confirms, 'Yes, this is truly where all the big Taliban leaders got their education, from the seminaries in Chaman and in the madrasas situated in nearby villages. Then they went to Akora Khatak in North-West Frontier Province, where they learnt higher religious education.' The Taliban and their supporting parties in Pakistan have invested everything in this region. At the time when the Taliban faced the crunch in Afghanistan (when they were driven out of power in late 2001 and forced to go on the run) their madrasas around Chaman remained well guarded against ideological impurity and outside influences. This investment has paid off as now the seminaries that dot both sides of the border provide the best fodder for the resistance movement."

This popularity of the Taliban and, by association, al-Qaida, in the tribal areas again demonstrates the Pakistan Government's difficulty in implementing the anti-terrorism program in regions where western propaganda cannot reach. Too tough an approach can easily lead to separatist movements and possible civil war, something the centre is very anxious to avoid.

Journalist Ahmed Rashid, an expert on Taliban and

Afghan affairs, wrote in *The Daily Times* on 28 January 2004 about the help Jamiat Ulema-e-Islam and its madrasas are extending to the Taliban in reorganising themselves and regrouping in Chaman and Quetta: "Pakistan's Jamiat Ulema-e-Islam (JUI) party now forms part of the governing coalition that rules Baluchistan. It is using its madrasas and mosques to house and mobilize thousands of a new, even younger, generation of Afghan and Pakistani Taliban to fight the Karzai government and terrorize southern Afghanistan. After prayers are over, the young Taliban – many of them in their teens – flood into the tea stalls of Pushtonabad, a Quetta suburb, in their distinctive black clothes, black turbans, long beards, and unkempt hair. They talk of the progress of the Taliban offensive in Afghanistan today. Taliban fighters, I was told, are better equipped than they were in 1994. They are buying Thuraya satellite telephones and hundreds of Honda motorbikes to carry out guerilla raids; they are also importing night-vision equipment from the Arab Gulf states."

President Karzai and other Afghan leaders have been harshly critical of the support the Taliban receive from the JUI and elements in the ISI. Even though Pakistan's military regime arrested some five hundred members of al-Qaida in Pakistan, it has still not arrested a single Taliban leader.

The Alliance of Pakistani Jihadi Groups with the Taliban

Pakistani jihadi groups and the Taliban are inextricably linked. Several training centres in Afghanistan were

used by Pakistani jihadi organisations during the
Taliban regime. These included the Sarobi and Jyora
camps in Khost, the Ghazni training centre in the
Shahshgoo Hills, the Mohammad training centre in
Bangarbar, the Rashkor camp to the north of Kabul
and the Karaga camp to the west of Kabul. It would be
too much to expect that they would have no continued
relationship after the fall of Kabul.

One member, Farooq, of Tahreek-e-Khuddam-e-
Islam (Jaish-e-Mohammad), said that their aim was to
secure freedom for the entire Muslim population all over
the world who are now being ruled by others. To achieve
this aim, they were ready to co-operate with whosoever
would be of help to their cause. He said that Khuddam-
e-Islam has sent most of its mujahideen to Afghanistan
on the appeal of Mullah Omar where, along with the
Taliban, they were targeting American forces. Such
confessions are made by most of the jihadi organisations
matter of factly. In fighting against American forces,
Harkat-ul-Mujahideen lost 110 men, Harkat-ul-Jihad-
ul-Islami lost 270, and Jaish-e-Mohammad lost 90 of
their mujahideen and commanders. *Al-Irshad* (December
2001) of Harkat-ul-Jihad-ul-Islami, said that, up to
November, 67 of their Pakistani mujahideen had lost
their lives, 10 of whom were important commanders.
One of its commanders said in August 2003 that 270 of
their mujahideen had been killed and it was incumbent
upon them to take revenge.

Shamsheer (Hyderabad) in its April 2002 issue,
quoted one Pakistani mujahideen activist saying:
"Earlier, we were on the line of Pul Kumri where there
was less bombed but when we reached the Khwaja

Ghar front, we found this place was heavily bombardment. There were two fronts and thirty of us were posted there. All of us were Pakistanis. There were two Taliban fronts nearby and close to the Amu river were the fronts of the Arab mujahideen. On the Arab fronts there were no mujahideen from any other country. A little way from there were the Chechen fronts. There were not many confrontations with the Northern Alliance, but America used to bomb a lot which served the purpose of the Alliance."

Al-Irshad published the following message from the Emirs of Harkat-ul-Jihad-ul-Islami after the fall of the Taliban: "Maulana Qari Saifullah Akhtar, the Emir of the Markaz, Mohammad Omar, the Emir of Harkat-ul-Jihad-ul-Islami of Pakistan, Mohammad Ahmad Mansoor, the Deputy Emir of Harkat, issued an important message for the mujahideen and the Islamic world that the present condition of Afghanistan is the result of smart moves by the Taliban. The Northern Alliance forces were targeting the common citizens of Afghanistan, so the Taliban rightly decided that the people should vacate the towns. Governments come and go and that does not carry much weight with us; the main aim is waging jihad in the name of God. Kandahar is still in the control of the Taliban and the mujahideen must keep their spirits high. The American commanders have reached Kandahar heavily armed. Now, the real war between faith and non-faith has started. God will defeat the Americans as were the British and the Russians in the past. Let Muslims not feel disappointed. Victory shall be with those who are in the right (God willing). The mujahideen should work in a better manner now; they should sacrifice their lives and property to be dear to God. Harkat-ul-Jihad-ul-Islami is devoting all its strength on this occasion and we hope that the mujahideen and the workers too will do their best."

"An activist of the Harkat-ul-Mujahideen, who has been involved in Afghanistan since 1988, concurs with the contention that, 'Until the guerilla warfare begins, there is no point in jihadis being stationed within the country.' He adds that, 'Amireeul Momineen Mullah Omar has himself announced that for the moment they should prepare themselves, and that when the time comes, he will give the signal for the Pakistani volunteers to join the war.' However, he maintains that the Taliban have an extremely efficient intelligence system. Anyone with suspect intentions will be found out very soon. Sources within the militant cadres hasten to add that not all volunteers, when they make their way into Afghanistan, will be engaged in combat. 'They are recruited according to their abilities, some are doctors, engineers etc. We have an intelligence system in every locality (so) that the Jaish-e-Mohammad is the most well organised. These people check the background of each volunteer, process his recruitment, and facilitate his departure to the border.' They maintain that there are hundreds of thousands of people, particularly from Baluchistan, the Frontier Province and the tribal belt who have committed themselves to the jihad when the call comes. In fact, in many villages in the Frontier Province and Baluchistan along the Afghan border families deem it their religious duty to send a loved one to fight in the jihad. Many of the men such as Abdul Zahir are potential recruits for the jihad."

It is clear from these various reports that Pakistani jihadi groups are taking part in the new jihad against America and the Northern Alliance alongside al-Qaida and the Taliban. The prominent Pakistani groups making their contributions include: Harkat-ul-Mujahideen (Jamiat-ul-Ansar), Harkat-ul-Jihad-ul-Islami, Jaish-e-Mohammad, Jamiat al-Furqan, Jamiat-ul-Mujahideen, al-Badr Mujahideen and Lashkar-e-Taiba. Reliable jihadi sources admit that the Jihadi organisations are winding up their base camps in Azad Kashmir and moving them to the Afghan border regions. These mujahideen have moved especially to assist the Taliban.

The Jihadi groups' media clearly indicate these new activities of the mujahideen. *Shamsheer* (April 2002) published a detailed report on the activities of a commander called Saifur Rahman in Afghanistan: "The person who got fame in the war at Gardez and who is considered to be the central character in this confrontation is Saifur Rahman, the son of jihadi commander Nasrullah Mansoor. Everyone knows of the great services rendered by Nasrullah Mansoor in the jihad of Afghanistan. He is especially remembered for beating the Russian war helicopters, apart from others. When differences arose among the Afghan leaders at the end of the Afghan jihad, Nasrullah Mansoor also became a victim of these differences. He received his martyrdom in an accident. It is said that a well-known Afghan leader, Gulbaden Hikmetyar, had a role to play in his martyrdom.

"Commander Saifur Rahman reminds us of him. A man of strong build and high spirits, he has always been present in the Afghan jihad. Later, he worked in close association with the Taliban. During these activities, he received injuries several times and he was once brought to Karachi for treatment. Even though he is not more than thirty-five years old, he enjoys respect among the Afghan leaders. This may be gauged from the fact that the person who had a major role during the discussions between Ahmad Shah Masood and the Taliban before (their) entry into Kabul, was none else but Saifur Rahman.

"Those who have been with him on the fronts confirm his unique bravery and capacity to face the enemy fearlessly. Just a few months earlier, at the time of the fall of the Taliban, he was performing his duties as a commander on a line beyond Kabul. When the orders for vacating Kabul came, he was one of the last few to leave Kabul. Like other leaders, he too is out of the scene now. No one knows his whereabouts. His name came up only when the Gardez confrontation came up. According to reports received at *Shamsheer*, he chose a hilly region near Gardez called Shahi Kot, which is covered with snow these days, for testing the spirit of the American forces. Anyone who chooses to go there, chooses for his death actually and Commander Saifu Rahman made the Americans choose that."

The Jihadi Groups of Hikmetyar and Jamaat-e-Islami

Many of the mujahideen of Gulbaden Hikmetyar's

Hizb-e-Islami had joined the Taliban during their tenure in government. Later, Hizb-e-Islami became part of the Northern Alliance and Hikmetyar took refuge in Iran. When America announced its intention to invade Afghanistan after 9/11, Hikmetyar declared his unconditional support for the Taliban. As a result of this declaration, he was obliged to leave Iran too. After the fall of the Taliban, he started organising his mujahideen in the Pushton areas of Afghanistan and initiated action against American and Allied forces in association with the Taliban. Gradually, he broadened his area of operation to Pakistan. He participated in the annual al-Badr convention at Mansahra in February 2003 and exhorted Pakistani jihadi organisations to take part in the new Afghan jihad. Al-Badr, as a subsidiary jihadi organisation of Jamaat-e-Islami, had taken part in the jihad against Soviet forces along with Hizb-e-Islami. According to al-Badr sources, this relationship has been revived. There is also information suggesting that Hizb-ul-Mujahideen activists from the Frontier Province also joining the jihad.

According to *The Daily Times* (7 December 2003), Hikmetyar's Hizb-e-Islami established two new organisations, Fidayeen-e-Islam and Mujahideen-e-Islam to recruit mujahideen from the Pushton areas of Afghanistan. Hizb sources also say that these organisations are also active in Malakund division and northern areas, apart from the tribal areas. Hikmetyar is also in hiding like Osama bin Laden and Mullah Omar but he is in touch with the Jamaat-e-Islami leadership. When Liaqat Baloch was elected as the Emir of Jamaat-e-

Islami (Punjab), Hikmetyar sent him his congratulations on 10 November 2003 and appealed to Jamaat-e-Islami to organize its jihadi activities afresh and to help the other mujahideen who were waging jihad against America. As Hikmetyar has taken a vow of allegiance on the hands of Mullah Omar, it is fairly certain that Hizb-e-Islami has now become a part of the Taliban. It is said of Hikmetyar that he has established contacts with several disgruntled warlords, including the former head of the Northern Alliance and interim President, Burhanuddin Rabbani, Ismail Khan, the Governor of Herat in the west of the country, and Abdul Rasul Sayyaf, Afghanistan's leading proponent of Wahabi Islam. The Karzai regime is too weak to take action against any of them.

The Daily Times article continues: "Significantly, in the early 1980s, these Afghan leaders, including Hikmetyar, belonged to the Muslim Brotherhood which emerged out of the Arab world and was the precursor to today's more extreme Islamic movements. Hikmetyar is trying to revive those connections and propagate Muslim Brotherhood ideology which is stridently anti-Western and anti-democratic. He says; 'All true Muslim Afghans who want an Islamic government in their country must know it is possible only when the United States and Allied soldiers are forced out.'

"Hikmetyar is also trying to whip up the sentiments of Pushton nationalism. In cassettes sent to journalists, he accuses the United States and the Kabul government of beginning 'a genocide on the Pushtons.' He has a considerable network of supporters in

Pakistan. After the 1979 Soviet invasion, the ISI promoted Hikmetyar ruthlessly, until he was dumped in favour of the Taliban in 1995."

Foreign Assistance?

The way both al-Qaida and the Taliban have restored their strength during such a short period of time inclines some analysts to believe that, apart from the Pakistani religious and jihadi organisations, they also got some assistance from other countries. China and Russia are at the top of the list of such countries. Jawed Ibrahim Paracha, of the Frontier Province, claimed that he had evidence of the fact that China and Russia had come into contact with the Taliban and they are already providing full military assistance to them so that America would be forced to face the same conditions suffered by Soviet Russia during its occupation of the country. This was reported in *Nidai Millat* (19 September 2001). The Americans, however, have not made this accusation but the rumours persist and an active Afghan commander told *The Daily Times* in July 2003 that al-Qaida and the Taliban had acquired the latest technically advanced arms. He could not identify the suppliers, however.

Operations Against the Taliban and al-Qaida in Tribal Areas

For the Pakistan Government, the Afghan Government and the American Government the problem with the 'war on terror' and the suppression of a Taliban resurgence is the fact that the main region of terrorist bases and organisation lies on both sides of the borders between Pakistan and Afghanistan. After the American attack on Afghanistan, a considerable number of Taliban and al-Qaida activists took refuge in the tribal areas situated on the Pak-Afghan border. These Pushton people were always sympathetic to the Taliban and their areas were important centres of activity during the Taliban regime. Many of these tribals have joined the Afghan jihad against America. Smaller scale operations against the Taliban and al-Qaida in the Pushton areas started when it became known that they had sought refuge in these tribal areas although bigger operations were not undertaken until October 2003. According to sources in the tribal areas inside Pakistan, during the American attack on Afghanistan many of those associated with al-Qaida and the Taliban suffered death and injury at the hands of the Pakistan Army. The number of dead persons is given as 70 and those injured is 400. This apart, 15 local civilians have also been killed and 300 have been injured. On charges of providing shelter to Taliban and al-Qaida mujahideen, homes, markets and mosques numbering some 150 have also been demolished. These operations have also claimed 20 Pakistan Army fatalities. It is important to understand the geographical, political, and historical situation and conditions in these areas in order to understand the background to these operations and the problems faced by the Pakistan Government in particular.

The Federal Administered Tribal Areas (FATA), are located in a narrow belt which runs along the Pak-Afghan border. They have a chequered history and a strategically distinctive position. This border, known to the British as the Durand Line, was named after Sir Mortimer Durand whose survey established this division during the Raj in 1890.

The FATA is about 27,220 sq kms (10500 sq mls) in area. The population of the FATA, according to the 1981 census, was 2.2 million. It is divided administratively into seven political units (agencies): Bajaur, Mohmand, Khyber, Orakzai, Khurram, North Waziristan and South Waziristan, and there are four Frontier Regions (FRs): Peshawar, Kohat, Bannu and Dera Ismail Khan, the last two of these are further subdivided to create FR Lakki and FR Tank.

The Administrative set-up of Khyber, Khurram and Waziristan dates back to the times of British rule, while that of the other three agencies – Mohmand, Orakzai and Bajaur and the FRs was established after independence in 1947. Geographically however, FATA can be divided into three parts, the northern, southern and central regions. The northern region comprises Bajaur and Mohmand which lie between the Swat and Kabul rivers. The central region comprises Khyber, Khurram, and Orakzai agencies, and the FRs of Peshawar and Kohat. The southern region includes North and South Waziristan and the FRs of Dera Ismail Khan, Tank, Bannu and Lakki.

Under article 247 of Pakistan's constitution, the FATA comes under the executive authority of the Federation. This area is composed of 11 major tribes and several sub-tribes such as Utman Khel, Mohmand Safi, Afridi, Orakzai, Turi, Bangash, Dawar, Shelmani, Shinwari, Mulagori, Parachinar, Masozai, Saidgai,

Mehsud, Waziris, Bhittani, Kharasin, Gurbaz, Ustrana, Utmanzai, Ahmadzai, and Shirani. The people of this area are largely Muslims, dotted with a very small population of Sikhs and Hindus. The language of the tribes is Pushto. The major rivers that traverse this area include the Kurram, the Gomal Tochi, the Swat and the Kabul. Apart from the well-known Khyber Pass, other major passes in the high and harsh mountains of the FATA include Nawa, Peiwar, Kotal Tochi and Gomal. The climactic conditions vary slightly from area to area, but it is, generally, very hot in summer and very cold in winter.

The areas making up the FATA have played an important role in the history of the subcontinent. The harsh and steep mountainous land interspersed with many passes, Khyber being the most important of them all, has over the centuries been an easy gateway for invaders – Aryans, Turks, Mughals, Huns, Durranis, Sythians, Tartars, Sassanians, Mongols, Seljuks and also Persians and Greeks. One of the earliest references to this area and its people dates back to the invasion by Alexander the Great, circa 323 BC, in which a tribe called the 'Apurtae' was said to have inhabited the hills of the present day Khyber Agency. The existing name 'Apredai' in the local language makes it very easy to see the connection.

During British rule, because of its strategic importance, this region was demarcated as a buffer zone against Russia and the threat of Tsarist expansion. This was done as part of Lord Curzon's 'Forward Policy'. However, the British never quite controlled the region themselves, but they had made arrangements with local tribal leaders who gave nominal allegiance to the Raj.

The autonomous status of the FATA was accepted by Pakistan at the time of independence through the famous Instrument of Accession signed by Qaid-e-Azam, Mohammad Ali Jinnah, at the Bannu Tribal Jirga in January 1948.

Administratively, the Federally Administered Tribal Areas enjoy a unique position whereby they are governed at the grassroots level through tribal representatives known as Maliks and Lungi Holders. There are a total of 3,616 Maliks and 3,441 Lungi Holders in the FATA and FRs. A Malik/Lungi holder is recognised by the government as a person commanding greater authority and influence over his tribe and he is responsible for the maintenance of his respective district.

There is also the institution of Khassadars (local police) which bears responsibility for maintaining law and order in the tribal area. The law and order situation has always been much better in the FATA as compared to other areas because of a tight self-defence mechanism inherent among the tribes.

The FATA is policed through the Frontier Crimes Regulation, the notorious 'black law' introduced by the British in 1901, whereby appointed political supervisors acted as police and magistrates. At first they were British but this gave way to local chiefs being appointed, many of whom were regarded as abusers of power. However, today, the jirga is the cornerstone of the tribal system. A jirga is a group of a few elders, mostly uneducated, who sit together and solve problems in accordance with the tribal customs and traditions in as short a time as possible. This is in sharp contrast to the slack judicial system enforced in the rest of Pakistan. This quick delivery of justice has convinced the tribal people of the famous dictum that 'justice delayed is justice denied.' The tribes elect eight members to the National Assembly and eight to the Senate of Pakistan. Previously, this was done indirectly, now it is carried out directly through an adult franchise.

Agriculture is the mainstay of the local economy, However, the FATA is deficit in food supply and relies on imports from other parts of Pakistan, particularly the North-West Frontier Province, for its food requirements. Only 6.5 per cent of the area is cultivated with low crop intensity and low yields. Livestock plays a very important role in the local subsistence pattern but it cannot be an adequate substitute for cereals. The major crops are maize, wheat, barley, rice, rapeseed, peanuts, peaches, apricots, pears, apple, walnuts and vegetables, with the cropping pattern varying from region to region.

A large portion of the tribal population is engaged in the transport business and a considerable number is working abroad. The FATA falls far behind the rest of the country in almost all socio-economic comparisons. There is some mining for minerals but the economy is predominantly agrarian and the marginal nature of the land permits only subsistence agriculture. The backwardness of the FATA was recognised in the country's sixth five-year plan and it was declared to be the least developed area of Pakistan.

Some 19 different minerals have been identified in the FATA and the regions potential can be productively exploited with improved access for development purposes. The mineral resources, including gemstones, offer opportunities for commercial exploitation. The land between major rivers can convert into rich forests and pastures. The passes running through the mountains of the FATA can be used as overland trade routes to central Asia, western Asia, the Middle East and Europe. The people of these areas are hard working and their lot could be improved by the provision of proper skill training and development efforts. Therefore, any serious effort to win 'hearts and minds' in the war on terror in these areas would do well to recognise these economic facts.

It must also be kept in mind here that not all of the tribal people provide refuge to the al-Qaida network. The Shia tribal people in the Para Chinar area, because of their Sunni v Shia religious differences with al-Qaida and the Taliban, are helpful to Pakistani forces in actions against the mujahideen. According to reliable sources, five major operations in this area have been conducted on the basis of the information given by the Shia tribals.

The tribes that have rendered help to al-Qaida and the Taliban include those branches of the waziri tribe called the Zali Khel, the Kari Khel, the Yar Gul Khel, the Naziri Khel, apart from the Masood Zai and the Ahmad Zai tribes. The tribes are spread through North and South Waziristan, Bajaur Agency, Bannu, and Dera Ismail Khan. Most of the operations against al-Qaida and Taliban have also been held in these areas.

The al-Qaida and Taliban influx into the tribal areas started in September 2001. According to sources from these areas, the first contingent of Arab and other country's mujahideen numbering about 370 fighters entered Tora Bora after the American bombing of Afghanistan. Just after entering Pakistan, they had a clash with Pakistani forces. Tribal sympathisers buried ten mujahideen who were killed in this action. After this incident, the mujahideen travelled for three days to reach the Para Chinar tribal area. Some of these mujahideen were handed over to Pakistani forces by the local people. *Nidai Millat* (Lahore: 19 September 2002) published a report with reference to this event: "When the Americans bombarded Tora Bora at the very beginning of their aggression on Afghanistan, the Arab Mujahideen left the place and sought refuge with the tribals in Chinar tribal areas. They had to set out again after getting back to health but just two days later, another rival tribe came to know of their refuge there, and they informed the Americans and Pakistani forces of their presence there. According to the tribals of Para Chinar, just as they got this information, the Americans started pressurising the Pakistan government to interfere into the matter. According to sources, the Pakistani officials started holding talks with the seniors in the tribe. The Sunni tribal leaders agreed to hand them over on the condition they will be given to the embassies of the respective countries so that they could go back to their respective homes. According to tribal sources, the Arab mujahideen were aware of these discussions. According to a correspondent of an Arabic journal published from London, Mahmood Khalil, an eyewitness, without giving his name, said that the tribals were aware that the Pakistani officials might go back on their words. In spite of this doubt, they believed them so that the Arab mujahideen could go back to their homes. The Arab mujahideen were brought to the trucks which were brought to carry them to Kohat jail for two days before taking up further discussions with the embassies in Islamabad. A tribal eyewitness said that just as they started getting into the truck, some Pakistanis abused them, and beat them up. This enraged the Arab mujahideen and thirty of them snatched their arms and attacked them. This was quite unexpected for the Pakistanis. They sought help from the post nearby and several helicopters came to their rescue. This skirmish led to the death of ten Arab mujahideen and several Pakistanis. About eighty Arab mujahideen also fled towards the mountains in the meanwhile. According to Jawad Paracha, the rest of the mujahideen were arrested and brought to Kohat jail where they were handed over to FBI agents."

After this operation, such incidents became a part of normal activities in these areas. Nevertheless, the mujahideen still operate in areas where the local population are either sympathetic to their cause or else they simply mistrust foreigners and Pakistani forces equally.

Some Major Reasons for Operations in the FATA

The first objection tribal leaders have made against

anti-Taliban operations in their areas is that the Taliban are not on any list of terrorists in the world. In which case, they claim, providing them with refuge is legal. Many Taliban members are also related to them tribally and tribal loyalty is very strong among them. Nevertheless, they may co-operate with Pakistani forces in respect of Arab and other foreign mujahideen provided they are sent back to their homelands and not handed over to America.

The American have other reasons for wanting to conduct operations in these areas. The kidnapping of American and allied forces personnel by mujahideen groups is one. Pakistani forces started their operation against al-Qaida in Bannu on 4 September 2003. Some sources said that these operations were started after intelligence was received that Osama bin Laden was in the area but ISPR (Inter-Services Public Relations) said it was a routine army anti-terrorist activity. Regardless, tribal sources also said that Bannu was used only as a headquarters and the real operation was carried out in Aqa Khel Pass against Mehsud and Waziri tribesmen who had given refuge to those members of al-Qaida and Taliban who had been involved in the kidnapping of 12 Americans from an American military camp there. According to other sources, Pakistani forces secured the release of these Americans and sent them to Afghanistan from Bannu airport. This was not the first operation with respect to the kidnapping of American forces. Jihadi sources claim that the Taliban and al-Qaida had more than 50 such prisoners with them until November 2003 and they say that these military operations were carried out to rescue American personnel. The Quds Press (an Arab news agency) interviewed an Arab jihadi commander called Abu Suhaib-al-Makki near the Pak-Afghan border. The interview was published in the weekly *Nidai Millat* (23 May 2002). Al-Makki said in that interview that the mujahideen had captured 18 Americans in a confrontation at Gardez. He said that they would use these prisoners to seek the release of their men. He also added that he had carried on secret discussions with the Americans over this issue. Tribal sources, on the other hand, claimed that al-Qaida and Taliban fighters had kidnapped 20 American and other allied forces personnel and had taken them to the deep forests of southern Waziristan. These kidnapped people were of British, Italian, and American nationalities.

American and Pakistani military sources say they believe that both Mullah Omar and Osama bin Laden keep crossing into the tribal areas. Some Pak-US operations were carried out only after the receipt of such intelligence. It is worth mentioning here that Osama used to live in Tira, a village on the Afghan side of the border with Khyber, and that he had also constructed a personal house there. According to tribal sources, he used to live there with 400 of his men during the days of the jihad against the Soviets in Afghanistan. It is said on the basis of this information that the mountain and hilly terrain is not new to Osama and his men and they are very familiar with its topography. Abu Suhaib al-Makki also claimed that Osama and Mullah Omar never stayed at one place for more than three days and very few people knew of their movements. Newspapers carried reports in June 2003 that the secret services in America and Pakistan had come very close to trapping Osama but this was later denied by the ISI. A journalist from South Waziristan called Ibrahim Khan, said that Osama was present in the Red Mountains near Miran Shah in the last week of December 2002. He said that the hills there can easily be used to hide and it would be impossible even to trace a lost person or animal there. That is why the locals know this place as 'the thief's den'. Ibrahim Khan also said that Machadar Kharoti, a large fort-like house, is now under American occupation and it was there that Khalid al-Zawahiri, the nephew of Aiman al-Zawahiri, sought refuge along with 22 engineers. He said that Khalid al-Zawahiri sported a small beard and always had an army man's stick in his hand. He was an engineer by profession but he had been entrusted with the responsibility of buying arms from Afghanistan. They had shifted there from Kabul. Khalid, and his associates had their identity cards made in south Waziristan. Later, they shaved their beard and moved to Peshawar. Ibrahim Khan also claimed, on the strength of his own sources, that Khalid al-Zawahiri planned to enter India via Rahim Yar Khan and, according to him, he and his associates are in India now.

Agreements With the Tribal Chiefs

When the mujahideen accelerated their activities in the tribal areas and little came from regular military operations against them, the political administration and the Pakistani military looked for a means of rapprochement. They struck several deals with tribal leaders. One such agreement was reached on 27 June 2002 between the tribal chiefs and the Pakistan Army which said that if anyone was found giving refuge to a foreigner, his house and property would be destroyed. In spite of this agreement, the movement of al-Qaida and the Taliban continued in the area. The Pakistan Army continued minor operations with the assistance of American contingents during this period. These operations, however, gathered momentum in October 2003 when leaders of the Zali Khel and Karri Khel tribes flatly refused to handover al-Qaida and Taliban jihadis to the army. Thus, in operations carried out from 12 to 18 October 2003, some 22 al-Qaida members were killed. Seven tribesmen were also killed and had their properties destroyed. In these circumstances, the tribal chiefs had second thoughts and handed over about a dozen al-Qaida members to the Pakistan Army. *The Daily Times* of 16 October 2003 carried out a report on the reactions against Pakistani forces and the government in the tribal areas: "A 50-year-old man whose house was destroyed in Thursday's military operation against al-Qaida activists in the area told *The Daily Times* on Sunday that authorities in Islamabad knew where the al-Qaida operatives were hiding 'but still bombed innocent citizens.'

'The Pakistani government is infidel. If it wasn't, the army would not have bombed us. They also took away three of my sons,' a furious Nawab Khan said. 'They know where the Arabs are hiding, but they are not arresting them.'

"Khan said army gunship helicopters pounded his house moments after he had finished saying his morning prayers. 'When the first few shots were fired I thought there might be a wedding going on. But seconds later my house was under attack from all sides,' he said while describing the operation's initial moments. He showed empty shells fired from gunship helicopters and the bombs which fell on his house. His house is a few yards away from three other houses which were also attacked in search of the al-Qaida operatives.

"Khan said he had decided to leave Baghbar, a kilometre from the Pak-Afghan border for Wana, the South Waziristan Agency headquarters. 'They might bomb my house again someday, so I should shift to somewhere safer.'

"He denied that there were al-Qaida operatives in the area. 'War is waged in Afghanistan and they target us here,' Khan said, adding that nobody in his family was killed or injured during the operation.

"Anger against the army runs high among deeply conservative tribesmen in this tribal zone that both Kabul and Pakistan suspect to be safe havens for Taliban and al-Qaida elements, but tribal chieftains avoid open criticism of the army.

"However, younger tribesmen are more vocal about their feelings. 'Everyone is sad about the operation conducted against our people,' 28-year-old taxi driver Wahidullah told *The Daily Times*. 'Some day our people might attack the army if such operations continue,' he warned.

"He too denied the presence of al-Qaida and Taliban activists in the country. But he conceded that since the people in the tribal zones were religious, they had sympathy for the Taliban."

Muttahida Majlis-e-Amal also made protests in the parliament and its members insisted that Majlis-e-Amal would raise its voice in and outside the parliament against these operations. This made it clear that the political and tribal leaders did not want any Pakistani political interference in their affairs. In fact, the tribesmen sometimes mislead their political representatives also. "Who can get the secrets out of their hearts?" a tribal leader asked and answered himself; "It could either be money or trust but the government has failed on both counts."

Ibrahim Khan, a South Waziristan journalist, said that the American contingents had started their actions in the region in November 2001. While many tribesmen offer refuge to Taliban and Arab mujahideen, some chieftains serve the Americans as informants for the sake of money. However, much of the time, their information is not accurate. Khan said that Maulana Darya Khan, from a border village, was killed only for the reason that he was against the Americans in the area and used to speak against any tribesmen assisting them. Khan further said that American commandos units and investigators stayed in the border areas while their planning units were located near Dera Ismail Khan. He also claimed that the Americans announced their withdrawal from particular areas several times but the tribesmen always knew where they were hiding. These foreign contingents have American and British commandos from special forces divisions. According to Khan, they were being guided by a former Pushton mujahideen commander, Shabbir Ahmad, who was selected for the job on account of his knowledge of local routes and conditions. Ibrahim Khan further said that Osama was seen in this area in December 2002 and local people were very unhappy about the operations conducted by Pakistani forces to try to nail him. As a result, those tribesmen who were not in favour of providing shelter to al-Qaida earlier, were now doing so. In spite of the fact that some tribal people are helping the anti-terrorist forces for money or because of religious rivalry, most of the locals are very much with the Taliban and the mujahideen network cannot be driven out of this region even if the war continued for another fifty years.

From these accounts, it is clearly not possible for the anti-terrorist coalition forces to drive Taliban and Arab mujahideen out of the region in a few months. Therefore, on the one hand, Pakistani and American forces continue their military operations, while on the other hand, no doubt in recognition of the political reality, Pakistani political agents are trying to find solutions by encouraging tribal leaders to collaborate and to win the battle for 'hearts and minds'.

Because of these circumstances, Ahmad Zai, the Minister of Tribal Affairs called a meeting of interested parties in January 2004 which then assured the government of its support in operations against the Taliban and al-Qaida. It was also decided to form a tribal group to punish those who helped Taliban and al-Qaida activists. It is interesting to note that the tribal member of the Assembly, Maulana Abdul Malik, and former member, Maulana Noor Mohammad, of Muttahida Majlis-e-Amal also attended the meeting and supported the decisions.

Action Plan for the Spring Season

An American newspaper, *The Los Angeles Times*, published a report in February 2004 saying that American forces based in Afghanistan had plans to take action against Osama bin Laden and the al-Qaida network in the tribal areas of Pakistan that month. Pakistani officials denied this report but it took only two weeks for the situation to be clarified. The Pakistani forces started their actions in South Waziristan in a big way shortly thereafter and, in spite of denials from the government, both American and tribal sources claim that American military contingents provided full support to Pakistan's army in these operations. This support was not limited to satellite intelligence technology because American commandos were present and supervised the operations also. The Waziristan operation was carried out in the last week of February and was said to be the forerunner to a bigger campaign to be carried out in the spring season. Then the news came that, after the exposure of Dr Qadir Khan (the Pakistani scientist accused of revealing nuclear secrets to other Islamic governments) America had also sought permission to carry out unilateral operations in the tribal areas. In this connection, the American Commandant General in Afghanistan toured the GHQ in Rawalpindi and decided important details of the operation with Pakistani military chiefs. This further strengthened the impression that preparations for major military operation in the spring are in full swing.

According to *Asia Times* (2 March 2004): "Osama bin Laden will be 'smoked out' probably on a tip by an Afghan tribal leader willing to make a cool $25 million. And all credit will go to the secretive Commando 121 which is known to comprise Navy Seals and commandos from the army's Delta Force.

"The Pentagon has fired its first rhetorical Tomahawks of the season through a leak this past weekend by a 'US intelligence source' that bin Laden, Mullah Omar and about 50 top al-Qaida operatives had been located in Baluchistan. President General Pervez Musharraf was said to be on the brink of authorising an American intervention. According to the Pentagon script, the fugitives are 'boxed in' and packed in a tight group surrounded by an array of US and British Special Forces, and apparently with no chance of escaping." *Asia Times* claimed.

The report said: "The fugitives are now said to be in the isolated Toba Kakar mountains in Baluchistan and very far from the Afghan province of Zabol. They are supposed to be in an area between the villages of Khanozoi and Murgha Faqizai. There is an obvious escape route, a tortuous mountain trail towards the Afghan border village of Ala Jezah. And there are the not so obvious routes, known only to bin Laden and a few Arab and Afghans familiar with the country since the early 1980s.

"Pentagon chief Donald Rumsfield was in Afghanistan this week. Exasperated diplomats suggest to *Asia Times Online* that he may have personally negotiated the terms of the 'authorization' with President Musharraf. After all, these are the stakes that really matter for the Bush administration that when, where and how to spin the capture of bin Laden and Mullah Omar, it said.

"CIA chief George Tenet was on a secret mission to Islamabad in early February to discuss the modalities of the spinning concerning bin Laden's whereabouts. According to the CIA chief, bin Laden has 'gone deep underground.' He was not specific and unlike the Pentagon, he did not point to the exact global satellite coordinates of bin Laden and his crew of 50. Rumsfield clearly knows something that Tenet does not. Another key actor, President Musharraf, is duly following his script and is stationing 'tens of thousands' of Pakistan Army troops in the tribal areas and vigorously trying to smoke out the usual al-Qaida and Taliban suspects. President Musharraf's job is much easier now that the whole porous area has been declared off limits to the foreign press.

"Sources in Peshawar confirm to *Asia Times Online* that Pakistani and American forces are raising hell on both sides of the porous Pak-Afghan border, contributing with helicopter gun ships, paramilitary forces and regular round troops. This is the *hors d'oeuvre* for the already well flagged upcoming spring offensive. This American offensive at first will be concentrated in North and South Waziristan on the Pakistan side, and the province of Paktia and Paktika on the Afghan side. Pushton tribes in the Afghan province of Khost confirm to *Asia Times* that, after a bombing campaign, American forces and local Afghan allies brought with them the usual suitcases full of dollars and are also involved in house-to-house searches. This area used to be a stronghold of mujahideen commander Jalaluddin Haqqani. The Americans will be forced to start a real war in Paktika because some of the Paktika districts are now ruled by Hikmetyars' Hizb-e-Islami, others by tribal leaders hostile to the Karzai regime. Information minister Sheikh Rashid Ahmad confirms that the army was now deployed 'all over the tribal areas.' 'Our rapid action forces are there; they have sealed the border.' The information minister's assurance that 'no one is allowed to come in from Afghanistan' is part of the new official spin from Islamabad 'as part of Pakistan's commitment to the international community against terrorism.'

"Pakistan may have sealed the border with Afghanistan but how to unseal it for the Americans is a matter to be discussed face-to-face by Rumsfield and President Musharraf. The previous official Pakistani script saying that its army could not legally enter tribal areas has been reduced to dust.

"And what if bin Laden decides not to follow the script? According to reliable sources, bin Laden has made his seven bodyguards take an oath to kill him in the event of his being in any danger of being arrested. 'He will try to blow himself up.' according to reports.

"On the other hand, Western diplomatic sources who prefer to insist that if bin Laden is arrested according to the current Pentagon plan, the whole operation will be kept secret to be disclosed only a few days before the American presidential election in November."

The jihadi *Daily Islam* and the weekly *Zarb-e-Momin* based in Karachi, on the basis of special reports from Afghanistan, published a report on the same day, 27 February 2004, that a war of nerves had begun.

Successes Against al-Qaida and CIA Involvement

During the year 2003, some 1500 al-Qaida activists have been captured or arrested in Pakistan. However, official confirmation of only 600 arrests has been made so far. The number of Pakistani military personnel who lost their lives in operations against al-Qaida is said to be more than a hundred.

It seems fairly certain that the CIA has been playing an important role in arrests and counter-terrorists moves in Pakistan. It should also be clarified here that the name of the FBI is generally being used in the context of operations against al-Qaida but, according to informed sources, that is just a 'cover name'. No doubt, there must be some real FBI, and, maybe, DEA (Drug Enforcement Agency) personnel involved because of their urban policing experience and their files on international smuggling, criminal and terrorist groups but it is an open secret that the main operations are actually being conducted by CIA field-workers.

Since the beginning of the terrorist crisis after 9/11, the Pakistan Government has denied any assistance or role by the FBI (CIA) in operations against al-Qaida inside Pakistan. The government maintained that these operations were being conducted by its own intelligence agencies without assistance from American agencies. However, a member of a secret service institution involved in these operations revealed that he acted in various operations on information received from the CIA. He also claimed that American satellite technology was being used to carry out the programs. The Pakistani media did not buy the government's line about the non-involvement of American agencies in these operations inside Pakistan and, eventually, the government stopped making denials. Later, the relationship between the CIA and Pakistani intelligence agencies was given a formal shape by the formation of a joint working group in which all agencies, ISI, FBI (CIA), Military Intelligence, the Intelligence Bureau and the Criminal Investigation Department of the police operated in conjunction. After several successful operations against al-Qaida, the Pakistan Government decided to establish a Special Investigation Group (SIG). This group was established under the supervision of Home Minister, Faisal Saleh Hayat, but the formation was left to FBI (CIA) experts. Initially 50 officers were trained, 17 of them coming from the Federal Investigation Agency (FIA).

Apart from these measures, Pakistani police and security services have also played a significant part in the arrest of al-Qaida activists. The government has an easier task in arresting foreign jihadis and jihad organisers outside the tribal areas where there is less loyalty for them and where informers can more easily be found. The following list is interesting in this regard.

Abu Zubaida: who is believed to have served as Osama bin Laden's field commander, was captured in March 2002. The Americans describe him as a 'key terrorist recruiter and operational planner and member of Osama bin Laden's inner circle.' He has strong connections with Jordanian and Palestinian groups and was sentenced to death in his absence by a Jordanian court for his role in a thwarted plot to bomb hotels in Aman during the millennium celebrations. US officials believe he was also connected to a plan to blow up the US embassies in Sarajevo and Paris.

Khalid Sheikh: a very important member of al-Qaida, was arrested in Rawalpindi in March 2003. This arrest was claimed as 'a big success' against al-Qaida. This is understood from the reaction of President George Bush who said: "The man who masterminded the September 11 attacks is no longer a threat to the United States of America."

Ramzi Binalshibh: was captured in September 2002. A Yemeni national, he is alleged to be one of the most senior al-Qaida members to be· arrested. He is thirty and is said to have become a key member of the al-Qaida cell operating in Hamburg in Germany after seeking political asylum there in the late 1990s. He was alleged to be a co-planner of the 9/11 attacks on America. US intelligence officials believe he may have been involved in the attacks on the American warship *USS Cole* and on a Tunisian synagogue.

Yassir al-Jaziri, also known as Abu Yassir al-Jaziri, was among the men wanted by the United States. His name surfaced at a court hearing in Lahore for one of his associates. He is said to be a close relative of Osama's first wife. It was said that he had grown a beard and took pains to be well disguised but he was under surveillance by security agencies and, after confirming his real identity, his residence was raided and he was arrested. He was sent into American custody in Afghanistan later along with several of his associates.

Obaidullah, a Saudi national, was arrested in Peshawar in May 2003. He was in charge of communications for al-Qaida and he had links with the two leaders of Pakistan's big religious parties, Maulana Fazlur Rehman, head of a faction of Jamiat Ulema-e-Islam and now the leader of the official opposition in parliament and with Jamaat-e-Islami chief, Qazi Hussain Ahmad. He had recruited other al-Qaida activists in Saudi Arabia and sent them to Pakistan. He was high on the FBI's wanted list.

Haris bin Asim: was arrested in Kucch Garhi, Peshawar, after Obaidullah on 26 June. Three CDs were recovered when he was arrested which indicate that Osama bin Laden is alive and well. He admitted that he came from Saudi Arabia on the orders of Obaidullah and spent seven days with him at his Phase II residence in Hayatabad. Bin Asim admitted receiving three CDs from Obaidullah which had messages from Osama bin Laden originating from three different places and which had been filmed in May 2002. He also had US $40,000, 40,000 Saudi Riyals and 2,000,000 rupees in his possession. The news of his and Obaidullah's arrest was not made public. Officially, only Information Minister, Sheikh

Rashid Ahmad, and President Musharraf were notified by the arresting officers. Sources among them say that Musharraf gave the news of these arrests to President Bush personally and with great pride. After the investigations in Pakistan, bin Asim was sent to Afghanistan where a special team of the FBI interrogated him. The diary in his possession when he was arrested reveals that he was the teacher of Khalid Sheikh. These two arrests greatly increased the intelligence on the structure and operational methods of the resurgent Taliban and al-Qaida. Haris bin Asim was an expert in his area of operations and had performed his duties well over a long period of time.

Adil al-Jazeeri: an Algerian national, was arrested by Pakistani law-enforcement officers on 18 June 2003. Sources say he had links with al-Qaida and that he had been involved in terrorist activities in Pakistan also. He was arrested along with a Turkish national suspected of providing forged documents for use by al-Qaida operatives trying to evade arrest.

Apart from these more important arrests, secret service and anti-terrorist agencies claim that many other people from various countries were also arrested in Pakistan on suspicion of their links with al-Qaida. They were 40 from Algeria, 16 from Saudi Arabia, 20 from Morocco, 22 from the United Arab Emirates, 11 from Libya, 7 from Kuwait, 20 from Egypt, 28 from Indonesia, 18 from Malaysia, and 36 from the West Asian countries. Also arrested were 5 people from America, 2 from Australia and 11 from Britain. A total of 238, which does not include those suspected al-Qaida or mujahideen activists arrested in the tribal areas during police and military operations there. Not all of these were handed over to US authorities. Some were deported to their respective homelands. It should also be mentioned here that 22 other Pakistanis were also arrested on suspicion of having links with al-Qaida but they were released after investigations. Following is a list of wanted international terrorists. The Security Council of the UN released a list of wanted al-Qaida activists in November 2003. There is no Pakistani in the list. Released in two parts, it has a total of 34 names:

UN List Part I

1. Abdaqui Youssef (alias Abu Abdullah), born in Tunisia 1966, lived in Italy (Varese).
2. Aqli Mohammad Amine (alias Mohmed Amine Akli, Killech Shamir, Kail Sami), born in Algeria 1972, lived in Italy.
3. Amdouni Mehrez (alias Fusco Fabio, Hasan Mohmed, Abu Thale), born in Tunisia 1969, lived in Italy.
4. Ayari Chieb ben Mohamed (alias Hichem Abu Hichem), born in Tunisia 1965 lived in Italy (Bologna).
5. Baazaqui Mondher (alias Hamza), born in Tunisia 1967, lived in Italy (Bolgna).
6. Dumont Lionel (alias Bilal, Hamza, Broughre Jacques), born in France 1971, lived in Italy.
7. Essadi Moussa ben Amor (alias Dahdah, Abdelrehman, Bechir), born in Tunisia 1964, lived in Italy (Bresica).
8. Fettar Rachid (alias Amini del Beigio, Djaffer),

born in Algeria 1969, lived in Italy (Milan).

9. Hamai Brahim ben Hedefi, born in Goubellat Tunisia 1971, lived in Italy (Bologna).

10. Jarraya Khalil (alias Yarraya Khalil, Abdel Aziz ben Narvan, Omar Amrou), born in Tunisia 1969, lived in Italy.

11. Jarraya Mounir ben Habib (alia Yarraya), born in Tunisia 1963, lived in Italy (Bologna).

12. Jen Dobi Faouzi (alias Said, Samir), born in Tunisia 1966, lived in Italy (Bologna).

13. Mnasri Fethi ben Rebat (alias Amor, Abu Omar, Alic Fethi), born in Tunisia 1969, lived Italy (Bologna).

14. Ouaz Najib, born in Tunisia 1960, lived in Italy (Bologna).

15. Rarvo Ahmed Hosni (alias Abdallah O Abdollah), born in Algeria 1974, lived in Italy.

16. Saleh Nedal (alias Hitem), born in Yemen 1970, lived in Italy (Bologna).

17. Yandarvieh Zelimkhan (alias Ahmedovic Muslimovich), born in USSR (Khazakstan) 1952, lived in Russia.

UN List Part II

1. Ali Yusuf (alias Ali Galoul), born in Somalia 1974, lived in Sweden.

2. Ahmed Said al Qadr (alias Alkanadi, Abu al Rahman), born in Egypt. He is believed to have dual Egyptian and Canadian nationality but no other details are available.

3. Aquadi Mohammed (alias bin Belgacem, bin Abdallah), born in Tunisia 1974, lived in Italy.

4. Essid Eami (alias bin Khemals, bin Salah), born in Tunisia 1968, lived in Italy.

5. Ayadi Shafiq bin Mahomed, born in Tunisia 1963, lived in Germany, Austria, England and is now said to be in Ireland.

6. Bouchoucha Mokhtar, born in Tunisia 1969, lived in Italy (Milan).

7. Charaabi Tarek (alias Bachir bin Amara, Akassharabi), born in Tunisia 1972, lived in Italy (Milan).

8. Namoun Darkazanli (alias Abu Ilyas, Abu Ilyas, Ali Suri, Abu Luz), born in Syria 1958, lived in Germany (Hamburg).

9. Riad Muhammad Hasan Hijazi, (alias Hijazi Raed, Abu Ahmed, Al-Shahid), born in the US (California) 1968, of Morrocan descent, lived in Jordan (Aman).

10. Ali Ghalib Himmat, born in Syria 1938, lived in Italy.

11. Armand Albert Friendrich Humber (alias Huber Ahmed), Swiss national.

12. Zayn al-Abadin Mohammad Husayn (alias Abu Zubaida, Abd al-Wahab, Zayn al-Abidin), thought to be a Saudi national with Palestinian and Egyptian passports, a close associate of Osama bin Laden and facilitator of travel.

13. Nasreddin Ahmed Idris (alias Nasreddin Hadi Ahmed), born in Ethiopia 1929, lived in Italy, Switzerland and is now thought to be in Morocco.

14. Mansour Mahomed (alias Al-Mansour, Dr Mansour), born in Egypt 1928, a Swiss national, lived in Switzerland.

15. Nada Youssef Mustafa (alias Nada, Youssef), born Egypt 1931, lived in Italy.

16. Abdul Rahman Yaseen (alias Taher, Abdul Rahman, Abdul Yasin Said), born in the US (Indiana) 1960, has American and Iraqi passports and is believed to be now in Iraq.

17. Mansoor Fattoum Zeina, born in 1933, little is known about him, lives/lived in Switzerland.

In November 2003, American law enforcement agencies produced a list of Pakistani men wanted in the US for a variety of criminal offences; murder, drug trafficking, kidnapping, fraud, etc., but there were no terrorism charges and there were no Pakistanis on the UN list of wanted terrorists.

The FBI issued a new list of their most wanted men in November 2003:

1. Osama bin Laden (alias bin Mohammad, The Prince, The Emir Abu Abdullah, Mujahid Sheikh Haj, The Director). Age: 46 years. Place of birth: Saudi Arabia. Left-handed, walks with a cane. Languages: Arabic, Pushto and English. Osama bin Laden is wanted in connection with the August 1998 bombing of the US embassies in Dar-es-Salaam (Tanzania) and Nairobi (Kenya) in which more than 200 people, mostly local, were killed. Osama bin Laden is suspected of masterminding other terrorist attacks throughout the world.

2. Ayman al-Zawahiri (alias Abu Mohammad, Abu Fatimah, Mohammad Ibrahim, Abu Abdallah, Abu al-Muiz, The Doctor, The Teacher, Ustaz, Nur

al-Din, Abdel Muaz), Age 52 years. Nationality – Egyptian. Languages: Arabic and French. Al-Zawahiri is a physician and the founder of the Egyptian Islamic Jihad, an organisation that opposes the secular Egyptian government and seeks its overthrow through violent means. Al-Zawahiri is believed to serve now as an advisor and doctor to Osama bin Laden and is currently thought to be in Afghanistan. He has been indicted for his alleged role in the August 1998 bombings of the US embassies in Dar-es-Salaam and Nairobi.

3. Abdel Karim Ali Nasser. Born in Saudi Arabia. Languages: Arabic and Farsi. He has been indicted in Virginia for the June 1996 bombing of the Khobar Tower Military Housing Complex in Dahran, Saudi Arabia.

4. Abdullah Ahmad Abdullah, an Egyptian national born circa 1964. He has been indicted for alleged involvement in the 1998 bombings of the US embassies in Dar-es-Salaam and Nairobi. Abdullah fled Nairobi in August 1998 and went to Pakistan (Karachi). He is now believed to be in Afghanistan.

5. Muhsin Musa Matwalli Atwah, an Egyptian national born circa 1965. He is also wanted for the Dar-es-Salaam and Nairobi bombings. Atwa is believed to be in Afghanistan.

6. Ali Atwa (alias Ammar Masour Bouslim, Hasan Rostam Saleem). A Lebanese national born circa 1966. He was indicted for his participation in the June 1985 hijacking of an airliner which resulted

in assaults on various passengers and crew members and the murder of one US citizen. He is an alleged member of the Lebanese terrorist organisation, Hizbullah, and is believed to be in Lebanon.

7. Anas al-Liby (alias Anas al-Sabai, Nazih al-Raghie, Nazih Abdul Hameed). He is wanted in connection with the bombings in Dar-es-Salaam and Nairobi. He sought political asylum in the UK but is believed to be in Afghanistan.

8. Ahmed Ghailani (alias Ahmed Khalafan, Abu Baker Ahmed, Abu Bakary Ahmed, Ahmed al-Tanzani). A Tanzanian, he was indicted in New York in December 1998, for his alleged involvement in the 1998 bombings in Dar-es-Salaam and Nairobi.

9. Hasan Izz al-Din (alias Ahmed Garbaya, Samir Salwan, Said). He is said to be a member of the Lebanese terrorist organisation, Hizbullah, living in Lebanon. Was indicted for his role in the June 1985 hijacking of a commercial airliner.

10. Ahmed Mohammed Ali (alias Shuaib, Abu Islam al-Surir, Ahmed Ahmed, Ahmed the Egyptian, Ahmed Hamed, Hamed Ali, Ahmed Shieb, Amed al-Masri). He is wanted in connection with the 1998 bombings of the US embassies in Dar-es-Salaam and Nairobi. Ali may have formal training in agriculture. He lived in Kenya until fleeing that country in August 1998 to Pakistan. Believed to be in Afghanistan.

11. Fazul Abdullah Mohammed (many alias). A computer expert, he was indicted in September

1998 in New York for alleged involvement in the bombings of the US embassies in Dar-es-Salaam and Nairobi. Mohammed likes to wear baseball caps and tends to dress casually. Whereabouts unknown.

12. Imad Fayez Mugniyah was indicted for his role in the 1985 hijacking of an airliner. He is said to be the head of the security apparatus of the Lebanese terrorist organisation, Hizbullah. He is thought to be in Lebanon.

13. Mustafa Mohammed Fadhil (many aliases) He was indicted in New York in 1998 for his alleged involvement in the Dar-es-Salaam and Nairobi bombings and for conspiring to kill US nationals.

14. Sheikh Ahmed Salim Swedan (many aliases including Ahmed the Tall). He was indicted in December 1998 in New York for his alleged involvement in bombings Dar-es-Salaam and Nairobi and for conspiring to kill US nationals. Swedan once managed a trucking business in Kenya.

15. Abdul Rahman Yasin (alias Abdul Said Yasin, Aboud Yasin). He is wanted for his alleged participation in the terrorist bombing of the World Trade Centre in New York in February 1993, which caused six deaths many wounded. Yasin is epileptic.

16. Fahid Masalam (many aliases). He was indicted in New York in February 1998 for his alleged involvement in the 1998 bombings in Dar-es-Salaam and Nairobi. He is known to have been a shopkeeper in the past.

17. Ahmad Ibrahim al-Mughassil (alias Abu Omran). He was indicted in Virginia for the June 1996 bombing of the Khobar Towers Military Housing Complex in Dahran, Saudi Arabia.
18. Mohammad Atef (alias Abu Hafs, El-Masry, El-Khabir, Sheikh Taysir Abdullah, Abu Khadija). He was indicted for his alleged involvement in the 1998 bombings in Dar-es-Salaam and Nairobi. Atef is allegedly Osama bin Laden's second-in-command in al-Qaida.
19. Saed Ali El-Hoorie (many aliases). He was indicted in Virginia for the 1996 bombing of the Khobar Towers complex in Saudi Araba.
20. Saif al-Adel (alias Muhamad Ibrahim Makkawi, Ibrahim al-Madani). He is wanted in connection with the 1998 bombings in Dar-es-Salaam and Nairobi. Al-Adel is thought to be affiliated to the Egyptian Islamic Jihad and is believed to be an important member of al-Qaida. He is thought to be in Afghanistan now.
21. Ibrahim Salih Mohammed al-Yacoub. He was indicted in Virginia for the bombing of the Khobar Towers in Saudi Arabia.

Chapter 7

TOWARDS A SOLUTION IN KASHMIR?

The Muttahida Jihad Council (MJC), in a meeting in October 2003, gave final shape to its operational plans for 2004. The council decided that, in future, all operations would be conducted under the MJC banner and no affiliated organisation would be allowed to operate alone. Sources inside the MJC revealed that other important decisions were also taken and a prohibition was imposed on all of the component parties against them issuing any press statements or even to talk to newsmen. The MJC also decided that it would not issue any public statement regarding the ongoing Indo-Pak peace talks and that it would concentrate on jihadi operations.

Jamaat-ud-Daawa's (JD) weekly *Ghazwa Times* (30 January 2004) nevertheless, gave some details about the MJC plan for 2004. This weekly reported that the MJC had decided to start operations against the Indian Army in Kashmir in the summer and these would be the most ferocious for years. Actually this campaign is going on currently in spite of the Pakistan Government's denials.

According to a report in 2003, a lot of mujahideen fighters had crossed the borders and were now already in Indian-held Kashmir. Therefore, even if the MJC could not send new groups into Kashmir in 2004, it was claimed that this would not affect the proposed operation. A proposal from some hard-liner members of the MJC had stressed that the All Parties Hurriyat Conference (APHC) should expose the 'betrayers' (dissidents in the movement). According to the jihadi organisations code of conduct, betrayers also deserve the same fate as the Indian Army men. "But the idea was rejected and the MJC revised their support for Syed Ali Geelani's APHC and decided that all organisations would support Ali Geelani and his new party."

These decisions were, apparently, taken on one side but, on the other side, the scenario was changing. Reliable sources inside the MJC revealed, in February 2004, that jihadi leaders had discussed the changing situation with President Musharraf in a meeting which was, reportedly, held in January 2004. But the MJC leaders were not satisfied with President Musharraf's new stance on the Kashmir issue. "President Musharraf made clear to them that jihadi operation could not continue until the issue was solved. He asked that the MJC should give its support if the negotiations resulted in an agreement with India." The sources said that the MJC leaders agreed that General Musharraf had limitations but the MJC would hasten its operations against Indian forces. The sources added that the MJC had given the task to its operational commanders in Indian-held Kashmir.

However, after the President's meeting with the MJC leaders, the pressure built up on the jihadis to minimize their activities even further. "We already had launched only a few fighters into Indian-held Kashmir because of the pressure from the government and now, we have further pressure to minimize our activities." A Hizbul activist said.

Disappointment and Depression Among the Jihadi

It was spring 2004 in Azad Kashmir and, for the first time, this writer observed disappointment and depression among the jihadis. Readers of a previously published account of mine about the Kashmir jihadi groups (*Jihad – Gateway to Terrorism*) will remember descriptions of these mujahideen flying high on a diet of ISI patronage, massive financial subsidies and a high wave of popular support. On this occasion, most of those same mujahideen leaders who were still in the jihadi business were now idling away their time in their, almost empty, offices in Muzaffarabad. In February 2003, most of these offices had bustling with activity and had dozens of wide-eyed boys and young men entering and leaving in a constant stream. They had come from all over Pakistan, from inside Azad Kashmir and even from Indian-held Kashmir across the Line of Control to volunteer for the jihad. Wirelesses were continually receiving messages from mujahideen groups operating in Indian-held Kashmir. Jihadi anthems blared out across the streets to create emotional waves through the atmosphere. Posters and pamphlets were abundant. No longer. The bustle and blare and the feverish activity has gone. Now, there is an unusual quietness about the offices and streets.

"This year we have been asked to restrict our movements. I do not know whether or not these orders are permanent." A Harkat-ul-Jihad-e-Islami (Maulana Muzafar group) commander told this writer. He also said that they were not even being allowed to go back to their own homes to spend vacations. "After the attacks on President Musharraf, we are restricted to our offices," he said, rather bitterly. "We cannot understand what the government is trying to do. On the one side, it is promising that the jihad would not be ended but, on the other side, its compromising attitude on Kashmir is frustrating us," he said.

He was uncertain about his own future and expressed the fear that he would be arrested, as had 313 mujahideen of Harkat-ul-Jihad-ul-Islami (Ilyas Kashmiri group) who had been arrested during a Pakistani law enforcement raid on the jihadi training camp in Kotli in the first week of January 2004. "We cannot believe what the government promises, although in a meeting with jihadi leaders, President Musharraf had himself assured us that if we did not become involved in terrorist activities in Pakistan or supported the sectarian terrorist organisations, the mujahideen would not be restricted in their activities," he said but, added; "What he did with the mujahideen in Afghanistan, he could do the same with us."

According to this commander, the situation is not same for all the jihadi organisations. "Lashkar-e-Taiba, Hizb-ul-Mujahideen and some other groups are still busy with their business as usual. But on a smaller scale, and these are being imposed on us as the role models," he said.

There are many mujahideen in Azad Kashmir who, like this particular HUJI commander, are frustrated and not at all happy with the government's new stance after the 9/11 outrages. Many militants want to continue their jihadi struggle to liberate Indian-held Kashmir and these are most hostile to the new government restrictions. However, a significant proportion of mujahideen running through every jihadi organisation want abandon the gun, but they find themselves between the devil and the deep blue sea. Those from Indian-held Kashmir could not go back their homes for fear of arrest by the Indian security services, while the Pakistani mujahideen fear they may be arrested under the new anti-terrorism legislation if they return to their homes in Pakistan's districts, towns and cities.

Legally, because of the constitutional uncertainty concerning the status of Azad Kashmir, they are relatively safe if they remain where they are. As long as they are there, however, the threat of escalation of the conflict with India remains also. Clearly, the Pakistan Government has stalled, if not stopped, the jihad from operating against Indian forces on the other side of the LoC. If the Pakistan Government is sincere about its new peace proposals and policies towards India, and its anti-terrorism policies towards the rest of the world, it might be a good idea to offer an amnesty against arrests in return for promises of genuine future peaceful pursuits from the now disillusioned mujahideen who want to give up the gun. If India is also sincere in its desire for peace between the two nations, an amnesty allowing 'former mujahideen' to return safely to their homes in return for similar commitments to pursue peaceful lives could help to ease the situation even more. This sort of amnesty was used by the British when they released convicted terrorists from prison after the Good Friday Agreement with the IRA's political wing.

Those mujahideen who persist in crossing the border to fight Indian forces are the diehards who are mostly acting against the wishes of the Pakistan Government, and the ISI do not really have much control over these groups now. Be that as it may, there does seem to be a change going on and that presents an opportunity for a peace movement to become established.

The Jammu and Kashmir Salvation Movement

The growing feeling that exists among a large number of mujahideen that it is time to abandon guns and 'give peace a chance' include many jihadi leaders. "Guns in Jammu and Kashmir are going out of fashion. Most national and international players in the conflict appear to believe now that politics is the panacea for all the problems of the erstwhile princely state," said Arif Jamal, an expert on Kashmir affairs. According to him these feelings are much stronger among the militants on the Indian side of the Line of Control. After Mufti Sayeed, a Kashmiri Muslim, was elected and formed his government in Indian-held Kashmir he has continuously offered incentives to militants to give up their guns. He has also been favouring the release of detainees. Thus, the willingness of the Indian authorities to meet the Pakistan Government and the Kashmiri mujahideen in the middle on these issues seems to be a possibility.

Therefore, after such a long struggle, many Kashmiri jihad organisations and other important leaders had become disillusioned and dismayed. Their ideology was being challenged and their plans were being frustrated. The patronage of the ISI was withdrawn and their funds were less plentiful. Some of them adopted a political rather than a military approach while others seem to be ready to surrender or engage in a ceasefire if they could be sure of an amnesty. The late Hizb-ul-Mujahideen commander, Abdul Majeed Dar was a prime example of the new thinking that was influencing the Kashmir jihadi leadership even before the 9/11 attacks. He had conducted negotiations with the Indians and had announced a ceasefire in August 2000. That was, probably, the reason he was assassinated. But now, hundreds of former Hizb-ul-Mujahideen jihadi fighters have formed a new political party, the Jammu and Kashmir Salvation Movement (JKSM) dedicated to finding a peaceful solution to the Kashmir problem. Many of these former fighters spent their youth in Indian jails or in training camps in Azad Kashmir and Pakistan. Although a majority of the members of the new JKSM belonged to the Hizb-ul-Mujahideen, former fighters from other jihadi groups have also joined the movement.

Abdul Majeed Dar, who worked as the Chief Operational Commander of the Hizb-ul-Mujahideen, first proposed the idea of the new party several years earlier. He put the idea to the Kashmiri mujahideen after his offer to India of the ceasefire in July/August 2000 which had brought him to a confrontation, referred to earlier, with Syed Salahuddin, the supreme commander of the Hizb-ul-Mujahideen. Although Dar had agreed the ceasefire with the approval of Salahuddin, the supreme commander withdrew his support a few days later. But many of the Kashmiri mujahideen had been impressed by Dar's arguments for a political course rather than military one and the new JKSM is the result.

Dar had started enlisting everybody in the Kashmiri mujahideen who was ready to make the switch to a political struggle because of the changing international situation. He worked hard through 2001 and succeeded in getting a constitution for the new party by its founding members in May 2002. He then continued to organise political cadres from among the militants on both sides of the LoC through the following year. This created a lot of animosity and frustration among other Hizb-ul-Mujahideen leaders. They started expelling anybody who was suspected of being in touch with Dar and this led to a clear divide in the Hizb-ul-Mujahideen. Dar had decided to propagate the policies of the new party in other parts of Pakistan as well. Unfortunately, unknown killers assassinated him in March 2003 when he was bidding his family farewell before leaving on his proposed trip. The murder shocked the nascent political party. It was thrown into confusion and its activities stalled. However, in September 2003, the surviving leadership appeared to believe that the time had come for them to launch their party.

The JKSM wants to function under the umbrella of the All Parties Hurriyat Conference. According to the JKSM Chairman, Mohammad Maqbool Khan, the All Parties Hurriyat Conference has, in principle, agreed to accept the JKSM as a member. The JKSM leaders call themselves 'the abandoned mujahideen', but it is not a religious group in any sense of its ideology. The JKSM flag clearly reflects the ideology of the new party. The flag has four parts. A red part, which reflects the region's blood-soaked history. There is a white part, which reflects the Kashmiryiat, the peoples' love of peace and religious tolerance. Another part is green and, although it is a favourite colour of Muslims, the JKSM constitution defines it as a symbol of the greenery of Kashmir's country. The moon-like symbol with a green background symbolizes the captivity of the peaceful people of Kashmir.

The JKSM appears to have a promising future, for several reasons. First, there is a large number of 'abandoned mujahideen' in Jammu and Kashmir. They are highly politicised and have a desire to continue their struggle through non-violent means. No other political party or organisation has such a membership base and, because they have fought as jihadis, they are not easily intimidated by threats. Most importantly, the number of mujahideen fighters who want to abandon the armed struggle in favour of a political struggle is increasing steadily. The JKSM offers them a ready-made vehicle, with very strong Kashmiri credentials, to enable them to engage in a political struggle. This correspondent has spoken to dozens of Kashmiri fighters who are very enthusiastic about the new political party.

However, the Hizb-ul-Mujahideen generally, particularly those from Pakistan rather than Kashmir, were against the formation of the new Jammu and Kashmir Salvation Movement to begin with but, because of the radically changed conditions in Pakistan, it has itself come under pressure to be more political than jihadi in its own activities. The new situation is very challenging for Hizb-ul-Mujahideen because, currently, it also holds the chairmanship of the Muttahida Jihad Council (MJC). Its patron, Jamaat-e-Islami (JI), is no longer openly supporting it because of the internal and international pressure on Jamaat-e-Islami itself in turn. After the formation of the pro-mujahideen provincial governments in North-West Frontier Province and Baluchistan, Jamaat-e-Islami has been careful to qualify its relations with Hizb-ul-Mujahideen. The new JI attitude has increased the pressure on Hizb-ul-Mujahideen to such an extent that, as revealed by an important Hizb jihadi leader, whereas Jamaat-e-Islami had previously played an important part in lessening government pressure on them, now, JI was not trying very hard to protect them and, therefore, security agencies were dominant over the entire Hizb-ul-Mujahideen organisation.

The Transformation of the JKLF into a Moderate Party

There have been signs in the recent past suggesting that the Jammu and Kashmir Liberation Front (JKLF) might still be able to play a role in shaping the future of the disputed territories. Not for a long time have so many people in Kashmir wanted an independent state, the ideal for which the JKLF stands for. However, it is premature to say whether either faction of the JKLF would be able to take full advantage of this growing feeling. Both factions, the one led by Ammanullah Khan, and the other by Yasin Malik, sensed the change that is taking place in Kashmir. Islamic jihad, as opposed to Azadi (freedom), is definitely losing its appeal for the people of Kashmir. Ammanullah Khan responded by offering a 'roadmap' that would lead Kashmir towards true independence, while Yasin Malik has been running a signature campaign to the same end for his faction.

Although the JKLF had engaged in armed struggle against Indian forces in Kashmir in the early days it was never intended to have become the jihadi organisation into which it evolved later. It was not Islamist and it relied on a broad spectrum of Kashmiri people for its support, including Hindus and Sikhs. It was the only group which had some organisational structure on both sides of the Line of Control in the late 1980s when Muslims in the Valley of Kashmir took up arms against the Indian occupation. The JKLF happens to be the only organisation that willingly and formally adopted the armed struggle at that time.

The Jammu and Kashmir Liberation Front dominated the political scene in Kashmir between July 1988 and October 1989, the formative period of the armed struggle in Kashmir. "It was Ashfaq Wani and Yasin Malik who started the struggle in July 1988 and converted it into a mass resistance," said Emir Dawood chief of the Yasin Malik group, remembering the days of earlier glory. He recalled; "There was no sectarian colour to the freedom struggle at that time. Hindus, Muslims and Sikhs jointly started the movement and there was no mention of a Kashmir Alhaq (accession) to Pakistan." He said that, initially, Kashmiri youth crossed into Azad Kashmir in 1988 and 1989 as members of the Student Liberation Front and the JKLF's student wing. There had been an 'understanding' that the students would be sent back after training but, according to Emir Dawood, the ISI agencies trapped them and compelled them to form pro-Pakistan Islamist jihadi groups. "They were forced either to procure weapons and money or to involve themselves in recruitment or to become jihadi fighters. Half of them got side-tracked and a lot of jihadi organisations came into existence," he said. "Our commanders, Hilal Beg and Mustaq Zargar, established the Ikhwanul Muslimeen and the al-Umer Mujahideen respectively. Many of our fighters also joined Hizb-ul-Mujahideen," he said.

But the real history of the JKLF began in Birmingham in the United Kingdom. It was formed there on 29 May 1977. It established branches in other cities of the UK over the following two years. At the same time, it opened branch offices in several European and Middle Eastern countries. It opened its offices in Azad Kashmir and Pakistan in 1982 and in Indian-held Kashmir in 1987. Thereby, the founding fathers of the JKLF kept both Pakistan and India at an equal distance by launching their party in a third country. This enabled them to build an organisational structure on both sides of the Line of Control. This also gave them the advantage in mobilising Kashmiri expatriates in Europe from both sides of the Line of Control. They were expatriate Kashmiri people who had the money to finance their plan to liberate their homeland.

The early leaders of the movement in Kashmir were naive in their belief that Pakistan would help them. Pakistan would certainly help any group which wanted to fight the Indians but the whole of Kashmir is seen by Pakistan as part of Pakistan, period. Neither India nor Pakistan want an independent Kashmir. The ISI did not become involved in training guerilla fighters simply to help them to establish an independent state. The ISI wanted to engage the Indian Army on the cheap by formenting a Vietnam style war that would wear India down. It was intended to be a war fought by proxy, using Kashmiris as the cannon fodder. And later, secular-minded JKLF mujahideen were to be persecuted or assassinated if they did not conform to the ISI's Islamist agenda.

Most of the JKLF fighters in the early days were turned into Islamists and, giving the reasons for this, Emir Dawood stated that that was because of the involvement of the ISI. The inheritors of the original JKLF founded an Islamist organisation, called Hizb-ul-Mujahideen, in 1989. Many other Kashmiri Islamist organisations also emerged on the scene in 1989 and 1990. In this way, the secular freedom struggle of the JKLF became an Islamist cause about ten years after its formation.

Gradually, the Islamists, supported by the ISI, drove the secular-minded JKLF mujahideen out of the armed struggle by physically eliminating its entire command structure. According to the JKLF chairman, Ammanullah Khan, the Islamists killed more JKLF commanders than the Indian Army between 1989 and 1994. But the actual coup de grace came when the Indian Army attacked the local offices of the JKLF near Hazrat Bal in March 1996. Twenty-six JKLF activists were killed in that attack in spite of the fact that the remnants of the JKLF had announced the abandonment of the armed struggle and their transformation into a political party in 1994.

The new ray of hope for the JKLF comes in the wake of the split in the All Parties Hurriyat Conference. Pro-independence feelings have always existed on both sides of the LoC. However, they never dominated the political scene in the state. These feelings remained suppressed for many years until the 1999 Kargil crisis, followed two years later by the *volte-face* on jihad generally and the Taliban by the Pakistan Government in the aftermath of the 9/11 terrorist attacks in the United States, led to a resurgence of these feelings. These episodes were construed as an indication that Pakistan was unable to stand up for the rights of the Kashmir people under the Indian threat of wholesale war and mounting international pressure.

The split in the All Parties Hurriyat Conference surprised no one because a rift had been brewing for some time. Pakistan government support of the splinter group, led by Syed All Shah Geelani, is fast pushing other parties towards what is popularly known as the third option. Most watchers of APHC politics agree that a majority of the rival Ansari-led APHC component are most likely to embrace the cause of an independent Kashmir in future. It was, perhaps, this understanding which enabled Yasin Malik and Ammanullah Khan, in Indian-held Kashmir and Azad Pakistan respectively, to push their agendas forward. Yasin Malik ran a signature campaign for his political cause while Ammanullah Khan revived his independence plan with some modifications.

Under the first phase of the five-phase, optimistic, roadmap produced by Ammanullah Khan, the UN Secretary-General should take steps to form an International Kashmir Committee (IKC) under the UN's Security Council Resolution 1172. The Secretary-General should then discuss the matter with the governments of India and Pakistan and with the heads of the political parties on both sides of the LoC.

Among other measures, the IKC should try to convince the interlocutors that the resolution of the Kashmir issue is in the best interest of all the parties involved. The IKC should also request the United Nations to increase the number of UN military observers in Kashmir to facilitate the withdrawal of the Indian and Pakistani armed forces and the non-Kashmiri jihadist organisations.

In the second phase, assuming a bilateral agreement, the entire state of Jammu and Kashmir would be demilitarised. The armed forces and the intelligence agencies of the two countries would withdraw completely from the state. The borders between the two present parts of Kashmir would be cleared of minefields by the withdrawing forces. The armed militants of Pakistan and India would also withdraw during this phase and UN military observers would help the IKC in its task of achieving this peaceful situation.

In the third phase, the IKC would disarm armed rival factions among Kashmir's civilian population with the help of the Pakistani and Indian governments. After this, the IKC would facilitate the nationals of the new state of Jammu and Kashmir, who left their homes because of the jihad and who are living in India, in Pakistan, or in Azad Kashmir, to return to their homes. Those nationals of the state who left the state in earlier times would have to choose either India, Pakistan, or the state of Jammu and Kashmir as their permanent homeland. The UN military observers group would help local administrations to carry out this reconciliatory task.

In the fourth phase, the IKC would help local administrations to reopen all those roads, closed since 1949, connecting the present Indian-held Kashmir with Pakistan-administered Azad Kashmir. The IKC would then establish a national government at Srinagar. This government would include representatives from all of the regions, from the main political parties and from all religions. The legislative assemblies of Indian-held Kashmir, Pakistan-administered Azad Kashmir and the legislative council of Gilgit-Baltistan would form the interim national assembly. This national government would work under the supervision of the IKC.

This political system, it is proposed, would last for 15 years after which time a referendum would take place under UN auspices to determine the will of the people. This would be the last or the fifth phase. The people of Jammu and Kashmir would be asked whether they want to remain independent or join one of the contending states. Ammanullah Khan has always said that he would accept any decision of the people of Kashmir in free and fair plebiscite.

The new JKLF roadmap is flexible and detailed. It is also optimistic because its successful implementation depends on many regional and international factors, but it does offer a way out of the current crisis. Kashmir has been described by one observer as 'the bone between two dogs with neither willing to let go of the end they have between their jaws. India's fear, even paranoia, about splintering of the union is understandable because of its own regional, ethnic, religious and linguistic diversity and it dislikes anything that encourages claims to separatism. Pakistan wants Kashmir because it wants to expand in size and influence. Many Kashmiris, some since 1947 and many more since 1989, have wished 'a plague on both your houses' because the Indo-Pak power struggle over their unfortunate nation has led to wholesale murders, sectarian cleansing, and a fractured society, not to mention the economic distress, suffered by Kashmiri people generally. Where once there was the Kashmiryiat, the concept of peaceful co-existence with other religious groups and cultures, with a generally prosperous or at least economically sufficient people, now there is general misery. Any national political movement is attacked by Pakistan if it is not Islamist and by India if it wants to secede.

Yet the present situation cannot go on indefinitely. Neither side will yield if it means giving advantage to the other side. Therefore, the independence and military neutrality of Kashmir, guaranteed by the United Nations, possibly with some sort of condominium relationship with the two rival states, would solve the problem and ease tensions in the world generally. Like the Israel-Palestine issue, the lack of a solution leads to insurrections, terrorism and war which are ever present and vary only in intensity from time to time. The so-called 'war on terror' cannot be won until the causes of the terror are addressed.

At the time of the partition of the subcontinent in 1947, regarded as a black day for millions of people on both sides of the partition, Kashmir was intended to decide its own future. Alas, two powerful rival states decided otherwise and the seeds of past wars and the present conflict were sown. However, Indian objections to independence is invalidated by the fact that Kashmir was not included in its union in the first place, and Pakistan has no legal claim to the state either.

Grouping in All Parties Hurriyat Conference

On 12 July 2003 the All Parties Hurriyat Conference replaced its chairman, Abdul Gani Bhat with Abbass Ansari, a centrist politician. The decision was a sharp rebuke to the Islamist right, which had been seeking to reinvent the APHC as a militant pro-Pakistan and pro-jihad movement. With the installation of Ansari as APHC chief, Syed Ali Geelani, a pro-Pakistan and pro-jihad leader lost the first battle in his war to take charge of the organisation. Later, in August 2003, he announced the establishment of his own faction of the APHC and some small parties of the alliance joined his side.

The reason behind Geelani's factionalism was stated to be as he had wanted an organisation called Peoples Conference expelled from the Hurriyat as it had taken part in state elections in defiance of an APHC boycott decision. But the new chief of the alliance, Maulavi Abbass Ansari, had given a clean chit to the group.

But these differences grew even more sharply when new chairman Ansari announced in August 2003 that he was going to travel to Pakistan to persuade armed Islamist groups to; "Lay down their guns because a solution to the Kashmir problem can be found only through dialogue," he said.

Geelani's position was very week in the APHC at that time because he also had differences with his own party, Jamaat-e-Islami, which he was representing in the APHC. The Jamaat supported Ansari's candidacy and had retired Geelani from his duties, replacing him with Ashraf Sehrai. When Geelani formed his APHC faction he was not acting for his own party but, with the support of some smaller parties, he had become the head of this new APHC faction. He had only the support of 5 parties, none of which were in the APHC Executive Council. Some of Geelani's opponents made the accusation that the ISI was behind him and was playing a role to divide the APHC.

Geelani's Differences with Jamaat-e-Islami

Geelani differences with Jamaat-e-Islami came to the

surface when he was 'retired' as head of the Jamaat's political wing and as the representative of Jamaat in the APHC, and from all other duties. Guhlam Mohammad Bhat, of Jamaat-e-Islami, announced that Geelani's would no longer represent the organisation at the APHC. The decision, he claimed, had been made because of Geelani's poor health. But later it was proved to be a political decision and Geelani's supporters blamed the Jamaat leadership for marginalising 'Emir Jihad', as Geelani was known. His marginalization began in 1997, when his Emir, Guhlam Mohammad Bhat gave an interview that distanced the Jamaat-e-Islami from Hizb-ul-Mujahideen and called for an end to the 'gun culture'.

The Impact on Jamaat-e-Islami

Geelani vehemently disagreed with this policy. Geelani and his supporters in the Indian-held Kashmir's division of Jamaat-e-Islami and among jihadi groups were of the opinion that the All Parties Hurriyat Conference was inclining towards India and had adopted the anti-jihad policy because the new APHC chairman, Abbass Ansari, announced that he wished to travel to Pakistan in August to persuade jihadi organisations to terminate the armed struggle.

A Hizb-ul-Mujahideen spokesman in Pakistan, Abdul Saleem Hashmi, said that, according to the Jamaat-e-Islami constitution, anyone who passed the age of 65 years had to retire from the party. He said that another two of the party's leaders, Sheikh Guhlam Muhammad and Sheikh Abdullah, were also retired at the same time as Geelani. Hashmi also admitted that differences had started between Hizb-ul-Mujahideen and Jamaat-e-Islami about the Geelani issue and these became serious later. The Hizb leadership was unhappy about the Jamaat's decision to shift its offices from the Hizb office premises and was now apparently denying any links with it. The leadership also believed that the Jamaat was favouring the Majeed Dar group of Hizb-ul-Mujahideen, many of whom had moved into the Jammu and Kashmir Salvation Movement in pursuit of a peaceful solution to the states' problems.

ISI Support for Geelani?

Pakistan stopped supporting the APHC in the latter half of 2003 when Geelani decided to set-up a different alliance of separatist groups. Although Geelani had played a key role in the armed struggle in Kashmir from the very beginning, he succeeded in winning the support only of a few insignificant politicians for his new faction. So weak was this support that his own party disowned him by retiring him. The Geelani-led splinter group proved to be just a political wing of the Muttahida Jihad Council. At the same time, the APHC could not survive the crisis unscathed. Three of its seven-member executive council, representatives of Jamaat-e-Islami, the Jammu and Kashmir Liberation Front and the People's League, decided to stay neutral.

Unfortunately for Pakistan, the parting of ways between the APHC and its former patrons took place at a time when the Indian Government had more or less agreed to hold talks with the Kashmiri separatists.

After projecting the APHC as the sole representative of the Kashmiri people for more than a decade, Pakistan now has difficulty in convincing the world that the former no longer represented the people of Kashmir. Pakistan's policy of siding with the Geelani-led APHC splinter group has pushed the Ansari-led APHC away from the Pakistani position. However, it would be premature to say that the Ansari-led APHC was leaning towards the Indian position. Other critics maintain that the ISI still controls most of its constituent parties and jihadi groups. Geelani is regarded by them now as a mere tool of the ISI with the annexation of Kashmir into Pakistan as their goal. A sovereign state of Kashmir is not on the ISI's agenda. Too many early JKLF activists were murdered by the ISI's hit-men for there to be any doubt about that fact and Ammanullah Khan's roadmap for peace would not suit the ISI because it is fairly clear that the people of Kashmir, on both sides of the present divide, would very probably vote for real sovereignty for Kashmir. It is really a question of the Pakistan Government's true agenda that will determine the outcome of the issue and whether or not they can rein-in those ISI elements who persist in the purely Islamist cause.

Nevertheless, India took advantage of the situation and did not waste any time in holding the first round of talks with the Ansari-led APHC because it would serve to show to the world that the Kashmir problem was a domestic issue. However, these talks between the APHC and the Indian Government have not yet yielded any tangible results, at least not in the short term. Pakistan has, apparently, abandoned its demand for tripartite talks in favour of bilateral talks with India which may indicate that it actually has lost its influence over the All Parties Hurriyat Conference.

Jihadist Backing Geelani

Not surprisingly, Pakistan-based jihadi groups responded to Geelani's dismissal with outrage. The United Jihad Council (MJC) and other Kashmir based jihadi organisations had announced support for Syed Ali Geelani in August 2003, and urged him to form his own party. Geelani accepted the jihadi's request and assigned Guhlam Ullah Safi, Guhlam Nabi Noshari and Hizb-ul-Mujahideen Supreme Commander, Syed Salahudin, to contact different jihadi groups and Kashmiri parties, especially elements within Jamaat-e-Islami, who were not satisfied with the APHC's current policies in Azad Kashmir and Pakistan. Geelani was also himself in contact with different jihadi leaders in Pakistan for their support. Al-Badr Mujahideen spokesman, Janissar Akhter, confirmed that Geelani had contacted their Emir, Bakhat Zamin, and Jamaat-ul-Ansar's Maulana Fazlur Rehman Khalil looking for their support. Geelani also contacted Jamaat-ud-Daawa's Emir, Hafiz Mohammad Saeed. All of these jihadi groups announced their support for Geelani.

Jamaat-e-Islami Allows Geelani to Form His Own Party

When these jihadi groups announced their support for Geelani, Jamaat-e-Islami (Pakistan) Emir, Qazi Hussain Ahmad, reviewed the matter and called for a meeting of the Kashmir Committee [which consists of Jamaat-e-Islami (Pakistan), Jamaat-e-Islami (Azad Kashmir), Jamaat-e-Islami (Indian-held Kashmir) and Hizb-ul-Mujahideen] in October 2003. To avoid serious differences, Geelani was allowed to form his own party and Hizb-ul-Mujahideen was allowed to support him.

This decision was contradictory because Jamaat-e-Islami (Indian-held Kashmir) was allowed to stay in support of the Ansari-led group of the APHC. One Jamaat insider, commenting on the situation, told this correspondent that Jamaat-e-Islami had been under pressure from 'the agencies' (ISI) to announce support for Geelani, but Jamaat-e-Islami (Indian-held Kashmir) was saying that it was a matter of party discipline and Geelani's position would weaken the party in the valley. So, Qazi Hussain Ahmad pleased both factions, while he himself supported Geelani.

Geelani No More

When the Pakistan agencies (ISI) were lobbying for Geelani in his dispute with the APHC, the situation regarding Pakistan's relationship with India was uncertain. But, after August 2003, developments had started regarding the normalization of that relationship. In the new scenario Geelani would be of help to the Pakistan case to balance-off the APHC Ansari group, which had lost the confidence of the Pakistan Government.

But Pakistan also has need of a Kashmiri leadership that would represent the Pakistani stance on Kashmir and which could support the Pakistan Government's decisions whether or not these turned out to be against the jihadis' wishes. Geelani would not have been a suitable candidate in this regard because of his jihadi loyalties. Now efforts are on going to bring a moderate Kashmiri leader to the front who would, when required, be acceptable to India at the negotiation table.

Muttahida Jihad Council Transformation

In October 2003, the Muttahida Jihad Council (MJC) had also been restructured with six smaller alliances within it representing various groups that would no longer use the words; jihad, lashkar, jaish or mujahideen as part of their names so that they would appear more political than militant. Only Hizb-ul-Mujahideen was allowed to use its original name.

These new alliances are; the Kashmir Resistance Forum (KRF) designated in three groups, 1, 2 and 3, and the Kashmir Freedom Forum designated in two groups, 1 and 2. "We have been told that these names are damaging Pakistan's image abroad as well as the Kashmiri freedom movement." a jihadi leader had told this writer. Asked why the Hizb was allowed to use its original name, he replied, "Hizb-ul-Mujahideen also holds the chairmanship of the jihad alliance and quarters abroad consider it representative of the Kashmiri freedom movement alone." This new structure of the MJC was implemented in January 2004. KRF (1) represents Lashkar-e-Taiba, Brigade 313 (a Harkat-ul-Jihad-e-Islami faction lead by Ilyas

Kashmiri), Lashkar-e-Islam and al-Badr Mujahideen, while KRF (2) is an alliance of al-Jihad, al-Fateh, Hizb Ullah and Muslim Janbaz Force. KRF (3) consists of Harkat-ul-Jihad-e-Islami (Maulana Muzafar group), Jamiat-ul-Mujahideen and Jamiat-ul-Ansar. KFF (1) is an alliance of Jaish-e-Mohammad and al-Umer Mujahideen and KFF (2) includes Islamic Front, Jamaat-ul-Furqan, Tehreek-e-Jihad, al-Barq and Tehreek-ul-Mujahideen.

This new 'adjustment' is called, muwakhaat (an Arabic word meaning agreement on the basis of brotherhood), and sources said this would also reduce the jihadi groups' internal differences. The thinking behind this restructuring of the militant organisations is that the new names will improve their image, making them look more like political groups.

The Muttahida Jihad Council previously had consisted of 15 organisations all of which were Kashmir-based. The five Pakistan-based organisations including Lashkar-e-Taiba, Brigade 313 and al-Badr Mujahideen were not part of MJC but they have been included in the new structure. "The MJC constitution barred Pakistan-based organisation from the alliance but circumstances have changed. We need unity and no one can deny their role in jihad," a jihadi leader had said. Syed Salahuddin, chief of Hizb-ul-Mujahideen, was elected Chairman of the MJC for five more years and that was acceptable to all concerned.

There were suggestions that the MJC's restructuring was brought about by Pakistani agencies (ISI) because the main purpose was to try to bring all jihadi organisations on to one platform. So, when any consensus was needed on Kashmiri issues, no group could oppose it. Pakistan-based groups had now, in effect, joined the MJC and this was not the first time that the council had been restructured. In January 2002, a formula for a merger of the different groups was proposed but some smaller Kashmiri and Pakistan-based organisations refused to accept it. They wanted to maintain their independent identities and most Pakistani jihadi leaders were not prepared to become subordinate to smaller Kashmiri organisations, sources claimed, and added; "This structure is an extension of the 2002 formula and now leaders of these organisations will not share responsibilities with others." The sources also said that these smaller alliances would launch operations against Indian forces in Kashmir, but only after getting permission from the MJC leaders.

However, currently, the Pakistan establishment is not looking too successful with the experiment because the MJC is not agreeing with Pakistan on many different issues. These will be discussed later.

Towards a Solution

Kashmir-based jihadi and political parties had formed a Joint Policy and Planning Committee (JPPC) in March 2004 to prepare a roadmap for a ceasefire in Indian-held Kashmir and the resolution of the Kashmir dispute. "The Muttahida Jihad Council and political parties, especially those belonging to the All Parties Hurriyat Conference (referring to the Ansari and Geelani groups) have been given a deadline to join the JPPC by August 2004," this author's sources had said.

A meeting of representatives of political and jihadi parties, held in Islamabad in March 2004, had led to the formation of the JPPC with Tajammul Sheikh as its head. He is a journalist and had not played any prominent role in Kashmiri politics before. The executive committee members were, Mehmood Sager, vice president of the Jammu Kashmir Freedom Democratic Party, Maulana Ghulam Nabi Noshari of Jamaat-e-Islami (Indian-held-Kashmir division) and Rafiq Dar, Professor Nazir Shal, Ghulam Rasool and Malik Abdul Majeed of the Jammu and Kashmir Liberation Front (Yasin faction).

Reports carried by the local press included the name of the MJC Chairman, Syed Salahuddin, in the new JPPC but a Hizb-ul-Mujahideen member said that Salahuddin was not present at the meeting. "He was in the border area and the local press published his name erroneously as one of the participants of the meeting," he said, and it is true that Salahuddin was under pressure from the MJC's component parties not to join the new Joint Policy and Planning Committee because it was regarded as a forum that could weaken the jihadis by forcing them to accept a ceasefire decision. So it is unlikely that Salahuddin was a party to this development. "The forum is created on directions from the United States and the government is taking special interest in the JPPC," one jihadi leader commented. Another jihadi insider said that the jihadis were confused because, on the one hand they were asked not to stop the jihad, but on the other, they were being pressurised to join the JPPC forum created, they say, to announce a ceasefire.

Professor Nazir Shal, one of the executive committee members, had said publicly that the JPPC was basically a 'think tank' formed to work out a possible resolution to the 55-year-old dispute. Asked why this exercise started only after thousands of Kashmiris had been killed, he replied angrily, "We have to resolve the problem and this is not a proper time to raise such questions." He continued; "Kashmiris had thought about the solution to the problem at different stages of the freedom struggle and now we shall prepare a roadmap on the issue which will be acceptable to Kashmiris."

Emir Dawood of the JKLF (Yasin group) stated that the JPPC could be an alternative to the APHC because the Pakistani government was not happy with its leaders. "It is against the establishment's desires, which wants Kashmiri leaders to follow its dictates." Dawood had said. The APHC (Ansari group) convener in Pakistan, Syed Yousaf Naseem, said that if Pakistan, India and Kashmiris agreed to a ceasefire, it would be acceptable to everyone. But he refused to accept the JPPC as an alternative to the APHC. "We shall not become a part of it and will condemn it at every forum. The United Nations gave the roadmap on Kashmir and we are bound to it, but if the new roadmap is imposed on the Kashmiris through its puppet leadership, we shall not accept it," he said.

Meanwhile, official sources had confirmed that Pakistan and India had discussed on a six-month ceasefire between Indian forces and Kashmiri militants in Indian-held Kashmir. According to these sources, the ceasefire decision was discussed at a meeting between India's and Pakistan's respective Foreign Secretaries in February 2004 to pave the way for the reopening of the Muzaffarabad to Srinagar bus service linking the two parts of the divided state. "The summit-level talks between the two countries is conditional on the ceasefire between the Kashmiri fighters and Indian troops. The foreign ministers of the two countries will meet again in August to announce the start of the Muzaffarabad-Srinagar bus service and the date for the summit meeting. Both sides have agreed that the ceasefire will provide a basis for confidence-building measures to start the Muzaffarabad-Srinagar bus service and the summit talks," these sources said.

The sources also said that both countries were preparing the ground for the longer ceasefire but Pakistan had the biggest problem with this because they had to try very hard to persuade the Kashmiri jihadi leadership to join-up. "The Joint Policy and Planning Committee created by Kashmiri political and jihadi parties is also a part of the agenda to convince Kashmiris to agree to the ceasefire. Many jihadi leaders had expressed concerns about whether the ceasefire would be permanent or temporary. Another question facing the jihadi leadership is who would announce the ceasefire first, the Indian Army or the militants," the sources said and; "The restructuring of the Muttahida Jihad Council is part of the agenda to give it a political face," the sources also revealed.

From this, it appears that the Pakistan Government

was instrumental in the formation of the JPPC and in the restructuring of the MJC. The sources say that jihadi groups have been ready to announce the ceasefire for quite some time and wanted a role in the whole peace process.

The Kashmir Bus Service

Pakistan and India had agreed to restart the bus service between the two capitals of divided Kashmir (Muzaffarabad and Srinagar) but both sides have some reservations. India fears this bus service could enable jihadi infiltration if a visa policy is not applied, while Pakistan is insisting that the bus service must be started under an international agreement in which Kashmir is considered to be a disputed territory.

India wants to secure all possible doors against militants before the bus service starts. The service would be a major step in Confidence Building Measures (CBM) between both countries. "The whole peace process depends on it." A senior official had told this writer. "The bus service would mean the end of infiltration completely and a permanent ceasefire, not only on the Line of Control, but also generally from the mujahideen and the Indian Army in occupied Kashmir." said this official, adding; "If this happens, its mean nothing could sabotage the peace process." According to this source, both countries agreed to announce the starting date of the bus service in August 2004 but the process was proving very difficult to sort out all issues. If the visa condition is applied for Indian and Pakistani citizens and was lifted only for

Kashmiris, it would present legal problems for India because the Indian Constitution declares Kashmir to be an integral part of India. Opposition parties in India could makes this an election issue. Pakistan's position is also very sensitive on the visa issue. Pakistan believes that if it agrees to the visa condition for Kashmiris, it would contravene the United Nations Resolution on Kashmir, in which the Line of Control is stated to be a temporary border and would mean that Pakistan had accepted it a permanent border.

However no international or local law ever existed for Kashmiri nationals to use visas or other documents for travel within Kashmir. Until 1956, Kashmiris were free to cross the LoC and they needed only Kashmir nationality certificates. Pakistan offered India a revival of this process to relieve this sticking point. Both sides are also working on other possible solutions for the visa problem. Pakistan has also suggested that United Nations Military Observers could be involved in this process, according to which the observers would be able to issue passes for Kashmiris after consulting local authorities.

While, between themselves, India and Pakistan are talking about the Muzaffarabad-Srinagar bus service as a confidence-building measure, Kashmir-based militant groups are talking about attacking the bus service and, consequently, are trying to sabotage the peace overtures. The general view of this situation in Muzaffarabad was that militant organisations on both sides of the LoC want to scare people away from the bus service because they want to sabotage the peace negotiations. "Akhwan-ul-Muslimeen, Jaish-e-Mohammad and

Jamiat-ul-Ansar have warned the public not to take the bus because they will hit it when it starts," a jihadi leader had said. He added that such sabotage was likely on Pakistan's side of Kashmir as well as India's. Knowledgeable people in Muzaffarabad confirm that the militants are succeeding in frightening people away from the new bus service. Most political parties and people will not accept visas or other such conditions on travel between the two parts of Kashmir.

Emir Dawood, of the Jammu and Kashmir Liberation Front, said there were hundreds of divided families anxiously waiting on both sides of the LoC for the bus service to begin but the JKLF's stance was that no visas or permissions should be necessary because it believed both sides of Kashmir were one region.

Aysha Afroze Butt, the women's wing president of the Jammu and Kashmir National Liberation Front said: "The jihadis will be out of business if the divided families meet." She also hoped Kashmiris would act to would thwart the militant's conspiracies against peace in spite of their fear of them. However, a Hizb-ul-Mujahideen commander defended the militant's position. He said: "The bus service could damage the Kashmiris' freedom struggle. They are fighting for their right to self-determination and the bus service would mean that Pakistan has withdrawn from its position." He went on to say that the militants would not allow the bus service until India acknowledged Kashmir as disputed territory and resolved the issue according to the United Nations Resolutions. A Harkat-ul-Jihad-e-Islami militant claimed that the Kashmir freedom struggle was about to 'bear fruit' and the bus service and other such reconciliatory measures would demoralize the militants. "People from neither side will support the bus idea till they are guaranteed the Kashmir issue will be settled according to their wishes," he said.

This militant did not elaborate on what result had actually been achieved by the jihadi freedom struggle. Outside observers might think it had led to the destruction of Afghanistan, Iraq and Kashmir, the death of many thousands of Muslims and the development of Islamophobia in many parts of the world. Nevertheless, the gun will prevail and may well see the destruction of other countries in due course. No country is too big to be massively disrupted by internal conflicts whether they be ethnic, religious or class based and if there is a minority willing to engage in violence who do not want any social conditions except those they dictate, the future for every country becomes uncertain. Pakistan is replete with such minority groups.

Chapter 8

JIHAD INTERNATIONAL?

"Prince Turki al-Faisal, the head of Saudi Arabia's security services, says that al-Qaida came out of Afghanistan, not from Saudi Arabia. If it did, we in Pakistan did not know it. In fact, a number of our religious and political leaders and Urdu columnists have suggested that al-Qaida did not exist before the Americans coined the name to punish Afghanistan. Many authoritative voices in our religious circles actually think that no Muslims were involved in the 9/11 terrorism and that the World Trade Centre was destroyed by the Jews. There is even less knowledge about the members of al-Qaida and their links with our jihadi organisations. Names like Abu Zubaida, Khalid Sheikh Mohammad, and Ayman Al-Zawahiri mean nothing to most of us. Indeed, most of the jihadi leaders, the likes of Maulana Masod Azhar and Fazlur Rehman Khalil, who virtually ruled Pakistan for ten years, don't ring a bell with Pakistanis. And if you refer to Maulana Abdul Jabbar and his terror against Christians in Islamabad, Taxila, Jhika Gali, and Sheraton Karachi, you are sure to draw a blank. And this among people who engage you seriously on the subject of jihad and international terrorism!" wrote Khalid Ahmad, in *The Friday Times* (5 August 2003)

In February 1998 a press conference was held at

Khost in Afghanistan where the Osama bin Laden-led International Islamic Front for Jihad Against Jews and Crusaders (IIFJAJC) was introduced to the world via the Pakistani media. A team of Pakistani journalists covered the venue which was organised by the ISI. Just one year earlier, *The Herald* (January 2002) revealed that Pakistani intelligence agents, (the ISI), were instrumental in introducing Osama bin Laden to Mullah Omar. The meeting led to the reactivation of Osama's former guerilla training facilities in Khost, a portion of which was handed over to Harkat-ul-Mujahideen, a Pakistan based jihadi group, to set-up their training camps. When these camps were hit by America in 1998, al-Qaida allowed Pakistani militants to shift to its camps at Rishkhor and Kargha near Kabul and at Daronta near Jalalabad. Created in 1989 to serve Arab mujahideen and their families in Afghanistan, al-Qaida became obsessively anti-American following the Gulf War of 1991 and it conducted a number of terrorist acts against US troops stationed in Saudi Arabia. After a decisive crackdown on extremist outfits by the governments of Egypt and Algeria during the mid-1990s, those Egyptian and Algerian militants gravitated towards Afghanistan and al-Qaida, paving the way for the formation of the International Islamic Front for Jihad Against Jews and Crusaders.

Information provided to US interrogators by the American Taliban recruit, John Walker, indicates that al-Qaida gave its members a choice, to fight alongside Islamic forces in Afghanistan, Central Asia, Chechnya, Kashmir or the Balkans, or of becoming a part of its worldwide terrorist network. While the number of these al-Qaida volunteers in these fronts runs to over 10,000, the strength of its terrorist network remains a matter of speculation.

US authorities suspect that al-Qaida has from several hundred to several thousand members drawn from over thirty countries of Africa, Asia, and the Pacific who run terrorist cells in 66 countries around the world including Europe and North America. A Harkat-ul-Mujahideen commander claimed that; "No one could recognize al-Qaida men because they live like ordinary people and mix with them. They are doctors, teachers, engineers and businessmen and never look like the mysterious terrorists."

Their activities are funded by commercial front organisations. In addition, some of the charitable donations made by wealthy Saudis, Arab businessmen and mosque funds from the oil-rich Gulf states are being siphoned off and sent to al-Qaida cells for carrying out terrorist acts.

To trace-out the al-Qaida worldwide network is not an easy task but Pakistani intelligence agencies have the edge because these were closely engaged in the jihad against the Soviets in Afghanistan and had the closest relationship with al-Qaida operatives. Al-Qaida had established its network in Pakistan and Afghanistan during the anti-Soviet jihad and afterwards it maintained these to operate its worldwide network and allowed it to also play a subversive role the internal politics of Pakistan. The post 9/11 arrests of al-Qaida operatives in Pakistan clearly indicate how strong it was in the country.

Al-Qaida in Pakistan

Osama bin Laden was a regular visitor to Pakistan, especially Peshawar, during the Afghan jihad against the Soviets. During this war, he established links with Pakistani jihadi leaders including, Hafiz Mohammad Saeed, of Lashkar-e-Taiba, Maulana Fazlur Rehman Khalil, of Jamiat Ulema-e-Islam, Qari Saifullah Akhtar, of Harkat-ul-Jihad-al-Islami, and others. These Pakistani jihadi groups had not only supported Osama but also other Arab mujahideen, which later jointly formed an international terrorist network.

A most carefully researched book written by Jason Burke; *Al-Qaida: Casting a Shadow of Terror*, reveals details about Osama and the Arab mujahideen in the pre-Taliban era. Burke is meticulous in piecing together his portrayal of al-Qaida to avoid allegations of prejudice and 'civilizational hostility'. He reveals that Benazir Bhutto has been claiming that Osama bin Laden had inspired Ramzi Yusuf to assassinate her. When Ramzi Yusuf returned to Pakistan after trying to blow up the World Trade Centre in New York in 1993, he was asked to kill Pakistan's first woman Prime Minister, Benazir Bhutto. At that time he was staying in Peshawar in a guest house run by Osama and he was renewing his contacts with a sectarian organisation with whom he had trained in an Afghanistan camp. Burke says that some Pakistani Gulf-involved businessmen funded Ramzi Yusuf to do the job. There was also a Kuwaiti donor called Khalid Sheikh Mohammad, Yusuf's uncle. Yusuf's assistants for the assassination job were boys who had taken training with him at the al-Farooq camp in Afghanistan. The material for the bomb was sent from Pabbi, the training camp run by Abdur Rub Rasul Sayyat, an Arab from the Afghan jihad who had worked closely with Osama. Yusuf tried to blow up the Bhutto residence in Karachi but the bomb went off in his hands, injuring him seriously. The people who visited him in hospital were said by Burke to be 'senior figures in the Pakistani terrorist group, the Anjuman Sipah-e-Sahaba (Pakistan).' Burke did not link Ramzi Yusuf with Osama bin Laden directly although his uncle, Khalid Sheikh Mohammad, who funded the 1993 attack on World Trade Centre, was later to become the most important channel of funds to al-Qaida from rich families in Kuwait. There is other evidence of a connection between the two.

However, the people who bombed the World Trade Centre in 1993 were, reportedly, all trained in Afghanistan; Mahmoud Abouhalima, Ahmad Ajaj, Siddiq Ibrahim Siddiq, Ibrahim al-Mekkawi and Mahmoud al-Sabbawy. Pakistan was forced to hunt down these Arabs of the Afghan jihad after this. Pakistani law enforcement agents arrested Ramzi Yusuf and Ali Bid, who was a surviving leader of the Egyptian group that had assassinated President Sadat, and they were extradited to America. Most of the Arabs from the Afghan jihad went to ex-Soviet Islamic states and to Chechnya. Chechen leader Jauhar Dudyaev sent his volunteers to Afghanistan to train as fighters before he started the revolt against Russia. Osama bin Laden and his Arab mujahideen left Pakistan and went to Sudan but they were also in

Somalia killing American troops in Mogadishu. Osama boasted about this himself in an interview with Abdelbari Atwan of the al-Quds al-Arabi of 27 November 1996.

Burke explains why he did not connect Ramzi Yusuf with Osama bin Laden, in spite of the fact that Muhammad Jafal bin Khalifa, husband of one of Osama's half-sisters, went with Yusuf to establish a branch of the International Islamic Relief Organisation (IIRO) in the Philippines where Ramzi Yusuf was in contact with Janjalani who, in turn, had set-up the Abu Saiyaf terrorist group with money possibly contributed by the IIRO. Abu Saiyaf was named after the great jihadi leader of Afghanistan, Abdur Rub Rasul Sayyat. Osama's brother-in-law, Khalifa, was arrested in Jordan for funding two bombers from the Philippines. He admitted in court that he had given them IIRO money for 'past services'. Khalifa has since returned to Saudi Arabia and denounced Osama, which leads Burke to conclude that he could not be a part of al-Qaida! He doesn't connect Ramzi with Osama and al-Qaida also because Ramzi's rhetoric is free of the thought content of Abdallah Azzam, Osama's teacher at Jeddah University. The demand note he had delivered after the 1993 bomb attack in New York contained a leftist message, not the threat of a 'salafi' apocalypse associated with al-Qaida.

After New York and the failed attack on Prime Minister Bhutto, Ramzi Yusuf next tried to undertake a major bombing attack in the Philippines with Janjalani but, once again, he burnt himself with the bomb-making material in a hotel room. On this occasion, he was again funded by his mother's brother, his uncle Khalid Sheikh Mohammad, who had funded his failed attempt to kill Benazir Bhutto. Benazir Bhutto had got the ISI to register all the 'foreign' mujahideen, mostly based in Peshawar, after Egypt complained that Mohammad Shawky al-Islambouli, a brother of the killer of President Sadat, was being sheltered in Peshawar. The ISI came up with some 5000 names: 1142 Egyptians, 981 Saudis, 946 Algerians, 771 Jordanians, 326 Iraqis, 292 Syrians, 234 Sudanese, 199 Libyans and 102 Moroccans. Then, in 1995, the year the Egyptian embassy in Islamabad was bombed, Egyptian President Mubarak was almost killed by the Peshawar-based terrorists in Sudan.

The man who blew up the Egyptian embassy in 1995 was Ayman al-Zawahiri, who Lawrence Wright profiled in *The New Yorker* (16 September 2002) under the title; *The Man Behind bin Laden*. He is an Egyptian doctor linked to Islamic jihad. He was one of the accused in the assassination of President Sadat in 1981. He planned the al-Qaida attacks in Somalia in 1993, the bombings of the American embassies in East Africa in 1998, the USS Cole in Yemen in 2000 and the World Trade Centre on 11 September 2001. He has a $25 million bounty on his head. He had escaped to Jeddah in 1985 and met Osama bin Laden there. Both were under the tutelage of Abdallah Azzam, a Palestinian who reconciled Syed Qutib's concept of jahiliyya (fanaticism) with terrorism to produce the rationale for al-Qaida. Syed Qutib's brother, Mohammad, was also at Jeddah University at that time. Abdallah Azzam was murdered in Peshawar in

1989. Burke is unsure who did it but Lawrence Wright says it was Zawahiri who had him killed because of their rivalry for attention and money from Osama bin Laden. It is interesting to note that Ayman al-Zawahiri got into the Islamic jihad because his brother, Mohammad, was in it and Khalid Muhammad Sheikh got into the Peshawar based jihad because his brother Zahed was in it.

What has caused the latest upheaval is the book; *Sleeping With the Devil* written by former CIA operative, Robert Baer. It connects the Saudi ruling family with the activities of al-Qaida but also reveals details about some very sensitive, lucrative, American commercial contracts with the royal family. Baer, a decorated officer, revealed some of his findings in an article entitled; *The Fall of the House of Saud* published in *The Atlantic Monthly* in May 2000. After King Fahad's near fatal stroke in 1993, his favourite wife Jawhara, who is pushing her 29-year-old son, Abdul Aziz, in competition with nearly 12,000 other princes for Fahad's attention, began to run the royal palace. To exert leverage on his rivals, Abdul Aziz began funding the Wahabi Islamic movement which had become increasingly critical of the Saudi rulers and openly inclined to support the views of Osama bin Laden. Abdul Aziz was discovered to have funded the Taliban in Afghanistan and terrorist operations in Russia, apart from some dubious charities in the United States. But Baer also reveals details about American connections to Saudi Arabia, especially big contracts with firms such as Carlyle and Haliburton with which former Secretary of State, James Baker, and current Vice

President, Dick Chenney, are involved. The Saudi royal family has invested approximately $1000000000000 (one trillion) in the American stock market and keeps an equal amount in cash in American banks to offset the American budget deficit. Baer reveals that Pakistan also gets half a billion dollars worth of free oil annually from Saudi Arabia. Needless to say, jihadi propaganda neglects to mention the massive extent of Saudi, Kuwaiti, and Gulf states' investments in the Great Satan when they are whipping up a fervour of anti-Jewish and anti-Christian passions through their media.

Khalid Sheikh Mohammad, Yusuf's uncle from Kuwait, had gone to Peshawar as had the Palestinian, Abu Zubaida, to continue their activities from a safe base. When Osama bin Laden fled to Sudan in 1992, Yusuf's uncle went to Karachi to live there posing as a Saudi businessman. Abu Zubaida stayed in Peshawar together with another devotee, Omar Sheikh, overseeing the training of more young men in the camps in Afghanistan. During his stay in Karachi, Yusuf's uncle reorganised various jihadi terrorist factions taking forward what his nephew had begun in 1995. Pakistan was regarded as the best primary breeding ground for new recruits for al-Qaida. Along with Abu Zubaida, a key al-Qaida commander, and Ramzi bin al-Shibh, Khalid Sheikh Mohammad set about reorganising factions of the Sipah-e-Sahaba, Lashkar-e-Jhangavi, and Harkat-ul-Mujahideen-al-Alemi, along with the banned Lashkar-e-Taiba and Jaish-e-Mohammad under a unified organisation called Lashkar-e-Omar. It is claimed by knowledgeable security agents that the American journalist, Daniel Pearl, was actually pursuing Khalid Sheikh Mohammad in Karachi for an interview when another al-Qaida operative, Omar Sheikh, abducted him. Omar Sheikh was convicted for the murder and is now under death sentence in Pakistan. Daniel Pearl's murder, (he was beheaded), was said to be Khalid Sheikh Mohammad's angry reaction to being 'discovered' by the American press.

Osama bin Laden returned to Jalalabad in 1996. After the American invasion of Afghanistan, Khalid Sheikh Mohammad coordinated the financing for al-Qaida operations from Karachi, increasingly seeking support from Jamaat-e-Islami rather than from the Deobandi organisations. Abu Zubaida was finally caught in Faisalabad. Burke says he was caught in an ASSP (a local militant splinter group) stronghold but, in Pakistan, jihadi circles say it was from a 'safe house' belonging to Lashkar-e-Taiba, the most significant Ahl-e-Hadis connection with the Arabs. Khalid Sheikh Mohammad arranged for Omar Sheikh, who was in the Peshawar guesthouse of Osama bin Laden, to kidnap Daniel Pearl in 2002. A Yemeni jihadi beheaded Pearl in Karachi where he was being held. Khalid himself was caught in a house Rawalpindi in 2003.

The house in which Khalid Sheikh Mohammad was arrested belonged Dr Abdul Quddus, an elderly microbiologist, whose wife Mehlaqa Khanam is a Jamaat-e-Islami leader elected to a local government office. Dr Abdul Quddus, a married man with children, apparently did nothing wrong and was considered by his sister to be of unsound mind. But he is said to have been charged with involvement in the ambush and murder of an Iranian air force cadet in Rawalpindi some years ago. According to one report, Dr Quddus had a brother, Adil Quddus, who was a Major in the Pakistan Army. He was detained in Kohat by the investigation team looking into the Fokker air crash near Kohat in which the chief of the Pakistan Air Force was killed. It is speculated that the crash was actually an al-Qaida operation.

However, the command of the al-Qaida international terrorist network always remained in the hands of Osama bin Laden and the Arabs. Militant and jihadi organisations around the world have always been under their control. A former jihadi leader of the Kashmiri based organisation, Harkat-ul-Mujahideen, on condition of anonymity, revealed that, despite the devotion and commitment of the Arab mujahideen to the jihad, they always use Pakistani and Kashmiri jihadi groups for their missions. He said that the Arab mujahideen always tried to meet the requirements of the jihadi groups and provided money, training, and weapons but, in return, they use their manpower in different parts of the world and use their hideouts when needed. Giving as an example, he said that after the US forces attack on Afghanistan, some Arab mujahideen had gone to Kotli in Azad Kashmir and remained hidden in Harkat-ul-Mujahideen safe houses until they had a safe way out. He added that there was a threat on Harkat and other militant organisations by Pakistani and American agencies that if any Arab jihadis were found in their offices or camps, strict action would be taken against them (the organisations).

It is claimed that the key backers of al-Qaida are some twelve prominent Saudi businessmen, all of whom have extensive business and personal connections with the royal family. They are said to have ties to such ministers as the Saudi Defence Minister, Prince Sultan bin Abdul Aziz, and the Governor of Riyadh, Prince Salman. A report by the New York-based Council of Foreign Relations said al-Qaida's global fund-raising network leans heavily on Saudi Arabia. The report said that the al-Qaida network is built upon a foundation of charities, non-government organisations and internal patronage in Saudi Arabia to operate its worldwide organisation.

The Chinese Jihad

In December 2003, the Chinese Government sent a list and profiles of terrorists and terrorist organisations which were of concern to China. It wanted them investigated by the Pakistan Government. According to a report published in *The Daily Times* on 17 January 2004, this list of Eastern Turkestan terrorist organisations and terrorists compiled by the Chinese Ministry of Public Security was sent through diplomatic channels to Pakistan with a request for it to be forwarded to the relevant security departments.

Earlier, a most wanted separatist leader of the Uighur jihadi movement, Ismail Qadir, was caught by Pakistani authorities while he was meeting underground Muslim groups in Azad Kashmir. China claims that more than 1000 Uighurs were trained by Osama bin Laden's forces in Afghanistan during the

Taliban era. About 110 returned to China in recent years and were captured there. US forces captured about 300 in Afghanistan and about 20 were killed. Another 600 or so were thought to have escaped into northern Pakistan. China believes that most of the Uighur mujahideen could be present in Pakistani jihadi hideouts. Pakistani officials say that Ismail Qadir was handed over to China in March 2002 and is the third highest leader of the East Turkstan Islamic Movement. Beijing claimed that his group had connections with Osama bin Laden and a Pakistani jihadi organisation, Harkat-ul-Mujahideen.

Chinese officials believed that Qadir's accomplices are still in Pakistan and they may enter Xinjiyang province any time to start terrorist activities there. According to these official Chinese sources, Pakistani agencies had tried hard to capture the Chinese mujahideen hidden in Pakistan and had been successful in finding out their network in the northern areas of Pakistan. Another important Uighur jihadi, Hasan Mahsum, was killed in an operation against terrorists in December 2003. Reportedly, Hasan also had links with the al-Qaida network and had fought with the Taliban in Afghanistan against America.

However, separatist tendencies in China's north-western Xinjiyang-Uighur autonomous region are part of the area's history. The element of violence in the movement goes back to 1986 when Uighurs from the southern Kashgar area of the province joined the anti-communist jihad in Afghanistan, apparently incited by Uighur Islamists. Widespread rioting broke out a town called Baren, near Kashgar, in 1990, and again in

Yining town near the Kazakh border in 1997. Observers say there was a considerable number of casualties.

The East Turkestan movement had been active since the early 1990s, carrying out bombings, assassinations, and acts of arson, poisoning and assaults with the objective of forming a breakaway state. So far the movement has carried out more than 200 terrorists incidents in Xinjiyang which resulted in 162 deaths and injury to more than 440 persons. China says the Uighur separatists had developed ties with Pakistani jihadi organisations during the Afghan jihad because the liberation of the Chinese province of Xinjiyang is also a goal of some Pakistani jihadi organisations, namely, Harkat-ul-Jihad-ul-Islami, Jamiat-ul-Ansar, and Lashkar-e-Taiba. This predominantly Muslim territory in China's northwest shares borders with Pakistan, Afghanistan, and the central Asian republics. Pakistan is one of the few countries to have backed Beijing in their efforts to curb the Uighur jihadi groups. On his last visit to China, President Musharraf promised to 'wholeheartedly support' China's efforts to crush Uighur separatists. Since then, China and Pakistan have collaborated to combat terrorism. Sources said Pakistan had handed over about 100 Uighur separatists to China between August 2001 and March 2003.

The list that China sent to Pakistan in December 2003 recorded details of at least two terrorist organisations, the Eastern Turkestan Islamic Movement (ETIM) and the Eastern Turkestan Liberation Organisation (ETLO) as well as other jihadis attached to these organisations. It also claimed that these two organisations are still well connected to Osama bin Laden's al-Qaida organisation and receive training as well as funding from them.

The head of the Eastern Turkestan Islamic Movement, Hassan Mahsom, was one of the eight jihadis killed in a Pakistani forces operation against al-Qaida and Taliban fugitives in South Waziristan in 2003. Hassan's presence in the tribal areas was not the only example that proved the Uighur separatists are using Pakistan as a base and that they have links with the al-Qaida network.

A New Game Plan of the US in China?

An important al-Badr Mujahideen commander, Ameer Hamza, disclosed in a meeting that the Americans had succeeded in arresting some mujahideen fighters in Afghanistan and they are now using them against China. He has said that these mujahideen were captured during the war against the Taliban and al-Qaida and, after 'brainwashing' by US agents, they prepared these mujahideen to be sent into Xinjiyang. He also disclosed that these mujahideen were mainly from Afghanistan and Pakistan and that they had close links with the mujahideen.

China has consistently accused America of promoting terrorism in China. This appears to be a hangover policy from the cold war when America, according to many knowledgeable people, used terrorists to undermine any governments of which they did not approve. In their official remarks, Chinese authorities had been cautious in identifying the elements responsible for these acts, putting the blame generally on 'reactionary forces in the west, separatists and religious extremists'. But a German expert, Dr Gudrun Wacker, quoting Chinese officials in a seminar in Peshawar some time ago, said: "They have reported that the American CIA is formenting trouble and weapons for the purpose come from Central Asia, Afghanistan, and probably Pakistan."

China sent top security officials to Washington within two weeks of 9/11, and it has stepped up consultations with American agencies on the counter-terrorist programs. The Chinese officials also said that they are asking the US to return 3000 members of China's Muslim Uighur ethnic minority they said were captured fighting with al-Qaida network in Afghanistan. But Chinese officials did not get a positive response from America on this. The American Deputy Secretary, Mr Armitage, said he had mentioned the need to respect the Uighurs in his talks with the Chinese.

However, Mr Armitage said nothing about the rights of any other captured Muslims from anywhere else in the world. To many observers in Pakistan, there is American Government duplicity in the 'worldwide war on terror' designed to enable them to keep some terrorists 'up their sleeve' for use later in the same way that they used Osama bin Laden and the jihadi movement to attack the Soviets. They turned a blind eye to the activities of the jihadis in Kashmir and Uighur until 9/11 jolted them to recognise the fact that, once created, Frankenstein's monster always has a habit of attacking its creator. It appears that, regardless of 9/11, the international game plan goes on. In this case, critics believe, they wanted to surround China through the occupation of Afghanistan and by gaining military access to Tajikistan and other former Soviet Muslim states, and they want to keep a useful anti-Chinese Uighur insurrection force at their disposal. Thus, the claim that 9/11 was an American/Jewish conspiracy is, on the surface, too ridiculous for words, but the evident duplicity in America's foreign policies over many years, its persistent blind-eyed approach to Israeli atrocities against the Palestine people over the past fifty years, its support for the Contras in Nicaragua, its refusal to extradite Uighur terrorists, and the invasion of Iraq on spurious grounds, to name a few, enables the jihadi propaganda machine to make ridiculous claims and point to these facts as proof of the veracity of their own claims. Many Muslim people around the world believe the jihadis rather than Americans or western propaganda. Needless to say, the issue is easily resolved. If America actually likes terrorism and terrorists, provided they do not attack America, then they should say so. That is very unlikely but, at least, the American people should question their own government's behaviour as well as the behaviour of other Muslim government's around the world when matters of war or vital national interests are at stake.

The Bangladesh-Burma Connection

In October 2002, Bangladeshi police and intelligence agents raided an Islamic charity organisation, the Al-

Harmain Foundation, which had members from Algeria, Yemen and Sudan, and they took into custody seven members suspected of having links with al-Qaida.

The Bangladesh Government believe that the Al-Harmain Islamic Foundation is actually a terrorist organisation disguised as a Non-Government Organisation. The Al-Harmain Foundation offered diplomas in Arabic and Islamic studies for sixty students from various madrasas who were selected for a three-month course. After the course, the students went on to Medina Islamic University in Saudi Arabia for higher education. In addition to the diploma courses, students were provided with skills in computer technology. While the Al-Harmain foundation provided funds to Harkat-ul-Jihad-al-Islami (Burma wing) and had set-up camps for the refugees from Burma in Kaksus, the Burma wing of Harkat had used this district of Bangladesh as a base for its militant activities in Burma. Reportedly, it had also established a militant training camp in that area. Harkat-ul-Jihad-al-Islami also had close links with al-Qaida and its mujahideen had fought against the Northern Alliance and America with the Taliban and al-Qaida.

The Chechnya Connection

Separatist jihadi movements in other countries in the region did not use their own soil to train their Islamic fighters for the jihad. They looked to the Taliban Government in Afghanistan and Pakistan for such facilities, and 9/11 and the fall of the Taliban, to areas controlled by the Taliban and to the Pakistani tribal areas and, more recently, to former Muslim Soviet republics. The most recent of these camps is a training centre south of the Amu Darya (Oxus) river which runs along the border of Uzbekistan, Afghanistan and Turkmenistan, reportedly set-up by the Islamic Movement of Uzbekistan (IMU) to train militants from Uzbekistan, Tajikistan, Kyrgistan. In addition, al-Qaida provides sanctuary, funds, training in guerilla warfare and the manufacture of explosives to Arab dissidents from Egypt, Somalia, Sudan, Algeria, Saudi Arabia, Kuwait, Yemen, Jordan, and Iran. Afghan, Pakistani, and Arab militants were believed to have been involved in the August 1999 campaign led by the Islamic Movement of Uzbekistan (IMU) which captured about 20 villages in the south of that country. The IMU incursions into parts of the autonomous Russian republic of Dagestan sparked-off the second Chechen war.

In August 1999, Afghan, Pakistani, and Arab jihadis, trained in the camps of the militant organisations of various Islamic religious persuasion and nationality in Pakistan, are understood to have participated, along with Chechen commander Basayev, when they stormed some areas of Dagestan in Russia. This led to the second military intervention in Chechnya. These Islamic militants saw themselves as; 'warriors performing a divine duty to carry out the will of God'. Ultimately, Russian forces threw them out of Dagestan. In February 1999, the late Zelim Khan Andarbayev visited Pakistan on his way to Afghanistan.

He was granted a Pakistani visa. He carried out a tour of Pakistan to garner support for the Chechen militants. Qazi Hussain Ahmad of Jamaat-e-Islami was instrumental in winning support for him in many mosques and he met leading jihadi leaders during his visit. Jihadi groups in Pakistan donated three million dollars to Zelim Khan. He was killed in a terrorist incident in February 2004.

American and European Jihadis

Jihadists have spread their influence all over the globe, even in the United States and Europe. In October 2000, *The New York Times* reported that Ali Mohammad, an ex-army sergeant of European origin pleaded guilty before a US district judge to a charge of plotting with Osama bin Laden to kill Americans anywhere they were found, to attack US military personnel in Somalia and Saudi Arabia, to kill Americans at unspecified embassies and to conceal the conspiracy. He said that the object of the conspiracy, which he joined in the late 1980s, was to force the US out of West Asia.

According to *The New York Times*, Ali Mohammad left the US army in 1989 after three years of service. During his military career, he had earned a parachute badge and an M-16 expert marksman badge and was teaching soldiers from US Special Forces about Muslim culture. He also admitted that he had helped to move Osama bin Laden secretly from Pakistan to Sudan and had trained members of al-Qaida. Mohammad's case focused attention on the efforts being made by Pakistani and Afghanistan-based jihadi groups to recruit members from the Muslim communities in North America and the Caribbean. They were initially intended to attack US interests in West Asia and then later for a jihad in the US itself.

American Taliban recruit, John Walker, who was arrested in Pakistan and is now in detention in Guantanamo Bay, also disclosed details about the jihadi network in America and Europe. The story of the Australian Taliban recruit, David Hike, which follows, gives an insight into why some Americans and Europeans joined al-Qaida to become jihadis.

The ISI and Foreign Taliban

"My son was like 'Indiana Jones'. He moved from job to job seeking adventure before finding Islam two years ago," said Terry Hike, the father of the Australian Taliban member, David Hike. Terry had arrived in Pakistan in June 2003 to make a documentary about his son. David changed his name to Mohammad Dawood after converting to Islam and had started his jihadi life in Pakistan after his attachment to different jihadi organisations. He was one of the two Australians captured fighting with al-Qaida and the Taliban. He is also among the first of six al-Qaida suspects due to face trial by the US Military Tribunal Court. He was captured by Northern Alliance troops in December 2001 and was later transferred to US custody with at least four other prisoners, including the American John Walker, who was also found fighting with the Taliban.

David Hike (aka Mohammad Dawood) also allegedly threatened to kill an American upon his arrival at Guantanamo. Terry wants to save his son and the documentary on David's life was a part of his effort. Terry wants his son, if found guilty, to face trial in his own country but the Australian Government rules out rewriting the necessary legislation to allow him to be tried at home. Terry accuses the Australian Government of ignoring human rights abuses and effectively washing their hands of any concerns for his son. He also denied ever having admitted that his son was a terrorist and believes that David was not a senior member of the al-Qaida terrorist network. "After the disappointment from my government, I came to Pakistan to find some solid evidence that would prove that David was not a senior member of al-Qaida," he said. When he came to Pakistan, he had twenty letters with him which David had written from different places. Eight letters were from Pakistan and Terry wanted to visit very place from where his son had written these letters. These letters not only describe David's jihad journey but they also reveal some astonishing aspects of the jihadi organisations.

Letters

David converted to Islam in November 1999. According to his father, some of his friends had introduced him to Islam. He went to Lahore to participate in the Tablighi (Islamic preaching convention) in Raiwind. David wrote the first letter from the Tablighi Markaz in December 1999 and the letter shows that he was inspired by the environment of the Markaz. He informed his family that he was going on a tablighi tour for four months. His second letter was written in Peshawar and shows that he was very excited and inspired by Pakistan's progress. He gave details about his visit to the Nuclear Agriculture Institute in Peshawar and said that Pakistan had become an atomic power and was using nuclear technology for the betterment of humanity and for Muslims all over the world. He believed that Pakistan would become a major power in the world in the coming years. His next letter was also from Peshawar. This letter showed that he was very inspired by the Taliban and the ideas of jihad and told his father that Afghanistan was the only true Islamic state of the world, where Islam was practised in its original form. He said that Europe and America had reservations about the Taliban because of their jihad against the Northern Alliance, which is fighting the Taliban on behalf of America and India. After this, he wrote another five letters which have almost the same content.

On 14 February 2000, David wrote from Quetta and he talked about jihad for the first time. He wrote that the Taliban were fighting the real jihad to establish a true Islamic state and he revealed his view that the jihad in Kashmir was being fought as part of an American and Chinese plan to maintain a hold on the region. He explained that America was using India and China was using Pakistan to preserve their own interests in the region and that innocent mujahideen had lost their lives in an un-Islamic war. In this letter, he said he had decided to join the Taliban.

Tablighi Jamat records show that he was on the Tablighi tour but that he left the tour incomplete on 17 February. It may be assumed that he had met Deobandi jihadi leaders, especially Harkat-ul-Jihad-ul-Islami, which held the same peculiar views about the jihad in Kashmir and had concentrated on Afghanistan. But the very next letter, which he wrote from Afghanistan on 18 February, shows that his experiences in Afghanistan were not good and he told his father that it was not what he had expected. He also said that some of the Taliban fighters had threatened him with guns, but he did not mention the reasons.

David's next letter was from the Lashkar-e-Taiba militant training camp in Azad Kashmir, which was written on 4 March 2000. This letter was surprising because he now appeared to have different views about Kashmir. About this change, he did not say a word but wrote about his new vision that, after the independence of Kashmir was won, Pakistan, Afghanistan and Kashmir would become one state and a true Islamic system would be established in the world. Then America, China or Europe would not think of depriving Muslims anywhere in the world. He also wrote about the Inter-Services Intelligence (ISI) role in this regard and said it was doing a great service to Islam by helping to establish an Islamic state in the region. It may be presumed from this letter that, after a bitter experience with the Taliban, he joined Lashkar-e-Taiba to continue with his jihad activities.

On 4 June 2000, his letter, sent from the Line of Control in Azad Kashmir, said that he was waiting for his 'launching' into Indian-held Kashmir. This letter showed that he was quite happy to be in the battlefield for the first time. He wrote about two incidents in which an old lady and a young shepherd were killed by Indian forces. He was a witness of the events and, in his letter, he showed his hatred for the Indian forces. But David did not get an opportunity to cross the LoC because the circumstances for launching were not favourable. He returned to Quetta and on 10 August 2000, he wrote that it was quite hard for him to keep waiting for his launching. So, he decided to go back to Afghanistan to join the jihad there. In Afghanistan, he met Arab mujahideen and became familiar with their jihadi service.

He wrote his last letter from Karachi in which he related his battlefield experiences against the Northern Alliance. He informed his father that as he was in a Lashkar-e-Taiba office and that he had decided to get a proper religious education to become a better Muslim.

The Father's Experiences in Pakistan

Terry Hike went to Pakistan in the hope that he would meet with David's friends and the jihadi organisations' leaders who, he hoped, would welcome him and help him with the documentary to prove that his son was not an important operative in any jihadi organisation or al-Qaida. He first went to Sahiwal, to the home of a young man called Asim who was, apparently, David's closet friend. However, he was shocked when Asim's father flatly refused to meet him or allow him to talk to his son. He told him to go back home and not return. Later, Asim's neighbours told Terry that, a few weeks earlier, Asim and his male family members had been under investigation by an unknown agency and the family had broken all relationships with neighbours afterwards. They did not disclose why they were under investigation. When Terry reached Raiwind with his camera crew, the administrators of the Tablighi Markaz did not allow them to film even though their general attitude was co-operative and hospitable. They helped him find David's record and everybody was anxious to please Terry and his crew with food, cold drinks and tea. A volunteer serving tea said that he had prayed that all these foreigners would save themselves from the fire of hell by accepting Islam. Two other Muslim foreigners preached to them about Islam. The record showed that David had gone to Raiwind on 9 December 1999 and in February 2000 he had left Markaz without completing his tablighi tour.

The leaders of Jamaat-ud-Daawa, Lashkar-e-Taiba's patron organisation, also refused to help Terry or recognize David. They said immediately that they did not know anything about Dawood (David's new name) even after they had seen David's letter which was written on Lashkar-headed notepaper. Later, it was revealed by a Jamaat-ud-Daawa leader that Dawood (David) had been attached to Lashkar-e-Taiba but, in mid-2000, he had left them and got admission to the Jamia Banuri (a place of religious study) in Karachi.

Terry also went to Jamia Akora Kohtak in Nowshara and tried to find some clues about his son there. A local teacher offered to arrange a meeting with some Arab mujahideen in Afghanistan who, he claimed, definitely knew David because during the Taliban era all foreigners, including Arabs, lived in special residential areas in Kabul and Kandahar and were not allowed to live in other localities. But Terry was unwilling to walk into such a dangerous situation.

In Peshawar, every taxi driver he met offered Terry help if he wished to meet any Taliban or al-Qaida leaders. Luckily for Terry, he did not take up any of these taximeter offers. In fact, the taxi-men run a business on the side by arranging meetings for foreign journalists with Taliban and al-Qaida leaders in Peshawar. When the money changed hands, possibly hundreds of dollars, the entrepreneurs arrange a meeting with a fake Taliban, easily recruited from a nearby Afghan refugee camp.

In Lahore, when Terry went to the Lashkar-e-Taiba foreign office department, unhelpful people gathered around him and told him that the Lashkar foreign office had moved. Although there were several foreigners among the crowd, everybody denied any knowledge of David (Dawood). Terry also contacted many religious leaders who he expected would co-operate but nobody was ready to admit knowledge of Dawood. When Terry went to Karzai's Afghanistan to complete his tour he said that all those persons about whom David had written did not co-operate with him; they even refused to recognise him. He wondered if this was the Muslim brotherhood about which David used to write about in his letters.

Afterword

Regardless of his conversion to Islam or his change of name, David's, or Dawood's, story is not very different from the story of many thousands of young mujahideen born into the Islamic religion and with Islamic names who had also left their homes to become another Indiana Jones in a heroic adventure. An adventure that they believed had the blessing of God. The jihad.

Too many never returned to their homes. Their families wait, hoping their beloved sons, brothers, husbands or fathers have not been killed. There are just so many despairing families in Pakistan still in what, for most, is a futile vigil. Each such family represents a tragic human story. I met a father in Shangiar who thought that his son would come back one day. He is a regular visitor to the jihadi organisation's office where his son had volunteered after listening to and being persuaded by the propagandists of the jihadi movement. He does not yet know that his son was killed in Afghanistan. Luckily for Terry Hike, at least his son is still alive.

The fate of this unfortunate unnamed Pakistani Indiana Jones and that of the Australian Indiana Jones reveals the most important aspect of the jihadi network and its leaders. Without these young men, they are nothing. The jihadi movement in the world thrives on the inconsistencies and duplicity evident in the international affairs of powerful nations so that their conflicts of interests can be exploited by irrational dogmatists, often self-seeking, who can paint a perverse view of the world to encourage naive young men, from all parts of the world and from all religious communities, to take up arms for the 'just cause', their jihad, their liberation or their revolution. And, as history teaches, if their war for their just cause is successful, they themselves, invariably, become war mongers, or tyrants, or equally repressive or equally corrupt.

I hope readers will appreciate the importance of the struggle for the hearts and minds of young men in the Islamic world today. That world is, for the average young man, a poor world where economic and educational opportunities are thin on the ground. It is a fertile breeding ground for fanaticism, for irrational religious or political belief systems propagated by ideologues who use a few facts, often distorted, and a good deal of fiction to create a sense of injustice and anger among the population. That is how so many young men are encouraged to volunteer to fight for the jihad, the liberation or the revolution.

The Muslim world was, relatively, quiescent until 1947 when the plantation of Palestine began. When jihadis claim that America and the west is trying to destroy the Muslim world, they point to the fifty year persecution of the Palestinian people by the Zionists and America's role in supporting a plan for the creation of a Greater Israel as their proof. This running sore in the Middle East has alienated millions of Muslims all over the world from any possible reconciliation with the west.

There was no serious conflict between Muslims and Hindus in Kashmir until Afghanistan became a battleground for competing foreign powers. It was the Afghan jihad, promoted by America, Saudi Arabia and Pakistan, which led to the turmoil and terror and the potential nuclear-war situation which exists in the subcontinent today. Pakistan is riven with internal dissensions and conflict where the country's leaders are now under constant threat of assassination and with a possibility of civil war developing.

America's decision to invade Iraq has now added significant firepower to the jihadi propagandists. They do not have to try too hard to persuade young men that the Ummah is under attack. Muslims from all over the world, including Pakistan, have and are becoming eager volunteers in a new jihad against the Americans and their allies in that new conflict. As demonstrated in Pakistan, a dedicated foreign mujahideen, once they have gained a base of home-support, can prevent reconciliation in any country. The future for Iraq looks bleak.

Yet, all of these conflicts are capable of resolution. In this humble correspondent's opinion, an American change of tone in its relations with Israel would encourage, if not compel, Zionists to moderate their ambitions and accept a sovereign state of Palestine, an acceptance of the general will of its indigenous people for a sovereign state of Kashmir by Pakistan and India, and a withdrawal of all non-Muslim forces from Iraq would leave the jihadis with little to complain about and might allow people in the west to be free of irrational Islamophobia and real Muslim terrorism.

Appendix I
LIST OF MILITANT RELIGIOUS PUBLICATIONS IN PAKISTAN

The following newspapers and magazines are published and distributed in Pakistan by various religious and militant groups and organisations and they are generally supportive of the world jihadi movement. They are hostile to Pakistan's new anti-jihadi/pro-American policy and to American, Christian, Jewish and western influences in the Islamic world. They reflect the jihadi view of the world and carry appeals for funds for Islamic 'charities' and organisations which finance jihadi groups. They are accessible to the poorest of people in Pakistan, costing from as little as 5 to 50 rupees in price and they run from 6 to 50 pages in extent. Most of them are very professionally manufactured and printed.

Daily Issues

Title	Affiliation	Pages	Price	Location
Islam	Deobandi	8	5	Karachi
Jamaat Islami	Jamaat Islamai	16	9	Karachi
Insaf	Jamaat Islami	6	5	Lahore
Ummat	Rafeeq Afghan	16	7	Karachi

Weeklies

Title	Affiliation	Pages	Price	Location
Al-Hilal	Deoband	6	6	Karachi
Asia	Jamaat Islami	---	15	Lahore
Zarb-e-Momin	Al-Rasheed Trust	8	7	Karachi
Deen	Barelavi	4	4	Karachi
Ghazwa Times	Jamaat Al-Dawaa	4	3	Lahore
Shamsheer	Jaish-e-Mohammad	44	10	Hyderabad
Zarb-e-Raza Tehreek	Sunni	---	6	Karachi
Hizb-e-Islam	---	6	6	Karachi
Al-Hadis	Jamiat Ahl-e-Hadis	24	7	Lahore
Tanzeem Ahl-e-Hadis	Jamaat Ahl-e-Hadis	20	5	Lahore
Al-Mutaquam	Jamaat Ahl-e-Hadis	32	5	Lahore

Fortnightlies

Title	Pages	Price	Location
Jaish	52	13	Karachi
Al-Islah	44	13	Karachi
Sahifa Ahl-e Hadis	30	10	Karachi
Hizb-e-Mujahid	8	3	Rawalpindi
Jihad-e-Kashmir	54	15	Rawalpindi

Monthlies

Title	Pages	Price	Location
Al-Sabana	80	12	Lahore
Al-Abrar	66	16	Karachi
Al-Balagh	68	---	Karachi

Title	Pages	Price	Location
Al-Hamad	68	15	Karachi
Al-Ahrar	68	15	---
Al-Irshad	52	15	Islamabad
Mujalla al-Dawaa	60	12	Lahore
Al-Rabat	---	---	---
Zarb-e-Haq	4	3	Karachi
Al-Makhzan	60	6	---
Haq Char Yar	68	12	---
Zarb-e Taiba	---	---	---
Taiyyabat	---	---	---
Voice of Islam	---	---	---
Al-Sayeed	52	52	Mansahra
Sunni Tarjuman	52	10	---
Anwar-e-Madina	68	13	Lahore
Al-Ashraf	---	---	Karachi
Sadai Jamiat	38	15	Karachi
Ashraf	---	---	Peshawar
Mishkatul Misbah	48	10	Lahore
Al-Khatim	38	10	Lahore
Nusrat-ul Uloom	60	---	Gujranwala
Masihai	54	20	Karachi
Bazm-e-Qasimi	52	16	Karachi
Jaridatul Ittehad	84	15	Lahore
Jannatul Mawa	52	---	Gujranwala
Al-Murshid	68	25	Lahore
Tarjuman Ahl-e-Hadis	54	10	Faisalabad
Sadai Hosh	34	10	Lahore
Laulak Sahizada	60	10	Multan
NaquibKhtam-e-Nabuwwat	76	15	Multan
Sirat-e-Mustaqeem	52	10	Karachi
Al-Akhuwa	58	15	Lahore
Sada-i-Mujhid	52	15	Karachi
Naghmai Tauheed	60	15	Gujarat
Tadbeer-e-Nau	---	12	Lahore

Title	Pages	Price	Location
Al-Hareer	50	15	Lahore
Khilafat-e-Rashida	52	15	Faisalabad
Munaqib	44	10	Bhakar
Al-Huda	28	8	Miyanwali
Al-Numan	36	5	Charsada
Khairul Amal	---	---	Lahore
Shahadat	54	10	Islamabad
Al-Badr	54	15	Karachi
Banat-e-Aisha	110	25	Karachi
Al-Masood	28	10	Rawalpindi
Tanzeemul Islam	52	20	Lahore
Lisan-e-Sidq	68	15	Islamabad
Al-Maarif	50	12	Lahore
Al-Muntazir	52	15	Lahore
Mahaz-e-Kashmir	52	15	Muzaffarabad
Rizwan	72	15	Lahore
Al-Sayeed	62	35	Multan
Al-Hamid	60	20	Multan
Dawat-e-Islam	54	15	Karachi
Lasani Inquilab	44	16	Faisalabad
Noor-e-Islam	---	9	Sheikhopura
Daawat Tanzeem-ul Islam	46	10	Gujranwala
Kanz-ul Iman	52	10	Lahore
Ahwal-o-Aasar	68	15	Lahore
Al-Jamia	60	15	Jhung
Qutub-e Madina	52	15	Karachi
Nidai Ahl-e-Sunnat	52	15	Lahore
Minhajul Quran	68	12	Lahore
Saqlain	220	25	Islamabad
Khabarnama	52	15	Karachi

Publications Representing Jihadi Organisations

S N	Publication	Periodicity	Circulation	Representing	Medium	Important Writers
	Islam	Daily	Al-Rasheed Trust	Sipah-e-Sahaba/Jaish	Urdu	Maulana Fazl Mohammad
	Zarb-e-Momin	Weekly	---	---	"	---
	Al-Hilal	Monthly	15,000	Harkat-ul-Mujahideen/ Jamiat-ul-Ansar	"	---
	Ghazwa Times	Weekly	30,000	Lashkar-e-Taiba/ Jamaat-ud-Dawaa	"	Qazi Kashif, Abdullah Muntazir
	Shamsheer	Weekly	---	Jaish-e-Mohammad/ Tahreek-e-Khuddam-e-Islam	"	Ibn Ahmad Sheikh, Imtiaz Ahmad
	Jaish-e-Mohammad	Fortnightly	---	Jaish-e-Mohammad	"	Publication suspended
	Al-Khatim	Monthly	---	Tahreek-e-Jihad	"	Abul Hasan Jihadi, M Azim Inquilabi
	Mujalla al-Dawaa	Monthly	50,000	Lashkar-e-Taiba	"	Naved Qamar, Qazi Kashif N
	Shahadat	Monthly	10,000	Tahreek-ul-Mujahideen	"	Hafiz salahuddin, Z Zaki

LIST OF MILITANT RELIGIOUS PUBLICATIONS IN PAKISTAN

S N Publication	Periodicity	Circulation	Representing	Medium	Important Writers
The Message	Monthly	2,000	"	"	---
Al-Badr	Monthly	10,000	Al-Badr Mujahideen	"	Abdullah Azam, N. Zahir
Al-Masood	Monthly	2,000	Jamiat-ul-Mujahideen al-Alemi	"	Maulana Abdul wahid, Azhar Masood
Mahaze Kashmir	Monthly	5,000	Jamiat-ul-Mujahideen	"	M Abdul Rafey, Abdullah Haroon
Al-Irshad	Monthly	5,000	Harkat-ul-Jihad-al-Islami	"	Maulana M Ahmad, M Wasi Mateen Fikri
Zarb-e-Mujahid	Fortnightly	5,000	Hizb-ul-Mujahideen	"	Maulana Siddiq Arkani, M Ayyub
Al-Ribat	Bi-monthly	1,000	Harkat-ul-Jihad	"	
Jihad-e Kashmir	Fortnightly	7,000	Hizb-ul-Mujahideen	"	Abdul Hadi Ahmad, Sagheer Qamar
Tadbeer-e-Nau	Monthly	5,000	Jamat-ul-Furqan	"	---
Ah-Hareer	Monthly	5,000	Deobandi jihadi org.	"	---
Dawaat-e-Tanzeemul Islam	Monthly	2,000	Sunni Jihad Council	"	Sahabzada Faizul Hasan, Mufti M Khan Qadri
Kanz-ul Iman	Monthly	1,000	Lashkar-e-Ababeel Mujahideen/Jamaat Ahl-e-Sunnat	"	M Nayeem Tahir Rizvi, Tariq Mahmood
Ahval-o-Aasar	Monthly	1,000	Harkat Inquilab-e-Islami	"	Khalid Mahmood Qadri
Bedar Digest	Monthly	1,000	Deobandi policy	"	Malik A Sarwar, Abu Hamza

349

Important Journals Published by Religious Seminaries

S N Publication	Periodicity	Medium	Affiliation	Circulation	Rep. Imp. Writers
Al-Abrar	Monthly	Urdu	Deoband	7,000	Jamia Ashraful Madaris, Karachi Maulana Hakim M Akhtar, M Ibrahim
Al-Balagh	"	"	"	10,000	Darul Uloom, Karachi Maulana Taqi Usmani, Mufti Rauf
Al-Hamad	"	"	"	---	Jamia Hamadia, Karachi Maulana M Yahya, Mufti M Jameel
Al-Makhzan	"	"	"	3,000	Jamia Makhzanul Uloom, Khanpur Shabbir Ahmad Mewati, Iqbal A Siddiqui
Al-Sayeed	"	"	"	1,000	Darul Uloom Sayeedia Mufti Hafizur Rahman
Anwar-e-Madina	"	"	"	3,000	Jamia Madina, Lahore Maulana Naimuddin
Al-Numan	"	"	"	1,000	Darul Uloom Numania Mufti M Muslim, Khna Sayed

S N Publication	Periodicity	Medium	Affiliation	Circulation	Rep. Imp. Writers
Ashraf	,,	,,	,,	1,000	Jamia Ashrafia, Peshawar
Al-Hamid	,,	,,	Barelavi	1,000	Jamia Islamia Khairul Maad, Multan Khalid Perwez, Sahibzada Ahmad Mian
Bazm-e-Qasmi	,,	,,	Deoband	---	Darul Uloom Farooq azam, Karachi Iqbal A Siddiqui, Mufti M Ziaul Haq
Tarjuman Ahl-e-Hadis	,,	,,	Ahl-e-Hadis	1,000	Jamia Salfia, Faisalabad Mian Naim Tahir, Arif Shahzad
Al-Jamia	,,	,,	Barelavi	2,000	Jamia Mohammadi Sharif, Jhung Maulana M. Rahmatullah, Hafiz Ziyauddin
Nusrat-ul Uloom	,,	,,	Deoband	2,000	Madrasa Nusratul Uloom, Gujranwala
Jannatul Mawa	,,	,,	Ahl-e-Hadis	1,000	Jamia Rahmatullilaalameen Gujranwala Bashir Ansari, Ch. Asghar Ali

351

The Seeds of Terrorism

S N Publication	Periodicity	Medium	Affiliation	Circulation	Rep. Imp. Writers
Al-Muntazir	"	"	Shia	2,000	Jamia Al-Muntazir, Lahore Maulana M Afzal Haideri
Rizvan	"	"	Barelavi	---	Hizb-ul-Ahnaf, Lahore S. Mahmood A Rizvi
Munaqib	"	"	Deoband	---	Madrasa Darul Huda, Bhakar Maulana, M Abdullah, Dr F Rahman
Al-Huda	"	"	Deoband	---	Jamia Hanifia Ashraful Uloom, Harnauli Maulana M Yaqoob

Publications of Religious Organisations

S N Publication	Periodicity	Medium	Representing	Circulation	Major Writers
Al-Siyania	Monthly	Urdu	Majlis-e-Siyanat-ul Muslimeen	5,000	Wakil A. Sherwani
Al-Ahrar	,,	,,	Mjlis-e-Ahrar-ul Islam	1,000	Maulana M Yusuf Ahrar
Asia	Weekly	,,	Jamaat-e-Islami	5,000	Prof. Ayyub Nayyar
Al-Murshid	Monthly	,,	Tanzeem-ul-Ikhwan	,,	Maulana Akram Awn
Qutub-e-Madina	,,	,,	Dawat-e-Islami	25,000	M Amin Qadri
Al-Hadis	Weekly	,,	Markazi Jamiat Ahl-e-Hadis	10,000	Rana Shafiq, M Bilal Hamad
Tanzeem-ul Hadis	Weekly	,,	Jamat Ahl-e-Hadeeth	5,000	Maulana M Asfan salfi
Jaridatul Ittehad	Monthly	,,	Jamiat Ittehad-ul Ulema	5,000	Maulana Gauhar Rahman
Sahifa Al-Hadeeth	,,	,,	Jamiat Ghurabai Ahl-e-Hadeeth	3,000	Maulana Abdul Jabbar Salfi
Sirat-e-Mustaqeem	,,	,,	Ahl-e-Hadeeth Janbaz Force	2,000	---
Haq Yar Char	,,	,,	Tahreek Khuddam Ahl-e-Sunnat	4,000	Maulana Habibur Rahman
Khilafat-e-Rashida	,,	,,	Sipah-e-Sahaba	15,000	Tahir Mahmood

353

The Seeds of Terrorism

S N Publication	Periodicity	Medium	Representing	Circulation	Major Writers
Al-Maarif	,,	,,	ISO	5,000	Raza Abidi
Sadai Hosh	,,	,,	Jamiat Ghurabai Ahl-e-Hadeeth	500	M Afghan Salfi
Sadai Jamiat	,,	,,	Jamiat Ulema-e-Islam (S)	--	General (R) Hamid Gul
Masihai	,,	,,	Jamiat Ulema-e-Islam	1,000	Ahmad Khairuddin Ansari
Mishkatul Misbah	,,	,,	Jamiat Tulaba Arabia	5,000	--
Tanzeem-ul Islam	,,	,,	Majlis Tanzeem-e-Islam	1,000	Raziuddin Haider
Al-Akhuwa	,,	,,	Markazi Jamiat Ahl-e-Hadeeth	2,000	Rana Tanweer Qasim
Naghmai Tauheed	,,	,,	Jamiat Ishat Al-Tauheed-wal-Sunnat	2,000	Maulana Ziaullah S Bukhari
Al-Sayeed	,,	,,	Jamaat Ahl-e-Sunnat	2,000	Sayeed A Kazmi
Sunni Tarjuman	,,	,,	Sunni Tehreek	5,000	M Iqbal Qureshi
Dawat-e-Islam	,,	,,	Barelavi	2,000	Nasir A Jahangir
Lasani Inquilab	,,	,,	Tanzeen Mashaikh Azam	1,000	M Rashid Naqshbandi
Nidai Ahl-e-Sunnat	,,	,,	Jamat Ahl-e-Sunnat	1,000	Rashid A Rizvi
Genius	,,	,,	Millat-e-Islamia	5,000	--
Laulak	,,	,,	Aalami Majlis Khatm-e-Nabuwwat	5,000	Maulana Zahidur Rashidi
NaquibKhatm-e-Nabuwwat	,,	,,	Tahreek Tahaffuz Khatm-e-Nabuwwat	--	Abdul Latif Khalid Chima

354

LIST OF MILITANT RELIGIOUS PUBLICATIONS IN PAKISTAN

S N Publication	Periodicity	Medium	Representing	Circulation	Major Writers
Lisan-e-Sidq	,,	,,	Darul Tableegh-al-Jafaria	2,000	---
Saqlain	Quarterly	,,	Aalami Majlis-e-Ahl-e-Bait	----	Mohsin Ali Najafi
Minhajul Quran	Monthly	,,	Tahreek Minhaj-ul Quran	15,000	Allama Tahirul Qadri
Zarb-e-Raza	Weekly	,,	Sunni Tehreek	10,000	---
Zarb-e-Islam	,,	,,	Barelavi	2,000	---

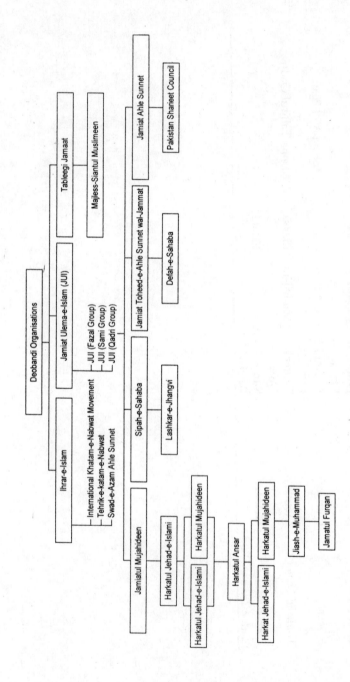

Appendix II: Chart of Deobandi Organisations in Pakistan

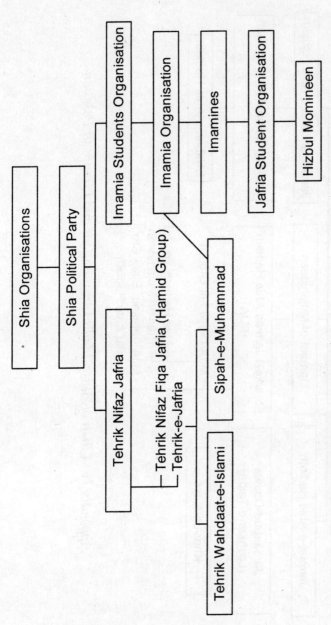

Appendix III: Chart of Shia Organisations and Groups in Pakistan

357

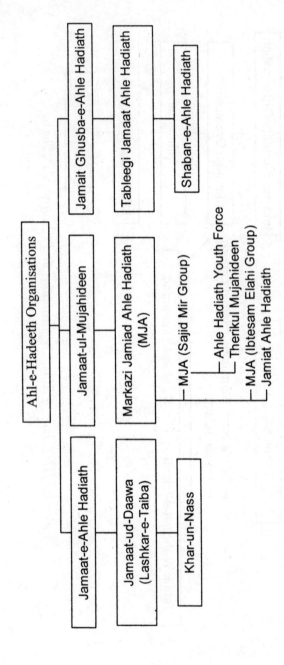

Appendix IV: Chart of Ahl-e-Hadis Organisations and Groups in Pakistan

INDEX OF NAMES OF PEOPLE

Ahmad Omar Sheikh
Ahmad Sayeed Sheikh
Ahmad Shah Masood
Ahmed Ghailani
Ahmed Mohammed Ali
Ahmed Said al Qadr
Ajab Gul
Akhtar Mohammad Usmani
Akhter Muawiya
Akram Durrani
Akram Lahori
Akram Wali Mohammad Badani
Ali Atwa
Ali Ghalib Himmat
Ali Yusuf
Allama Iqbal
Almas Khan
Amanat Ali

Amdouni Mehrez
Ameer Ali
Ameer Hamza
Aminullah
Amireeul Momineen Mullah
Amjad Farooqi
Amjad Wadaich
Ammanullah Khan
Anas al-Liby
Aqli Mohammad Amine
Aquadi Mohammed
Armand Albert Friendrich Humber
Asghar Ali
Ashfaq Pervez Kiani
Ashraf Dar
Asif Ramzi
Aslam Muawiya
Ayadi Shafiq bin Mahomed

Maulana Asif Qasmi
Maulana Azam Tariq
Maulana Bhai Maqsood Ali Shah
Maulana Dr Sher Ali Shah
Maulana Fazlur Rehman
Maulana Ghulam Nabi Noshari
Maulana Inayatur Rahman
Maulana Jalaluddin Haqqani
Maulana Khalil
Maulana Masud Azhar
Maulana Misbahullah
Maulana Murtuza
Maulana Muzafar
Maulana Naseeb Ali Shah
Maulana Noor Mohammad
Maulana Omar Farooque
Maulana Rahmatullah
Maulana Salimullah Khan

Maulana Samiul Haq
Maulana Shah Ahmad Noorani
Maulana Yusuf Shah
Maulavi Abdul Kabeer
Maulavi Aijaz
Maulavi Ghulam Murtuza
Maulavi Hamdullah Zahid
Maulavi Jalaluddin Haqqani
Maulavi Masood
Maulavi Mohammad Khan Shirani
Maulavi Mohammad Salam
Maulavi Noor Mohammad
Maulavi Obaidullah Anwar
Maulavi Wakeel Ahmad Mutawakkil
Michael Chossudovsky
Mir Zafrullah Jamali
Mnasri Fethi ben Rebat
Mohamad Usman

Mushtaq Zargar
Mustafa Mohammed Fadhil
Nabi Mohammad
Nada Youssef Mustafa
Nadeem Usmani
Nadir Magasi
Najibullah
Namoun Darkazanli
Nasir Shirazi
Nasirullah Babur
Nasreddin Ahmed Idris
Nasrullah Mansoor
Naved Butt
Naved Farooqui
Nawabzada Nasrullah Khan
Omar Karrar Khawak
Omar Sayeed Sheikh
Omar Sheikh

Osama bin Laden
Osama Rizwan
Ouaz Najib
Pari Gul Agha
Prime Minister Hikmetyar
Prof. Burhanuddin Rabbani
Prof. Hafiz Mohammad Sayeed
Professor Abdul Ghafoor
Professor Sayeed
Qari Abdul Baas Siddiqui
Qari Abdul Hai
Qari Abdul Majeed
Qari Asad
Qari Saifullah Akhtar
Qari Zarar
Qari Zawar Bahadur
Ramzi bin Shaiba
Ramzi Binalshibh

Tufail Altaf
Usman Zakaria
Ustad Abdul Ali
Yandarvieh Zelimkhan
Yasin Malik
Yassir al-Jaziri
Yusuf Azhar

Zafar Fateh
Zafar Iqbal Memon
Zakiullah
Zalmay Khalilzad
Zayn al-Abadin Mohammad Husayn
Zubair

GLOSSARY

Some of the Urdu/Islamic words which need to be explained in the glossary are as follows:

Al-Qaida	A terrorist organisation led by Osama bin Laden but now popularly used to describe all Muslim international terrorists
Ayah	A prayer
Baniyas	Cowards
Barelvi	A Sunni sect in the sub-continent
Communal/Communalism	Sectarianism
Crore	Ten million
Deobandi	A Sunni sect in the sub-continent
Emir	A title of various Muslims (mainly Arab) rulers
Fatwa(h)	A Muslim religious decree
Goondas	Vagabonds
Hurriyat	An Islamic organisation
Jihad/jihadi	The Islamic 'holy war' and its soldiers
Khilafat	The original model Islamic nation (Caliphate)
Lakh	One hundred thousand
Launching	The dispatch of

369

	mujahideen into Indian-held Kashmir
Madrasa	Islamic School
Maulana	A Muslim man revered for his religious learning or piety
Maulavi	A Muslim doctor of a law
Mufti	A Muslim legal expert who is empowered to give rulings on religious matters
Mujahid/mujahideen	Muslim fighters and their movement
Mulla (mullah)	A Muslim learned in Islamic theology and sacred law
Sahib	A polite title or form of address
Sharia(h)	The religiously inspired Islamic law and code of conduct
Shia	One of the major Islamic belief systems
Sunni	One of the major Islamic belief systems
Tribals	People of the tribal areas of Pakistan and Afghanistan
Ulema	Islamic scholars
Ummah	The Islamic world brotherhood